Advance Praise

"In this groundbreaking work, LaNail Plummer offers clinicians a powerful, informed approach to supporting and healing Black women clients. By exploring the historical context and lived experiences of Black women—and integrating these insights into solid clinical practice—she helps therapists engage clients with greater empathy. Both educational and inspirational, *The Essential Guide for Counseling Black Women* encourages therapists to deepen their personal and professional awareness as they build fluency in culturally attuned care. Plummer provides a needed, wise, and knowledgeable voice to the field of counseling."

—**Lynn Grodzki, LCSW-C, MCC**, author of *Building Your Ideal Private Practice* and coauthor with Margaret Wehrenberg of *Letting Go of the Work You Love: A Workbook for Therapists to Prepare for Retirement, Close a Practice, and End a Career with Integrity*

"This book offers valuable insights into the unique contextual factors influencing Black women's lives. Dr. Plummer's firsthand experience working with clients, therapist tips, and opportunities for therapists' introspection allow the reader to embark on a journey of clinical- and self-discovery alongside the material. The theoretical grounding, research-driven information, and emphasis on practical interventions make this book essential for any clinician looking to strengthen or refine their work with Black women clients."

—**Shavonne J. Moore-Lobban, PhD, ABPP**, coauthor of *A Black Women's Guide to Overcoming Domestic Violence: Tools to Move Beyond Trauma, Reclaim Freedom, and Create the Life You Deserve* and *Preventing Child Maltreatment in the U.S.: The Black Community Perspective*

"Dr. Plummer says the quiet part out loud—Black women are not being fully seen or understood by the therapeutic community—and provides a comprehensive framework for therapists interested in giving Black women what they deserve: to be seen in all of their complexity, lived experience, joy, and possibilities."

—**Pamela Fuller,** ICF-certified coach and bestselling author of *The Leader's Guide to Unconscious Bias*

"Within these pages is a sanctuary of affirmation for Black women. Dr. Plummer offers a validating overview of our achievements and testaments to our inner light, presented alongside a chronicle of the genuine challenges that persist within our community. For the clinicians who do not personally know this lived experience, this is a required read—an opportunity to more deeply understand the unique, expansive, and ever-nuanced lived experiences of Black women, and how to support Black women in reclaiming the wholeness they've always held inside."

—**Nityda Gessel, LCSW, E-RYT**, author of *Embodied Self Awakening*

THE ESSENTIAL GUIDE
FOR COUNSELING
BLACK WOMEN

THE ESSENTIAL GUIDE

for Counseling Black Women

LaNail R. Plummer
EdD, LCPC-S

Norton Professional Books

An Imprint of W. W. Norton & Company
Independent Publishers Since 1923

Note to Readers: This book is intended as a general information resource. It is not a substitute for appropriate training or clinical supervision. Standards of clinical practice and protocol vary in different practice settings and change over time. No technique or recommendation is guaranteed to be effective in all circumstances, and neither the publisher nor the author can guarantee the complete accuracy, efficacy, or appropriateness of any recommendation in every respect or in all settings or circumstances. All therapists and patients described in this book, and all session transcripts, are composites.

Any URLs displayed in this book link or refer to websites that existed as of press time. The publisher is not responsible for, and should not be deemed to endorse or recommend, any website, app, or other content that it did not create. The author, also, is not responsible for any third-party material.

Frontis © imagenavi / Getty Images

For information about permission to reproduce selections from this book, write to Permissions, W. W. Norton & Company, Inc., 500 Fifth Avenue, New York, NY 10110

For information about special discounts for bulk purchases, please contact W. W. Norton Special Sales at specialsales@wwnorton.com or 800-233-4830

Manufacturing by Versa Press
Production manager: Gwen Cullen

ISBN: 978-1-324-05347-7

W. W. Norton & Company, Inc., 500 Fifth Avenue, New York, NY 10110
www.wwnorton.com

W. W. Norton & Company Ltd., 15 Carlisle Street, London W1D 3BS

Authorized EU representative: EAS, Mustamäe tee 50, 10621 Tallinn, Estonia

1 2 3 4 5 6 7 8 9 0

This book is dedicated to my children, Alyssa Eve and
Bradshaw Jr., who made the ultimate sacrifice of time
to allow me to accomplish two dreams at once:
to be their mommy and to be a therapist.
Thank you, my kiddies. Together, we are breaking
cycles and creating new realities.

Whatever is bringing you down, get rid of it. Because you will find that when you're free . . . your true self comes out.

— Tina Turner

Contents

Acknowledgments   xi

Introduction: Centering the Lived Experiences of
Black Women in the United States   xiii

Part I: What Brings Black Women to Therapy

1. Choosing Nontraditional Lifestyles   5

2. Creating a Legacy Through Work   24

3. Breaking Generational Cycles   49

4. Understanding Friendships   72

5. Embracing Newfound Freedom   91

6. Moving Beyond Stereotypes   104

Part II: Working With Black Women Clients

7. Working With Emotions   123

8. Addressing Trauma   141

9. Addressing Mental Health Disorders via a Cultural Lens   160

Conclusion   185

References   189

Index   207

Acknowledgments

Thank you to:

My wife, Maegan, for always choosing me and allowing me to heal *within* our relationship. You are my safe haven.

My mother, who always made sure I had "a few dollars" to buy a book at the Scholastic Book Fair.

My daddy, who gave me all the goodness of his experiences and soul. You gave it all to me, Daddy. Thank you.

To Alyssa and Bradshaw Jr., who are both my kiddies and my teachers, my motivation and my accountability partners, my hopes, and my dreams.

To my girls, Ayana, Jonai, Deana, and Nikki, who cleaned up my imposter syndrome each time it set in and who reminded me of my purpose, power, and the need for patience while writing.

To the Cane (Bianca, Courtney, Ivanna, Shana, and Zanetta) and Ayris. Delta Sigma Theta Sorority, Inc. brought us together, but God knew we needed each other. Thank you for holding me down during the darkest times that came while also writing this book.

To my book club, Shunda, Pamela, Andrea, and Ayana. If we do not read, we do not write. Thank you for making sure we always read something fun, inspirational, political, or deep and have the best conversations about it.

To my editor, Deborah. You took a chance on me. I had and still have big goals, and you helped me make sense of it all. Thank you for being a partner in this work: mental health, writing, and dream catching.

To my God, my Orishas, and my ancestors. Thank you for choosing me for this day and time, for allowing me to be a vessel in the lives of many, for trusting me with this powerful message, and for making me, me.

Introduction: Centering the Lived Experiences of Black Women in the United States

I didn't learn to be quiet when I had an opinion.
The reason they knew who I was is because I told them.

—Ursula Burns

In every crisis there is a message. Crises are
nature's way of forcing change—breaking down old
structures, shaking loose negative habits so that
something new and better can take their place.

—Susan L. Taylor

Living in the moment means letting go of the past and not
waiting for the future. It means living your life consciously,
aware that each moment you breathe is a gift.

—Oprah Winfrey

I applaud you for picking up this book. Whether you were motivated by simple curiosity or a desire to expand your understanding and improve your clinical practice, I am proud of you for thinking outside the box and outside of all limitations. You are the MVP and your clients will appreciate you; I appreciate you too.

I became a therapist to understand people. As a young girl growing up in Southern California in the 1980s, I was witness to a wide range of human behavior. I observed that while some people around me were able to make decisions that resulted in the accomplishment of their dreams, there were others whose decisions did not match the goals they set for themselves, which resulted in difficult emotions and more maladaptive decisions. It was a lot for a young Black girl like me to comprehend. So, in my truest nature, based in inquisitiveness, learning, and the application of knowledge, I sought to learn more about people, about Black people in particular, and, even more specifically, about Black women. I think I did well.

I became a therapist because I wanted to help. We as therapists cannot fix any person. In fact, I am not sure people are required to be fixed. I believe that they can be enlightened, gain increased awareness, and learn to make decisions that are congruent with their goals of self-actualization. I see myself as a guide and a healer of wounds that are so significant that they cause people to fall into the abyss of trauma, which prevents them from being who they want to be.

For Black women, this experience is made even more painful by the fact that much of their trauma or pain is not a reflection of their decisions but, rather, that of societal norms that have marginalized them twice, as Black people and as women. I specialize in working with Black women because while they have big dreams, the barriers imposed on them often seem unbreachable, and the obstacles they face are unrelenting. And I believe that if anyone deserves a safe space to explore, gain awareness, and work toward self-actualization, it is the Black woman.

I became a supervisor and professor because I love to teach and help others apply knowledge. When students and novice counselors engage in supervision with me, they want to learn and apply their wisdom. They want to help. They want to grow. They are like you because they are curious and ready to explore concepts that were not taught in graduate school.

Most mental health clinicians are well intended. Our graduate-level education and our desire to enter into a healing profession generally yield clinicians with big hearts and an eagerness to help. In our personal lives, we're often known as the "person who listens" or the "person who gives great advice." As a result of these academic and behaviorally reinforced experiences, as well as inherent psychological and personality-related traits, most clinicians will behave with good intentions. However, those of us that work with marginalized communities know and understand that intentions do not overshadow impact. In other words, the negative impact of an intention that has been poorly executed can be greater than the intention itself. We must consider this when working with Black women. A well-intended therapist can cause damage if they are not culturally competent to the dualized, marginalized experiences of Black women.

The common impact of a well-intended but culturally incompetent therapist is that the Black woman does not feel seen, heard, and understood, and she will subconsciously realign with the stereotypes that prevent most Black women from entering therapy. The greater impact is that she may stop participating in therapy altogether and never get the structured opportunity to heal. An additional, parallel impact is that she may tell her friends and family members about her negative therapeutic experiences, which may result in them not wanting to seek or participate in therapy, either.

This book is rooted in the good intentions of the clinician who is working with a Black woman client who also needs more information and knowledge to reduce their ignorance. In other words, this book is written to make sure there is alignment between intention and knowledge, so that the therapist's impact is positive, which can not only directly aid the client but also positively impact generations to come. My goal in writing this book is for clinicians to feel celebrated in wanting to know more about their clients; to understand their cultural limitations, either as non-Black therapists or otherwise; to learn more about the intersections of race, gender, culture, and mental health and to apply this knowledge to their work with clients, without asking their clients to serve as both the client and the educator. For the Black women readers, who are also clients in therapy, my goal is for them to feel seen and to understand that they are worthy of mental health services, while being given the space to vent, reflect, introspect, process, and breathe.

Let's get grounded in some terminology so we can have the same operational definitions. It is important to provide definitions for some terms that will be used throughout this book. Our society has a proclivity for inclusivity, which overall is a positive thing, but it has had an unintended consequence of preventing us from highlighting uniqueness and individual or cultural identity formation. When the following terms are used in this book, it is within the context of identity rather than politics.

> **Woman:** An adult human being who lives and identifies as female, within and despite the sex-based identification rendered at birth (Cambridge University Press, n.d.).

> **Black women:** This is a political term that refers to women who have direct lineage to the African diaspora and identify based on their skin color, general culture, and/or experiences. This term is interchangeable with African American women but is not limited to women born in the United States (Collins, 2000).

> **Culture:** Culture is defined as a set of unique values, traditions, and beliefs that are transferred from one generation to the next through various methods of communication Kroeber and Kluckhohn (1952).

> **Intersectionality:** Intersectionality is a metaphor for understanding the ways that multiple forms of inequality or disadvantage sometimes compound themselves and create obstacles that often are not understood among conventional ways of thinking (Crenshaw, 1989). Intentionality addresses individual cultural identities of each person through an experience of interconnectedness and overlap.

In this book, trans women are included in the definition of women. Despite the political challenges that these women experience in this country, their current lived experiences are aligned with womanhood. The uniqueness of their identity may be included in the identification of the LGBTQ movement. However, while many of their lived experiences align with the experiences of traditional Black women, I also understand that their lived experiences may include a dynamic layer that is not specifically addressed in this book, particularly due to the socialization aligned with their biological sex and the fight to be seen as who they currently are, not who they were born as.

TO BE SEEN

When writing on lined paper, most people focus on writing within the margins, rather than along the page's edges. Keeping the content in the center of the page signals to the reader that it is significant—it's the main idea. The margins, on the sides, are narrower, so if a reader finds any content there, it will likely be comprised of fewer words, fewer full sentences, less full content, and thus, less significant and engaging content.

For many people within minority communities, this reflects their lived experiences. Their lives, community strengths, individual challenges, and overall existence are often pushed to the side, into the margins, and given less attention than the concerns of majorities. In a world where many issues, political policies, financial investments, and health-focused approaches are engaged with the centralized community of the racial and gender majority, many marginalized people are less seen and thus may become accustomed to being misunderstood, unappreciated, and devalued. However, there are some marginalized people who still fight back and use bold approaches in making sure that their lived experiences are seen, heard, and addressed with the same level of support and rigor that majority communities receive and experience.

In reading this book, you are taking a step toward fighting back, too. You are engaging in the process of learning, understanding, and realizing new things about the marginalized experiences of Black women. In living with two marginalized identities, many Black women are pushed even farther from the centralized issues of the majority yet remain hopeful and believe that one day they will be seen for who they are and their dynamic experiences will be recognized. For many Black women, the idea of being seen and valued is revolutionary. Being seen is worth the battle of presence, the work of building a seat at the table.

By reading this book and engaging with your Black woman client, you are better equipped to see her for who she is and not just her verbalized presenting issue or nonverbalized skill deficits or emotional challenges. In reading and engaging in this book, you will have context, strategies, and tips to elevate the therapeutic experience for your Black woman client. You will be able to see her, and she will appreciate you for it. While you may not have the power or systemic support to move your Black woman client from the margins to the majority, you will and do have the power to make a client feel that she is the center of attention without feeling a consequence, a negative engagement, or a less than ideal experience, simply because she is Black.

When you first meet with your Black woman client, ask her: What does it feel like to be seen? Take note of how she answers so that you can use this insight, along with the tools you will find in this resource book, to make your client feel seen when she is in sessions with you or in her trusted community. She is ready. And you will be too.

HISTORY x IDENTITY = A CULTURALLY RESPONSIVE APPROACH FOR CLINICIANS

While it is challenging to acknowledge and address the role of history in our current lives, especially since we (both the reader and the client) were not the makers of that history but instead are the recipients of its impact, we must take a stance in acknowledging how history has shaped our country and created the marginalization that we see in many repressed communities. When we consider the development of patriarchy from a political perspective that predated slavery and couple it with the racial divide that was used for economic growth and sustainability, we must acknowledge that women who were Black were the members of two major political structures that needed these women to sustain the structures. In other words, without women, patriarchy could not exist, and without Blackness, racism could not exist. Black women were needed and weaponized for the very systems that kept them oppressed.

Being in a powerless position, and at the same time being the very tool needed to maintain one's own marginalization, takes a massive psychological and emotional toll. The traumatic impact forced onto Black women is often beyond traditional words and has historical generational impacts. Acknowledging this, we can see that there are historical experiences specific to Black people, specific to women, and grandly impactful to the dualized identity of Black women. While this book is a guide for clinicians who work with Black women, this section will highlight the historical foundation of the uniqueness of the Black woman's identity, in a society that has chosen not to see her but absolutely needs her. Such a broad-based foundation is necessary for understanding the importance of a specific knowledge base for doing this work.

Identity-Specific Issues That Affect Black Women: Race

The term *involuntary minority* was developed by Nigerian sociologist John Ogbu (1978) as he explored the variance between minoritized groups and their relative successes and challenges. Ogbu defined an involuntary minority in two specific ways, the "nature of White American involvement with their becoming minorities and the reasons they came or were brought to the United States" (Ogbu & Simmons, 1998). Involuntary minorities are different from voluntary minorities because a voluntary minority has chosen to come to the United States to find opportunities and potential prosperity, while an involuntary minority did not have a self-determined reason or choice in being in the United States (Malone, 2023).

In consideration of Black Americans with ancestral enslavement, they are involuntary minorities. Their ancestors did not choose to be in the United States but, rather, were forced to be here because of slavery. Current day Black Americans who were born here did not choose to be here, but this is their home country. In moving to another country, they would still be a minority in that country. Even if they chose to move to a country that is highly populated by Black people, they will still be a minority because they are American. No matter where a Black American person goes, she will be a minority, voluntarily or involuntarily.

Even though forced to enter the United States, Black people fought in the Revolutionary War; their intent was to obtain freedom from slavery (Collins, 2013). Fifteen percent of the soldiers on both the American and British sides were Black people who desired independence for themselves and their families. At the end of the war, these nearly 5,000 people were forced back into enslavement; they realized that they had been deceived and used by both countries, neither of whom kept their promises (Collins, 2013).

Following the Revolutionary War, Black people, with the continued intention of independence, fought in the War of 1812. However, the outcome was the opposite of freedom; it was the denial of their participation and the committed decision to send them back into enslavement (History.com, 2022).

As further wars ensued, hundreds of thousands of Black people fought and died to protect the United States and those who had liberties to lead a life of freedom, justice, and prosperity, which despite their efforts did not include them. Counting the 12 wars the United States fought, including the Revolutionary War, Civil War, World Wars, country-to-country wars, and internal land wars, over 21% of the United States Army population has been Black (*Black-Americans: the United States Army*, n.d.). This equates to several million Black people who have fought and died for freedoms of Americans, which, due to segregation and systemic racism, did not include them. Yet, they themselves have not experienced the freedom that results from their sacrifice.

It was not until the Civil Rights Act of 1964 that Black Americans legally held the same rights as white Americans. Yet, while segregation is illegal, there continues to be overt and apparent discrimination that prevents true freedom in this country, specifically for Black Americans. This includes but is not limited to: disproportionate rates of education access and high-quality academic materials; disproportionate opportunities in safe and affordable housing and home ownership; a lack of access to wealth-building opportunities such as equal pay in jobs, access to corporate executive positions, investment in entrepreneurship and business ownership; and a lack of protection of life as proven by the disproportionate rates of death in health care, maternal and infant mortality, and murder by police.

As I lay the foundation for this book, it is important to understand the historical and racial context of what your Black women clients are facing. While this section is limited and focused on their ancestral and racial connection to fighting for freedoms that were not afforded to them, their present-day struggles are reflective of a continued fight for equality and the toll that takes on the mental health of Black Americans.

Identity-Specific Issues That Affect Black Women: Gender

While it is common knowledge that men served their communities as hunters and women were gatherers, there are periods of history that are overlooked when considering the strength that was required to tend large areas of land and some of the physical limitations that women experienced during pregnancies or other phases of their lives. History readings describe patriarchal societies originating as a matter of circumstance in which men tended to the land that produced products that were often sold or bartered for economic sustainability or advancement while women focused on childrearing (Saini, 2023). As older men died, they passed their land to their sons who they believed were most familiar with tending to the land or livestock (Ananthaswamy & Douglas, 2018). Through this culture, men obtained power because they maintained financial access. Women, most of whom did not own land or livestock, were subjected to legal marginalization and domination, thus preventing them from having a voice in issues related to voting, banking, homeownership, and even their bodies (Pierik, 2022). While patriarchal culture governs many societies, Surowiec et al. (2019) note that historically there have been no less than 160 matrilineal societies in which power and wealth were passed down from mother to daughter and women governed the laws and practices of that society. Present day matrilineal societies include the Khasi tribe and the Minangkabau people of Indonesia, the Mosuo people of China, the Bribri people of Costa Rica, and the Akan people of Ghana.

As we consider the role of patriarchy in the lives of women, it is important to note the foundation of religion and the spoken and unspoken rules, expectations, norms, structure, guidance, and limitations that religion places on women. There are no less than 45 biblical scriptures that impact the lives of women and which claim that the man is closer to God and the woman is closer to the man, the specifications of an ideal woman, the role of the woman in the home, and how a woman should dress.

Universally, religion has served as the moral and righteous path for one's being and one's path toward salvation. Many women lean toward these scriptures, despite the negative implications on their mental and physical health. In fact, there are many women who use these scriptures to justify pro-life principles, infidelity in the marriage, self-sacrificial behaviors, and the deferment of dreams.

When considering the role of religion in the lives of Black women in the United States, it should be noted that approximately 64% identify as religious with an adherence to biblical principles, versus 51% of Black men in the United States (Mitchell & Mitchell, 2024b). Thus, more than 50% of Black American women follow religious teachings despite the negative implications the teachings may have on their lives. I tread carefully around the concept that religion is both positive and negative because it is manufactured (Harrison, 1990). However, when anything compromises mental health, contextually it may be unhealthier than not.

Culture serves as a guardrail of status quo and the continuation of ideology. There is a culture to womanhood that dictates the meaning and behaviors of femininity, as well as the details of womanhood, mothering, wifehood, careers , and even when it is appropriate to aspire to and utilize legal and societal rights. In the 1986 journal article, "The Politics of Self-Respect," Diana Meyers writes that "women have traditionally been victimized by a mandatory right to play a distinctively 'feminine' role which has undermined their self-respect." Through further explanation, she says that culture sets morals and values for beings, categorizes each being into boxes, and then expects each being to operate based on a cultural rule. A variation from the rule can upset the structure of society and, rather than address the variegated needs of that being, that being is ostracized and given two options: Revert and follow the rule or stay on the margin and risk a loss of belonging and safety. Many women who may want to redefine womanhood for their individual selves are forced to make the overt decision between security within norms that they do not value or insecurity while creating and demanding an experience they deserve. For some women, this concept has formed the foundation of their feminist beliefs and values. Yet, for Black women, the strategic risk of an added experience of insecurity is a much heavier decision to make. Thus, many Black women have stayed the course toward security, in fear that entering another marginalized experience would compromise their mental health and even their physical safety. There are many times when Black women reluctantly lean into the ideas, notions, and created rules of womanhood and femininity simply to avoid an added push deeper into the margins characterized by social unacceptance and a lack of safety.

Intersections of Race and Gender for Black Women

From a research perspective, intersectionality is defined by Hernandez (2008) as

> an analysis of the dynamic interplay of one's gender identity, ethnicity, sexual orientation, religion, age, disability status, and other diversity characteristics upon multiple aspects of one's identity, including the resources and lack of

resources these differences convey in the individual within their current societal context. (p. 11)

To understand the intersections of race and gender for Black women, the clinician must take a qualitative approach through talking, interviewing, comprehending, synthesizing, and adding the information to their personal schematic frameworks. While quantitative data is important, it simply lacks the nuances of all those who live at the center of intersections.

Allen (1998) noted that she and Black women have an identity that is socially constructed and based on her physical salience and her awareness of being socialized as a Black woman. To her, this makes her an outsider within any majority-based group and creates challenges such as conflictual encounters and dialectic tensions in the ethic of caring. According to Allen (1998), Griffin (2012), and hooks (1989), the conflictual encounters and dialectic tensions in the ethic of caring have implications for both Black and non-Black women leaders. Conflictual encounters are experiences with others who, for example, directly express or imply that a Black woman is either undeserving of her position and is present in a company because of her double minority status (Allen, 1998, p. 578). In these encounters, a Black woman may believe she has to choose between her race and gender in situations of opposition by determining, for her situational survival, if she aligns more with defending and advocating based on her race or defending and advocating on her gender (Allen, 1998, p. 578). Unintentionally, a Black woman may also be placed in a position of being a representative of her race, gender, or both (Allen, 1998, p. 579). Black women may internalize these experiences, bury their feelings, and lose focus on their position or purpose within the organization. Allen stated that Black women are only embraced through structured stereotypes that limit how they can express their emotions. These limitations can influence a Black woman's perspective of self as well as how she chooses to interact with others. Direct conversations addressing these experiences in the safe, nurturing, and developmental space of clinical supervision can serve as a validation of her being and help the Black woman client reconnect to continue her purpose.

In order to address the re-empowerment of Black women and the complete restoration of a positive self-image, therapy is an important key. However, Hernandez (2008) noted that postcolonial thinking addresses the cognitive restructuring that must occur for helping professionals to examine their questions and statements, so they are better aligned with liberation versus continued oppression of marginalized groups. The Cultural Context Model (Almeida et al., 1998) was created and examined as a means of working with individuals who share similar experiences of marginalization because of culture. The model provided structure to address ways that systems and experiences relate to power and privilege. Through this understanding, Hernandez (2008) expanded on the cultural context model to make it applicable to psychology and clinical supervision utilization.

Hernandez (2008) proposed that the elements that challenge the socially constructed ideas of race and oppression become elements mental health workers use in their sessions with diverse clients. Through this approach, counselors benefit, because they will remain critically conscious of various issues and elements that address race and oppression. Hernandez and McDowell (2010) described the concepts of intersectionality, power, and relational safety within the context of mental health therapy and noted that the power structure allows a counselor to direct and guide a client's direction and perception of self. The influence of power needs to be addressed, specifically with clients of color who may be consistently subjected to being powerless in their lives. The counselor needs to initiate dialogues around intersectionality, power, and relational safety to strengthen the dynamics in the therapeutic relationship and lead to positive outcomes for the counselor, the clients, and the community.

Similarly, Yabusaki (2010) researched topics of diversity, privilege, and dialogue. Yabusaki used the emotions to create an experience of a dialogue around diversity helping the respondent to understand that emotions and responses are rooted in culture. Yabusaki concluded that culture plays a role in counselors' interactions with clients, and though it is often unconscious, it is important to build a structure of clarity so the counselor is aware and the client can learn and understand herself through the process.

Burnes et al. (2012) found clients expressed the importance of their clinician's ability to self-disclose, ask direct questions about their therapeutic relationship, and frequently explore the impacts of diversity in the group. The counselor's role, identity, and intentions must be clear, because they impact the client's learning experience, engagement, and safety in self-exploration. The impact of the Burnes study was that this approach often led to political activism because the clients explored culture, equality, women-centered variables, and relationship-centered variables. These areas were explored in depth through values related to self-care, nurturance, emotional connection, and consistent check-ins. Burnes et al. emphasized the importance of having clear and direct conversations when working with women. The conversations must be expansive and open to a range of feminist-based cultural experiences, but specific enough to have direct impact on the client in the session. In other words, counselors must be open to universal cultural truths, but also understand the impact such truths have on the individual client and the implications for her personal and professional identity.

Wong et al. (2013) explored themes of culture that had both a positive and negative impact on the therapeutic relationship. From the study, 20 themes emerged as factors that positively impact the relationship from a multicultural perspective. These themes ranged from counselors apologizing for mistakes to the client being open-minded and receptive. Additionally, 15 themes emerged as factors that hinder the therapeutic relationship such as the inability to create a safe and trusting space. Also, many of the clients felt that their minority status had a role in the difficulties they experienced in this unique setting. They said it impacted them personally and affected their ability to acculturate to the setting.

The abovementioned research should be used as a guide in understanding the role of cultural competency in counseling those with intersected identities, especially Black women. While there is research to address intersected and multicultural identities, the best approach in understanding your Black women clients is to purely listen to them. Listen objectively. Listen subjectively. Understand they are the experts in their lives and your job is to guide them to becoming the version of themselves they want to be. Address any of your own biases, challenges, and limitations without expecting your client to educate you or without you projecting onto them. Remember to listen. And listen well.

HOW TO USE THIS BOOK

Part I of this book centers on the lived experiences of Black women, the current and historical factors that motivate them to initiate and participate in therapy. Part II explores ways in which clinicians can support, help, and heal their Black women clients. This guide includes therapist's tips, catalyst questions, journal prompts, and case examples from my clinical practice that can be used by Black women.

Therapist's Tips

There are times when we, as therapists, are sitting in our offices, planning for our sessions, or researching one of our areas of need and we find ourselves stuck. The therapist's tips are on-demand strategies you can use when working with your client, especially within a specific topic or range of topics. The therapist's tips reflect evidence-based items that intersect at the point of thought and action. The goal of the therapist's tips is to provide a point of reference and a written consultation that can guide you as you guide your client.

Catalyst Questions

While we may have been trained in motivational interviewing, Socratic questioning, and therapeutic-aligned inquiry formats, there are times when we have the words in our mind but do not let them out because of our fear, insecurity in our roles, concern around misunderstanding, or simply doubting our skills and timing. There are other times when we are familiar with a topic, ready to engage a client, and do not have a starting point for the conversation. The catalyst questions are springboards into conversations around specific topics. They should be used as the entry point for a conversation or a redirection at a pivotal moment. I encourage you to review the questions prior to the session, write a few of them on your notepad, or have the book handy in case you need them as a reference.

Journal Prompts

Therapy requires clients to reflect by thinking about their past and to engage in introspection, which requires them to go inward, examine themselves, and see themselves for who they really are before they decide who they want to be. In our daily lives, we form rote routines that do not encourage reflection unless a problem has occurred. Rarely are we given the space to engage in introspection without being called selfish or self-centered. However, the journal prompts at the end of each chapter serve as the continuation of the session. One or more of the journal prompts can be assigned as homework too. These journal prompts can be used independently of therapy, either by the Black woman who is reading this book or by the Black woman client who is in therapy and would like to discuss a particular topic with their therapist. Some journal prompts are short and will resurface a memory, while others are a bit longer and may require several journal entries over multiple days and weeks. The journal prompts are a guide into reflection and introspection for the client.

Therapist's Introspection

The therapeutic alliance is a relationship between you, as the therapist, and your client. In every relationship, each individual influences the other. In the therapeutic relationship, the design is that you influence your client through the questions you ask, the statements you make, and the model you demonstrate. However, there are times when your client will influence you too. Most commonly this can be a form of countertransference, especially if it is not addressed. Yet, within the context of this book, both as a reader and one who is applying the content, you may find that your client, her experiences, her statements, and her behaviors may influence your thoughts and engagement. This will serve as a basis for your own introspection, examination, and interpretation. Therefore, at the end of each chapter, you will see a standard set of questions that will allow you to dive deeper into your personal and professional introspection, as a therapist working with a Black woman client.

Therapeutic Guide

The most insightful and informed therapists are the best therapists for Black women. Therapists do not have to be experts in the Black woman experience, but they have to be willing to learn about Black women and choose to be an expert in their own personal life. Intersections between curiosity, skill, and care are needed.

While this book focuses on the lived experiences of Black women and what they need, this book also requires you to be willing to explore the depths of who you are. It's not Freudian, in that the client is removed from us and we are removed from them. It is the opposite. We help Black women as we, independently and without their in-session guidance, help ourselves. While this is a guidebook, I can only give you the tools and I hope you choose to use them. Instead of telling you what to do each session with your client, I'd like to offer two main things in each guide section of each chapter:

1. After reading each chapter, there will be a series of questions you can ask yourself, to be used as a combination of personal and professional introspection.
2. After each chapter, I will highlight three therapies and how they can be used in relation to the chapter's content and your Black woman client.

CONCLUSION

You picked up this book because you were curious or because you decided that you want to increase your cultural competency. Thank you. I appreciate you. Your current and future clients will appreciate you. And the Black community will appreciate that you took the initiative to read more, learn more, and apply more.

While this chapter created a foundation for the information in the remaining chapters, please note that the content is sensitive and is dependent on your decision to engage with your Black women clients in new and powerful ways. Do not shy away from reading and do not shy away from applying the knowledge and skills immediately. The best way to learn is to apply. There is no need to wait. The time is now. Let's get to work!

THE ESSENTIAL GUIDE
TO COUNSELING
BLACK WOMEN

PART I

What Brings Black Women to Therapy

Choosing Nontraditional Lifestyles

The most common way people give up their power is by thinking they don't have any.

—Alice Walker

I think there are things for all of us to do as long as we're here and we're healthy.

—Gwendolyn Brooks

You are on the eve of a complete victory. You can't go wrong. The world is behind you.

—Josephine Baker

Clinicians who work with Black women must consider that many Black women have been raised to be conservative, as a matter of safety, history, survival, and religion. Yet, research finds that Black women are increasingly choosing to lead nontraditional lives (Carlton & Klassen, 2008). This may be because many Black women are no longer dependent on a spouse for financial support and security, as has historically been the case, because they earn sustainable salaries and are well educated. They do not feel pressure to have children because they can create legacies through their work. They are pursuing traditional spiritual practices that predate slavery and encourage a sense of freedom rather than fear. When they do choose marriage, they understand that they can be the primary breadwinner who does or does not cook, who can be but is not required to be sexy, who is or is not submissive, and so forth. This chapter will discuss the various cognitive, behavioral, and spiritual processes that lead a Black woman to therapy as she considers choosing a nontraditional lifestyle while already being in a marginalized category.

THE QUESTION OF MARRIAGE

Data from U.S. Census reports have shown that the rate of marriage among Black women has been dropping in recent years; in 2010, 75% of Black women were married, while by 2020, that percentage had dropped to 64.8% (U.S. Census Bureau, 2010, 2020). In national comparison data, Black women are the least likely demographic to get married and one of the demographics most likely to get divorced and stay divorced (U.S. Census Bureau, 2020). Many researchers have speculated about the causes of these trends, primarily through the lens of defeat, deficit, and concern. However, in working with Black women clients, one needs to consider that these rates reflect choice, not circumstance.

The power of choice is especially crucial for Black women, given that their ancestors and elders were not afforded the same liberties. These elders and ancestors were often forced into marriage due to religion, premarital conception, economic survival and determination, cultural standards, and mere social standing. However, as Black women are increasing their educational attainment, economic standing, career legacies, and preferred lifestyles, it is quite possible that they are making the active choice in determining if they want to be married, engage in a long-term partnership, or simply remain unattached.

With this consideration, therapists must also explore if an unmarried client has a desire to be married but feels unequipped, which is vastly different from fearing marriage or simply not wanting to be married.

While the data indicates that there are many Black women who are divorced or divorcing, one must consider that for some this may be an active and empowering choice, while for others it may be a matter of feeling or being unskillful in areas that are needed for a healthy marriage. These skills include but are not limited to effective communication, active listening, emotional awareness and regulation, trigger and sensitivity identification, core belief expression, and problem solving. As with any other skills, the client must be properly exposed to the information, ideally in a positive manner, and then given the opportunity to learn, practice, make inconsequential mistakes, practice again, communicate and process to determine strengths and obstacles in learning and implementation, practice again, and aim for refinement.

However, some people, including Black women, may not have had the best role models of marriage or traditional lives. As a result, some Black women may have lacked opportunities to practice relational skills or engage in inconsequential mistakes within the confines of a healthy parental, social, or romantic relationship. The lack of these skills and experiences may have an implication on the opportunity to learn and to practice and refine healthy and effective skills. Often, people engage in marriage because of a social standard but are unprepared to maintain a healthy, long-term partnership; have little patience for learning and mistakes; and may choose to opt out of the marriage rather than developing the skills needed to repair it. However, this does not mean that all Black women should stay married for the sake of being married. You, as the therapist, should initiate a conversation about skill-based learning, core beliefs, and childhood processing.

THERAPIST'S TIP: Creating an Environment for Skill-Based Learning

Throughout this book, you will continue to see the importance of skill-based learning and core beliefs. Skill-based learning specifically aligns with behavioral theory and the opportunity for clinicians to teach, review, reinforce, and reiterate skills with clients. Consider that skills are learned, not natural. Skill building requires the clinician to be intentional in when they introduce the skill, while creating a plan for review and reinforcement. This process is akin to a student who is taught a new algebraic equation. The teacher must introduce foundational lessons such as simple arithmetic, then algebraic concepts, followed by the introduction to the formula. After that, the teacher must give opportunities for the student to practice the formula such as worksheets, group assignments, and homework, followed by assessments of learning. In clinical practice, the client is the student and the clinician is the teacher. The skills that must be learned are aligned with relationships and interpersonal experiences. These skills include communication, problem solving, and restoration after an interpersonal rift. As you continue to read this book, please refer to Therapist's Tips for important skills—communication, problem solving, and restorative conversations.

There are many women who do not want to be married and have made an active choice to remain unattached. In these situations, therapists must ensure they are not engaging in countertransference, through the lens of misunderstanding a Black woman's choice or wanting her to change her choice to meet societal standards. The Black woman will benefit from therapeutic engagement that allows her to feel safe in her choice but also prepares her for imposing questions from family members, friends, colleagues, and even strangers. The safe haven of the therapeutic relationship can serve as the place of processing and the place in which a client can explore the various responses that she can and may make when people ask her questions, make statements, or misunderstand her reasons or rationale.

THERAPIST'S TIP: Managing Your Own Perceptions on Marriage

As a therapist, it will be important for you to take a moment and consider your personal, not professional, thoughts on marriage. Is marriage something you believe in and value? Do you believe all people should aim toward marriage? When you hear that a person is unmarried, do you question why? When you hear a person has been married for 50 years, do you celebrate? When you hear that someone has been divorced twice, do you judge or try to determine what happened?

By understanding our personal thoughts and values on topics like marriage, we become more self-aware to recognize when we are projecting our values on a client versus guiding them to figure out their own values.

As therapists, people place us in the position of being an all-knowing guru. But that is not true. We know how to lead therapy. We know how to utilize theory to help a client heal. We know how to be the best versions of ourselves for ourselves. But we do not know what is best for another person, for a client. That is for them to determine for themselves.

In the case of marriage, take 10 minutes and jot down your ideas. Let these ideas and beliefs remain your own and not the beliefs of your client. This will allow you to avoid countertransference and allow your client to live the life she wants to live.

THE QUESTION OF CHILDREN
INSIGHT FROM A CLIENT: SH

"I like being her mother. . . . I just do not like the mother I am when I am with him.

"I'm doing exactly what I am doing [getting a divorce] because I chose my child, not anyone else. I am doing what I want to do because I can and because I think it's what's best for her."

Client SH has been in therapy with for 6 years. She came to therapy because she was planning to get married, and her fiancé asked her to explore some of her childhood issues that were affecting their intimacy. Specifically, he wanted her to address her sexual trauma that was rendered at the hands of an older cousin. Her fiancé thought that this trauma was the source of her lack of engagement or excitement about him and their upcoming nuptials.

Two years into the marriage, they conceived a child, which was a positive addition to their union but also a source of new intrusive thoughts, rumination, and fear.

Through therapy, she explored the trauma of childhood sexual abuse along with the anxiety (and postpartum anxiety) related to having a child she was afraid she would not be able to protect. Additionally, she spent a significant amount of time addressing the trauma that was developing within her newly formed marriage. It was riddled with emotional and verbal abuse that escalated to physical violence.

Therapy served as a space for exploration and processing but also as a source of self-identification and empowerment. Following the decision to divorce her husband, SH endured a lengthy and troublesome divorce process, which was inundated with verbal assaults, threats, and a general environment of fear. She wanted better for herself, and her historical trauma and process propelled her to want better for her daughter too. She did not want to contribute to a repetitive cycle of abuse that could impact her daughter.

Once the divorce was finalized, SH took a year to explore who she would be as a woman, a worker, a business owner, and a mother. Oftentimes, she made statements about her daughter that were projections of who she really wanted to be. Her daughter served as a focus of motivation, discipline, and determination, but only within the realm of being a single mother. At one point in the process, she noted that she was a better mother because she chose to parent alone. In therapy, she was able to address and compartmentalize her relationship with her ex-husband and her ability to raise and parent her child. While the catalyst for therapy had been a suggestion by her then husband, therapy served as a tool for her to determine what type of mother she wanted to be.

Catalyst Questions: Exploring the Mother Role

Consider the following catalyst questions:

> What do you see in your daughter that you also see in yourself?
>
> How do you want your daughter to perceive you?
>
> When your daughter grows up, what do you want her to say about you? Use three adjectives.
>
> What are two things that you would like to change about yourself as a mother? Let's make it measurable and time-oriented so you can see your progress and celebrate your success.

These catalyst questions are important because they allow the client to explore who she wants to be. Often, the role of being a mother is portrayed as instinctual, easy, natural, and loving. But for many women, and especially for Black women, there may also be fears of isolation; concerns of being misunderstood about their rationale and decision-making when raising their child; difficulties in sorting out acculturation between the majority white culture and the legacy of the Black culture; concerns about balancing work disparities and the finances of being a parent; and challenges in prioritizing intimate relationships versus child-rearing. There may also be resentment and grief for the experiences that the woman lost when she made the decision to become a mother. While many people hesitate in initiating conversations about motherhood with women, fearing to offend the woman, it is important for you, the therapist, to recognize your unique position that allows you to ask questions others do not ask. You earned the privilege to probe; you need to take it seriously and ask the tough questions that will guide your client to self-awareness, cultural understanding, and healing.

For centuries, women have been socialized to take responsibility for having children. It was seen as a woman's duty, and women heard comments such as, "It's your job to build a family," "It is your job to support and expand the community," "God wanted you to have children, and that is why He made you a woman."

While these statements are now made less explicitly (though certainly women do still hear them), subliminal messaging continues to strongly reinforce the idea that a woman's primary purpose is procreation. As just one example, young girls are given baby dolls to play with, as a way of preparation for caring for and loving a child. In fact, there are baby dolls marketed to girls as young as 6 months old, with the average age of 2 years old. (Rabelo et al., 2014). Papalia and Martorell (2021) note that most children are highly sensory-attuned and emotional due to the early development of the limbic system and amygdala and less cognitive or verbally expressive due to the underdeveloped prefrontal cortex. Due to this, when a young girl receives a baby doll before age 5, she associates the baby doll with herself and her developing identity instead of recognizing the baby doll as an external object. To take it one step further, she is programmed from the moment she gets her first baby doll to believe that she is supposed to take care of herself by taking care of this baby doll, or rather that she is supposed to take care of the baby doll instead of taking care of herself.

Another example of the early maternal socialization of girls is through the discriminatory action of inviting young girls to baby showers and not inviting young boys or men. While there are recent changes in the inclusion of men at baby showers, men were historically excluded, making baby showers events that were exclusively for women celebrating other women. Through this process, young girls are invited to and expected to attend baby showers, as women celebrate other women's decision, option, or opportunity to birth a child. Young girls see and sense the grand celebration of bringing forth a child, having an entire party centered on the woman and her decision to have a baby and even fulfill a dream. The mother to be is engulfed with gifts, admiration, expectation, and joy. Success is portrayed as the decision and opportunity to have a baby.

Sadly, this is one of the few times that you see women being celebrated with so much intensity and consistency. Research from Aptaclub, an infant feeding company, finds that 64% of mothers in the United States have a baby shower (Trautwein, 2022). Additionally, ancient societies in Egypt, Greece, India, and parts of South America, Europe, and Africa created and celebrated pregnancies and births through a range of rituals centered on the mother and child.

Researchers and practitioners led by Carolyn R. Ahlers-Schmidt and colleagues (2019) noted that baby showers can also serve as a source of learning, understanding, and prevention of death, harm, and mistakes as mothers and other women share safety and care advice with the pregnant woman. However, the general expectation of the baby shower is to celebrate a woman and her decision to conceive and birth a child. The implicit communication is that girls are socialized and celebrated when they decide to have a child.

What happens when a woman decides not to have a child or postpones the process?

Between 1990 and 2020, the annual number of births in the United States dropped from 4.16 million to 3.66 million; in 2020, Black women accounted for 52% of all women who did not have children, making them the largest demographic of women without children in the United States (*Women in the Labor Force: A Databook*, 2022).

It is important to consider to what extent this trend represents Black women making an empowered decision to not have children, and to what extent it represents circumstances that may be preventing Black women from having children.

Circumstantial factors include but are not limited to not meeting a suitable partner or possible coparent; not being able to afford the rising costs of day care, child care, and basic child-based needs; living far from support systems and supportive communities; and encountering medical issues and challenges including a low number of healthy eggs, the presence of fibroids, endometriosis, and other uterine-based limitations; having a partner who already has children; having a partner whose physical or mental health is unable to produce enough sperm for conception; or fear of maternal death since Black women are four times more likely to die from maternal death than white women.

Choice-based factors are exceptionally interesting when considering Black women. Beyond the understanding that women are often socialized and conditioned to have children, Black women in the United States were historically forced to have children through the confines of enslavement or prevented from having children based on sterilization by the government.

Rachel A. Feinstein noted that rape-based pregnancy, slave breeding pregnancy, and product inventory–based pregnancy were common experiences for Black women who were enslaved (Feinstein, 2018). Oftentimes, these Black women did not have a choice between having a child or not having a child. It was more than socialization and conditioning. It was a requirement.

Researcher Adam Cohen (2017) found that in the 20th century, over 70,000 Black women were sterilized without their consent. With Supreme Court cases such as *Buck v. Bell* or state laws such as the Asexualization Act of California, it was permitted and authorized to medically sterilize Black women, starting with nonconsensual birth control, or ending with unknown hysterectomies. Upon finding out about these actions, the forced sterilization of Fannie Lou Hamer exposed the U.S. government and medical community; however, there were hundreds of thousands of missed opportunities for Black women to give birth to children they wanted to have and raise. My grandmother, Evelyn Carol Leisure, was sterilized at the age of 21, unbeknownst to her.

Given this history, when a Black woman in the embodiment of socialization, conditioning, and reinforcement makes a clear choice on her engagement in motherhood, it is one that should be processed, practiced, and supported in a nonjudgmental way. This applies to women who choose to have children and those who do not.

INSIGHT FROM A CLIENT: FY

FY loves her life. She travels around the world at least twice a year. She is a part of the elite circles in Washington, DC, is fashionable, hosts small dinner parties at her house, has a bustling career that she envisioned for herself, and dates successful men when she wants to. She is from a small town with traditional values for women and some restrictive perspectives for Black people. The intersection of restriction and tradition was the catalyst that propelled her to move out of her conservative town up to the vibrant and progressive city of Washington, DC.

Over the years, we have discussed and she has processed the decision to have children or not. While in therapy, she has had a few serious relationships in which the men wanted to marry and have children with her. However, she made a clear decision for herself that she did not want children. She wanted her lifestyle. The reality for her is, it is difficult to have a lifestyle like hers while raising a child, in America, as a Black mom. She noted that things change, people change, expectations change, life and love changes, when a Black woman has a baby.

The decision did not seem hard for her. There were many sessions that were concentrated on motivational interviewing, probing questions, sentence stem starters, and therapeutic silence, but once she landed on a firm decision that she believed in, she stood strong.

I waited several weeks to reintroduce the topic. I wanted to give her time to process alone while removing some of the intensity of her decision. When I mentioned the decision again, she remained consistent, which allowed us to discuss the various ways she would respond to people when asked about her status or desires in motherhood. She processed and created answers through question prompts, role play, and behavioral rehearsals, and she scaffolded conversations with her family and childhood friends. With the latter, she mentioned their answers in sessions, and we continued to explore her thoughts, feelings, and behaviors.

By the end of the process, FY had made a firm decision and had conversational language to explain her decision to men she would date in the future, as well as responses to questions and statements that others would ask simply because she was a woman.

Catalyst Questions: The Exploration of Having Children

Some of these questions included but were not limited to:

> When thinking about having a baby, what are the pros and cons?

> Would you be having this baby strictly for you? Or will this baby serve as a tool for something else, like quieting your parents, making new mommy friends or engaging with friends who already have children, satisfying a societal expectation?

> If you had to raise this baby alone because of some unforeseen circumstance with the father, would you still want to have the baby?

> In having a baby, what are three ways you can foresee your life changing? Considering each change, is it worth it to you?

> If you chose to not have a baby, what are three things you can expect to hear from your parents, coworkers, or men you choose to date? Let us take the next few weeks to process your thoughts and practice language you can use when confronting questions or statements about your decision to not have children.

> If you decide to change your stance on this topic, what are three things you can do right now that will allow for you to have children in the future? Let's start with egg-freezing. What other ideas do you have in mind?

- - - - - - - -

The insight from a client demonstrates the therapeutic work that is necessary when a Black woman decides not to have a child, particularly because women are socialized to have children and many Black women are making an active decision to break the mold of socialization and create a nontraditional life that supports their own vision and desires.

THERAPIST'S TIP: ALIGN YOUR THERAPEUTIC QUESTIONS WITH YOUR THEORETICAL ORIENTATION

When probing and exploring with clients, remember to use question prompts and ideas that are related to your specific therapeutic approach. Whether you practice therapy using cognitive behavioral therapy (CBT), rational emotive behavior therapy (REBT), dialectical behavior therapy (DBT), Imago, or feminist therapy, each therapy has solid and researched workbooks. Borrow a guidebook from the library, buy one online as an ebook, or check out your options at a bookstore.

Do not think you have to produce question prompts and activities alone.

Your learning does not stop after graduate school. Please continue to invest in your craft by reading books that are centered on your theoretical orientation and therapeutic modality.

Think of it this way: Would you want your physician to still use materials and research from when they graduated from medical school or would you want them to stay up-to-date and abreast of the new and innovative ways to treat you as a patient?

Your clients deserve the same dedication to your learning. They deserve to know and trust that their therapist is using research, tools, and guidebooks to navigate their therapeutic journey.

THE QUESTION OF ATTENDING CHURCH

According to the Pew Research Center religious landscape study (2025), while 79% of Black Americans identify as Christian, only 36% of Black Americans who identify as Christians attend church. Daniel K. Williams (2023) suggests that the great exodus from religious institutions is attributed to: a perception of these institutions' lack of empathy toward systemic suffering; the incongruity between physical health and mental health, specifically in the concept of praying away health issues that can be solved with the guidance of physicians, clinicians, and experts; religious institutions' lack of racial reconciliation; and simply not feeling seen. While the study is not exclusive to Black people, it includes their rationale and experiences.

Although there may be more factors contributing to a decrease in church attendance, the common thread is that Black Americans are becoming increasingly open-minded even while attending churches that may still practice from archaic positions, especially in the way in which they view congregants as one body rather than a collection of many individuals with their own thoughts, perspectives, and lifestyles. This phenomenon is even more present with Black women who, in their disrupted lives due to oppression, patriarchy, and racism, generally find hope and peace within the walls of their church and the words of their Bibles. Black women, who historically have comprised more than 50% of the weekly attendance and have committed actively to many of the committees and suborganizations within the church, are choosing to leave the church and find hope and peace outside traditional religion.

Spirituality, as defined as a way of interpreting one's experiences and the meaning of life, is an effective coping mechanism for many Americans (Park et al., 2017). While the terms *religion* and *spirituality* are often used synonymously, they are distinct concepts. Religion tends to focus on rituals, traditions, habits, and a canonical text, while spirituality tends to focus on one's way of being in and seeing the world. In other words, religion is focused on observable action and standard practice, whereas spirituality focuses on a relationship with a higher power that is neither seen nor measured.

In the *Psychology of Religion and Spirituality* journal, researchers Park et al. (2018) noted that, for Black Americans, there are far more positive tendencies associated with religion and spirituality than there are negative. Some of these tendencies include a higher sense of self-esteem, a greater sense of well-being, and decreased psychologically disordered symptoms. And yet, many Black people are still struggling with whether they should participate in church and religious practices, focus on spirituality and their relationship with God or a higher power, or forgo religion and spirituality altogether. This incongruence is especially present among Black women. When one is raised to be religious and yet feels unseen, unheard, and devalued within one's religious institution due to the historical and present practices related to patriarchy, it causes a sense of disconnect, which may or may not lead to mental health distress. Examples of patriarchal practices within religious communities include but are not limited to: women being forbidden to be pastors, preachers, ministers, or to participate in leadership roles; women being forced to wear dresses or long skirts, or cover their body so they are not assumed to tempt or distract the men in their church; women being unsupported when needing to divorce due to domestic violence, infidelity, or a misuse of family resources; women having to sit in separate sections of the religious building, either on back pews or another area; women being forced to marry at young ages or against their desire; women being encouraged to allow their sons to be with their fathers despite the character of the man; and women's voices seeming to not matter to anyone except herself. In short, she may ask herself, "What am I supposed to do now? Religion is not working. I cannot pray these issues away. And I do not want to spend my time, resources, and energy at a place that does not value me."

It is highly necessary for Black women to explore these thoughts, concerns, considerations, and incongruences. Exploration within the therapeutic environment is important because therapy is designed to be objective, safe, and client centered. While this topic could be addressed by the client with her friends and family, she runs the risk that her family is biased toward their religious practices or that her friends do not fully understand.

INSIGHT FROM A CLIENT: TR AND ZR

TR and ZR are a young couple who came to therapy for premarital counseling. They had been together for several years before deciding to get married and several more years before deciding to embark on therapy together. TR, the husband, participated in individual counseling as a matter of self-care, with a focus on managing his depressive symptoms and rumination. Therapy also served as an anchor to explore ways that he could be more flexible and less rigid. ZR, the wife, was a free-flowing person with a joyous smile, positive outlook, and fun solution for every situation. In fact, there were times in the sessions when she would benefit from grounding techniques to center her on a range of possibilities, not only positive and hopeful ones.

In the sessions, we spent a significant amount of time discussing the role of culture and cultural upbringing as it is interwoven in their lives. To the eye, both were Black Americans. However, TR's parents were from a Caribbean country, thus making him a first generation Black American and strongly rooted in the culture of his parents and extended family members. ZR's parents were raised in the United States for at least four generations. Their cultural difference was based on nationality versus race.

TR was raised in a very religious home. His parents were active in their church and religious holidays were an important time of the year. Through his young adulthood, he struggled with the pros and cons of engagement in religious practices. The identified pros included a sense of community, an outlet to his musical inclinations through the choir and band, messages of hope and direction, and development of identity within structures. The identified cons included toxic masculinity development, identifications of more limitations than possibilities, fear of failure, and the subsequent development of depression through the lens of not meeting cultural and religious expectations. At different points, he mentioned these challenges to me and his wife in our therapeutic setting. The conversation became extremely important when they started to plan their holidays, spending time with family, and determining if they wanted to set new traditions that would be centered on them as a couple and the possible children they wanted to have in the future.

ZR's thoughts on the dilemma were quite complex. While she did not grow up in a religious household, rituals and traditions were extremely important to her. She leaned into her husband's religion because of the rituals and traditions, along with the ways that it kept his family connected. She wanted these things for herself and their future children. So, while she did not struggle with explicit feelings around religion, she had difficulty with the ways to incorporate religious traditions into their new married life because she was inexperienced in the religious and cultural aspects that her in-laws expected of her. Additionally, while she wanted to learn more about the culture and religion, she did not want to fully acculturate because she found ease in her own family's practices too.

Through therapy, we set some preliminary options that included difficult and courageous conversations with their respective families. Additionally, they had to embark on a few activities that determined the priority of certain religious traditions while also considering replacement activities, too. While they have not had children yet, they have practiced these replacement activities and behaviors for 2 years and refine aspects of them annually with the goal that it fits their final desired outcomes.

Some of these replacement building activities were introduced through discussion prompts that included but were not limited to:

Discussing and determining what a *spiritual source* meant to them if it did not include God, Jesus, Muhammad, or any of the religious men who were outlined and promoted in religious texts.

Deciding how to engage with their spiritual source if that did not include prayer, collective worship, or text reading.

Discussing if they wanted a spiritual source, or if they had moved toward agnosticism or atheism.

Determining if they would still support religious activities with their families even if they did not engage fully in a religious practice. This included attendance at baptisms, christenings, and church-based weddings, while not planning those rituals for themselves.

It is important to note that when a client decides to remove one practice, ritual, tradition, behavior, action, or thought, there will be a relative gap in the emotional and behavioral space that the practice once occupied. Rather than leaving the gap open and running the risk that the client will add back what she just removed, it is best to explore and create healthy replacements. If a particular coping behavior is removed, a new replacement behavior should be added. If a thought is removed, a new replacement thought should be added. The additions of the replacement practices, behaviors, actions, and thoughts should be discussed with the client and collaboratively built between you and her. If the replacement is only built by you, it may be difficult for the client to have complete buy-in, apply the replacement, or evaluate its effectiveness. If the replacement is only rendered by the client, it may be difficult to assess immediately if it is healthy or if it's an extension of the previous ineffective behavior, action, or thought. The collaborative approach will promote more effectiveness, reinforcement, retention, and sustainability.

After several months of discussion, the couple reached agreement, with the understanding that what they had chosen could be temporary and subject to change when they decided to have children. However, encouraging them to engage in the discussion prompts created an opportunity to use skills in communication, problem solving, introspective and reflective processing, emotional expression, and team building.

ADDRESSING HETEROSEXUAL GENDER ROLES

Psychologists John Money and Anke Ehrhardt (1974) explored the natural behaviors associated with one's biological sex versus the social behaviors associated with one's sex. Their research concluded that most behaviors are set by binary cultural norms that children are socialized to from birth, based on the gender of the newborn and the cultural expectations from the family. Money coined the term "gender roles" (1955). Later research studied the development of gender-based toys and the analysis of how these toys and the environment influence conversations and the demonstration of gender roles (Davis & Hines, 2020). It was concluded that gender roles are socially constructed.

When we consider gender roles for Black women, who have always been in the American margins, the term and role are complicated and convoluted. Black women are on average more educated than Black men. Black women hold more professional roles and titles than Black men. Black women have a greater earning power than Black men. And Black women are opting out of traditional married life more frequently than are Black men. The environmental and social measures that drive gender roles may be less important to Black women than to others, and thus they must explore and determine how they want to engage in gender roles with their partners. Some of these roles include cooking, cleaning the house, paying for dates, taking care of children, traveling for work, being seen as the provider versus the nurturer, and dressing and grooming oneself in traditionally sexy ways or not. While some of these gender roles seem general or not worth addressing, a culturally responsive and aware therapist must understand that the intersection of gender roles and marginalized identities can be challenging, and there is a need to explore these topics, increase awareness and conversation for thoughts and decisions, and create an identity that can be expressed and shared with self, family, and potential partners or a current partner.

THERAPIST'S TIP: BE EMPOWERED TO ASK QUESTIONS THAT OTHERS WON'T ASK

Therapy is one of the few places where a person can engage in and be safely confronted with thoughts and questions they may have never heard or considered before they started therapy.

In our society, many people avoid certain questions or statements in alliance with being politically appropriate. Alternatively, some people are known to ask questions that can be direct and provoking, but lack safety for the listener and respondent. However, in therapy, it is expected that clinicians ask direct questions that create client introspection to yield greater self-awareness and transformative healing and action.

It is important for you, as the clinician, to ask questions, even questions that are politically incorrect, intrusive, or concerning. You must, of course, be sensitive, planned, organized, and clear. But do not avoid difficult questions; therapy may be the only place in which a client hears and thinks about something that is deeply rooted.

CONCLUSION

Today, Black women are offered more choices and options in their lives than any of the previous generations and their own elders. With the evolution of options, there is an evolution of decisions. While many Black women are choosing to stick with the norms and the traditions of their elders, there are quite a few who are deciding to pave a new path, rebel, revolt against old standards, and cultivate a life of their creation. For many, this may be exhilarating, powerful, exciting, and fun, while for others it may provoke anxiety or fear. There is a need to understand and process the decision to leave a traditional element of life while exploring the root causes for the change, the ways to respond when faced with curiosity or rudeness, and what it means to be a trailblazer, even in one's personal life. Be sure to explore the aligning questions, processes, and techniques that you can ask Black women and that they can ask themselves.

Therapist's Introspection

Personal	Professional
Before reading this chapter, what did you think about Black women and their engagement in nontraditional lifestyles?	Which clients came to mind while you read this chapter?
What were you taught or did you assume about Black women and their engagement in nontraditional lifestyles?	If you had an opportunity to redo a previous session with a Black woman client, what would you do differently, based on the information you learned in this session?
All of us have biases. What are two biases that arose for you while reading this chapter?	Whom do you need to talk to about this chapter's content? What do you want to say to them? How will you say it?
After reading this chapter, what did you learn and how will you put that information into application, both personally and professionally?	In thinking about your client's treatment plans, what new goals, objectives, and interventions need to be added?
What else did this chapter bring up for you?	

Therapeutic Guide

Therapy	Clinical Focus	Sample Therapeutic SMART Goal[1]	Technique or Intervention
Person-Centered Therapy	Congruence is a matter of accepting oneself (and another) without judgment and being self-aware Suffering/problems occur when one is incongruent. Problems occur when we lack awareness and acceptance and judge ourselves	Client will increase congruency in her life by identifying two elements of authenticity that she has chosen to hide, to be addressed and reassessed in 6 months. Client will remove two elements of incongruence between her thoughts and behaviors while replacing them with two healthy thoughts or behaviors, to be addressed and reassessed in 6 months.	Enhance the client's understanding of him or herself Eliminate or mitigate feelings of distress Identify where and in which conditions the client may feel judged Identify where and in which conditions the client may self-judge Identify and set clear boundaries Accept all elements about self; then decide what can and should be adjusted Utilize sand tray[2] table to address the onset of incongruence
Gestalt Therapy	People are capable of solving their own problems if given a chance to be authentic One shall not avoid emotions but rather walk into them, experience them, confront them, understand one's motivations and behaviors Use five senses to experience life and self	Client will identify and confront two negative self-perceptions that has prevented growth, to be addressed and reassessed in 6 months. Client will demonstrate the integration of past learned lessons with the development of a future ideal self, to be achieved in 6 months.	Increase awareness through confrontation of incongruencies Identify three problems and self-directed solutions Use feeling wheel to increase emotional awareness around choosing to live a nontraditional life Daily, assess one's engagement with the five senses (smell, sight, taste, touch, hearing) as a protective mechanism and a coping strategy

1 SMART Goal: specific, measurable, attainable, realistic, time-oriented goals. SMART goals are more detailed than standard therapeutic goals. The directness of SMART goals can add in client understanding, clinician direction, and the establishment of the therapeutic alliance.
2 Sandtray therapy is a therapeutic approach that involves the use of a sand tray and small figurines and objects that will allow the client to process and express complex emotions and thoughts without the use of words.

| Feminist Therapy | Examine oppressive systems that contribute to mental and emotional distress

Acknowledge societal norms and psychosocial factors that influence gender-based decision-making | Client will examine three societal norms and psychosocial factors that contribute to any emotional distress, to be addressed within 6 months.

Client will identify two systems that are counterproductive to the development of her personal ideal self. | Psychoeducation, especially using facts, statistics, and reading

Externalization in separating one's personal identity from how the world perceives them

Intersectionality identification. Temporary separation of identities to address root issues when possible or when needed

Resource identification and utilization |

Oftentimes, we, as clinicians, suggest homework assignments to our clients. Regardless of your theoretical orientation, homework assignments such as journal prompts serve as a bridge from one clinical session to the next. Additionally, homework assignments like journal prompts allow our clients to take time to be reflective and introspective. They can read the question and think about it during their chosen time such as on a walk, or while washing dishes, or driving to work, and running errands. At some point during the week, the client can sit down, write out her answers to the journal prompts and return to it later, to continue to process, to add more introspective thoughts, or to make changes. At the end of each chapter, there will be journal prompts that you can give to your clients as homework. These prompts are different from the catalyst questions. The catalyst questions are for you the clinician to use during sessions. The journal prompts are for your client to use outside of the therapeutic session.

Journal Prompts

Consider the messages you received while growing up:

- How was a traditional life defined? Do you fit within those standards?
- How was a nontraditional life defined? Do you fit within those standards?

Are you traditional in some parts of your life and nontraditional in other parts of your life?

- If so, list the areas.

Are there certain areas of your life that you wish you were more traditional or less traditional?

- If so, list the areas.

How has being traditional or nontraditional worked in your life?
- What are the pros?
- What are the cons?

If you identify as nontraditional, are there elements and experiences you miss about not being traditional?

- What does grief and loss look like for you since you are not traditional?

If you identify as traditional, are there elements and experiences you wish you could experience?

- What does grief and loss look like for you since you are traditional?

Regarding marriage, what factors contributed to your idea to be married or to not be married?
- Were those factors rooted in trauma, a negative experience, or a fear?
- Sometimes we call negative factors *lessons learned*. However, they are negative and counterproductive to our goals. If you removed those negative factors, would you change your position on being married or pursuing marriage or not being married or pursuing marriage?

As noted in the text, girls are often socialized to be mothers. Our first toys are usually baby dolls and we are encouraged to take care of these dolls as if they are real babies.

- What factors contributed to your decision to be a mother or to not be a mother?
- What have been the pros and cons of that decision?
- Based on your decision, do you believe you are missing anything?
- How are you treated as a result of your decision to be a mother or your decision to not be a mother?
- How has your decision to be a mother or not be a mother affected your mental health?

While having children can be celebrated and rewarding, what are some of the private and concerning thoughts you have about being a mother?

- What have you compromised to be a mother?
- What elements and experiences do you believe you lost?
- Where have those thoughts and feelings settled?
- Has resentment formed?
- Have other concerns arisen?
- Under what circumstances do you center yourself versus your children?

How do you identify your religious or spiritual practice?

- Why is this identification important to you?
- How is it similar to or different from how you were raised?

As you have identified your religious or spiritual practice, what are three new things you learned on your journey?

2

Creating a Legacy
Through Work

*It's not about knocking on closed doors. It's about
building our own house and having our own door.*

—Ava DuVernay

*Greatness is not measured by what a man or
woman accomplishes, but by the opposition he
or she has overcome to reach his goals.*

—Dorothy Height

*As a Black Woman with responsibility, I have to be emotionally
well because I am going against a 400-year racist narrative.*

—Viola Davis

In a 2020 article in *Time* magazine, Kimberlé Crenshaw, who coined the term
"intersectionality," explained what intersectionality means in our current day
versus when she created the term 30 years ago. She stated, "It's basically a lens,
a prism, for seeing the way in which various forms of inequality often operate
together and exacerbate each other. We tend to talk about race inequality as
separate from inequality based on gender, class, sexuality, or immigrant status.
What is often missing is how some people are subject to all of these, and the
experience is not just the sum of its parts" (Steinmetz, 2020).

This chapter addresses the lived experiences of work for Black women whose
engagement with work is not comparable to their racial counterparts or their
gender counterparts. Black women are the descendants of enslaved persons who
were brought to this land to work, and, after slavery ended, their relationship
with work was different from that of Black men and different from that of white
women. This highlights the nuance of intersectionality in their forced migration process, their race, and their gender.

There are more women in the United States than men and more white people than Black people (U.S. Census, 2023); however, these same statistics note that there are more Black women in the workforce, proportionately, than any other intersected identity. In diving deeper, Black women have a higher educational attainment rate than any other intersected identity group, thus creating the situation that many Black women are working and creating legacies through work (Anthony et al., 2021). While there is only one Black woman CEO of a Fortune 500 company, the U.S. State Senate Committee on Small Business and Entrepreneurship finds that most enterprising small businesses are created by Black women (Cardin, 2023). Many Black women are adding to traditional legacy routes through marriage and child-rearing and leaning into opportunities that create legacy through their work. Yet, there are several obstacles that arise in the process of trailblazing, being the most educated person within a family, and steering away from traditional legacy paths. In this chapter, we will note the pros and cons of being the most educated intersected population, having access to more money than the previous generation, being "the only" in a workplace, and trailblazing in industries, offices, and on teams. This chapter will also discuss the intrapersonal dynamic of Black women not being supported by other Black people and how this can affect the sense of community, stability, and safety.

MOST EDUCATED IN THE UNITED STATES: PROS AND CONS

The Civil Rights Act of 1964 and Title IV of 1972 coincided. At the time, all citizens of the United States were amid political turmoil based on international wars, educational and academic variance, and economic pressures related to recession. Marginalized citizens were fighting to be seen, heard, included, and ideally, valued. In her book, *Unbought and Unbossed* (1970), Shirley Chisholm, the first Black congresswoman stated, "Tremendous amounts of talent are lost to our society because that talent wears a skirt." Two decades later, author Alice Walker (1989) wrote an adjoining sentiment that reflected the thoughts of many Black women, stating, "Activism is the rent I pay for living on this planet." For Black women, this period of history was transformative in several ways that would affect them, their descendants, and the trajectory of the future, particularly through the powerfully persuasive perceptions of Black women in the workforce. During this period, women—and especially Black women—experienced a shift in their self-determination, which for the first time allowed their careers to be the foundation of their legacy, rather than the prescribed notion of children and families.

Since the 1960s, the consequences of the Civil Rights Act of 1964 and Title IV of 1972 have been largely positive. However, these intersected movements also created a cultural shock for the Black community, particularly for Black women. Between the era before the intersected movements (the 1940s) until two generations after the intersected movements (the 2000s), the data related to

Black women and their intersected cultural identities is aggregated, particularly because many researchers did not capture the data for Black women. There is data for Black people and data for women, but Black women were not the center of much research or of data-collection points. However, it is clear that between the 1940s and the 2000s, there was a 13% increase in Black women going to college (2% to 15%); a 100% increase in Black women owning legally registered businesses; a 24% increase in Black women homeowners (23% to 47%, aggregated); and a 20% increase in Black women leading independent or single lives (36% to 56%) (Besharov & West, 2002; McDaniel et al., 2011; U.S. Census, 2004, 2005). In noting a 100% increase in business ownership, it is important to acknowledge that prior to the intersected movements of the Civil Rights and Women's Liberation movements, Black women were not legally permitted to own or register a business. During that time, their businesses were legally registered under a male family member's name or were not legally registered at all (Women's Business Ownership Act of 1988).

Many Black women were able to make transformative change for themselves and their descendants due to the increase in educational access that included a high school diploma, undergraduate and graduate degrees, or a technical skill certification and credential. Black women were able to use educational success to increase the probability of career opportunities, opportunities that would allow them to make more money and have a different sense of freedom beyond the restrictive limitations of poverty. There are positive aspects to that reality, and for many Black women, there are consequences aligned with that reality, too.

Positives

- Increased alignment to the American dream (bigger house, nicer car, etc.)
- Higher quality health insurance
- Planned and paid vacations
- Increased perception of self-worth
- Possibilities of higher social status and acknowledgment
- Perception or reality of more freedom

Negatives

- The experiences and harm of being "the first"
- Few or no mentors
- Little or no relational and cultural guidance
- Remaining as "the only" for an indeterminate period of time
- Being the revolving resource for family members and coworkers to include giving them loans, being asked to do more than other members, and not being treated equally
- Being the spokesperson for one's race, gender, or intersected identity

Many of your Black women clients may be trying to reconcile their past and ancestral history (through the socialization and stories told to them by their elders) with the possibilities and vision of their future that they earned through educational attainment. More specifically, when people are in the middle of two different cultural norms, they are often attempting to seek harmony, control, and balance that allow them to carry forth past norms and values with present vision. Your client is no different but may not have identified the unique phenomenon of her experience.

Many of your clients may be participating in therapy to process the traumas they endured, the sacrifices they made, or the losses they experienced on their educational journey, starting in elementary school and extending through college and even their present-day workplace and professional development experiences. One factor that some Black women contend with is being the first or only Black person, woman, or Black woman in an environment that is not ready for them. And while this may be true for Black women in various social and professional settings, it often becomes even more apparent in the educational and academic realm.

EDUCATION IN THE UNITED STATES

The educational system in the United States was designed for white men to educate other white men (McGiffert & Axtell, 1976). During this time, white women were seen as lesser human beings who were too fragile to endure the pressures of education or too ignorant to be able to retain and apply the information that was taught to them. Yet, in 1727, the Sisters of the Order of Saint Ursula established the earliest formal, non-homeschool-based school for girls. Later, it became the one of the earliest schools to formally teach women of color that included both Native American women and Black women (Robenstine, 1992).

During this same time, many Black people were enslaved, and Black women experienced the dual trap of being enslaved and giving birth to children who would also be enslaved. Black people were not taught to read and write because it was perceived as a threat to their enslavement and an opportunity to rebel and demand freedom at any cost (Williams, 2009). In an 1862 article of *Harper's Weekly*, it was noted that in many states it was illegal to teach enslaved Black people to read and write; antiliteracy state laws existed from the colonial era (Rush, 1773).

During the postslavery period, many educational obstacles were created to limit the educational advancement of Black Americans. Factors included: large distances between residences and schoolhouses, teachers with limited and unequal education to white teachers, the familial need of income over education, inadequate and antiquated textbooks and learning supplies, and many other more nuanced factors that are beyond the scope of this book (Patsides,

1998). Given these factors, many Black women continued to live the legacy that was passed down to them in the United States: being a servant to others and meeting someone else's needs before they considered or acted upon their own needs.

With the emergence of the Civil Rights Movement and Women's Liberation Movement, many Black women begun to imagine and forge a life and career that was not limited to serving others but involved gaining education and making informed decisions about how they wanted to live their own lives. While this is beautiful and the American way, it came with consequences to Black women, who were still not considered human, capable, or American by many. These consequences included but were not limited to being misunderstood and subsequently judged, being ridiculed for having dreams that were different from those of others, losing relationships with those who did not support their dreams, losing access to social supports, and questioning their own identity and purpose because of the lack of support. Some of these consequences were not only projected by the majority population through the media and interpersonal socialization, but also within the family to which Black women were birthed and by which they were raised and conditioned. Despite what their families may have passed as legacy to Black women, the intersection of the two civil movements allowed Black women to embrace or reject their socialized positioning in life and in education.

For some Black women, it remained their purpose to serve others, not as a servant but in service. Note that the difference between serving and a servant is generally a choice and sense of empowerment. The majority of servants are in that position simply for survival. However, those who are of service have a greater sense of empowerment in their position. They do not need to serve to survive. They serve because they want to and can leave the position when they are ready. In alignment with the empowerment of choosing one's position, other Black women imagined and acted upon a legacy that was completely new to them and their ancestors, outside the role of servitude or being of service. For many of these Black women, increasing their educational and academic attainment meant confronting (and continuing to confront) difficult realities such as: initiating or enduring very difficult conversations with parents, caregivers, and family members to convince them of their personal competence while also easing the other person's feelings; finding money and resources to afford school; finding and trusting others to write recommendation letters; moving away from home; micro- and macroaggressions of an educational system built for white men, losing the veil of protection that's needed for the vulnerability of being a racial and gender minority; and acknowledging, addressing, and combating the complex emotions of fear, insecurity, confusion, and doubt.

Yet despite these obstacles, many Black women have chosen a life and legacy that reflects their academic and career journey. Their new legacy is related to work. While the older legacies that were passed down to Black women included work of service, the new legacy may include work that embraces their personal identities, curiosities, vision, mobility, and satisfaction, which may or may not include a work of service—but not servitude. In these cases, we see Black women who forgo the traditional or early path of marriage and parenting and use their younger years to build a legacy around work, work performance, and capital gain while climbing ladders and excelling by traditional and nontraditional standards.

While this seems empowering, it can also be daunting for the Black woman client because she is usually creating something new. The National Center for Education Statistics reported that in 2021, 84,633 Black women in the United States earned an associate's degree, 130,482 Black women earned a bachelor's degree, 69,548 earned a master's degree, and 1,730 earned a doctoral degree. Overall, this notes that Black women earn 68% of all associate's degrees, 66% of all bachelor's degrees, 71% of all master's degrees, and 65% of all doctorate degrees (National Center for Education Statistics, 2024). Yet, there still are a significant number of Black women that are not using their education or work as the foundation of their legacy (National Center for Education Statistics, 2024).

These statistics are discouraging and yet many Black women still pursue education and careers as the foundation of their legacy. These statistics represent women who earn degrees; however, it is missing the contextual and lived experiences for these women after the degree has been earned. For many of these women, earning a degree comes with lots of personal and financial gains; however, there are losses too. For some Black women, earning a degree comes with mental health and emotional losses such as being "the only" at work, being the first within the family; earning and having more money without the full understanding and education to maintain, sustain, or grow their money; living with the expectation to open doors and provide opportunities for others; and feeling the pressure to add a spouse or child to their personal legacy. While these words seem easy to write and read for you and me, they may be difficult to identify, label, acknowledge, address, process, and heal for individual Black women, which may be one of the reasons they are your clients today.

INSIGHT FROM A CLIENT: DX

Imagine: Being in an environment in which you are ready. You have the education, skills, connections, confidence, and competence to excel. Yet you are held back because of something you did not determine and could not control.

DX was raised by loving and doting parents who were highly educated, astute, strategically connected, and intentional about what DX was exposed to and how she lived life as a young person. She was one of many children, one of whom had an impairing lifelong disability that would prevent him from living an independent life, and yet she was encouraged to dream big, do many things, and soar despite the known challenge that her sibling experienced.

She came to therapy as a young Black woman in her early 30s, looking to create an identity as a postgraduate adult in a busy city that offered many possibilities and few known limitations. She was stuck.

She felt pressure to live up to the legacy of her affluent and successful parents, which included obtaining multiple degrees, getting married, having multiple children, and being in a financial situation to take care of her disabled sibling. She came to me to address and accept her decision to focus on her career and financial standing instead of marriage and children. It was a tough decision that involved egg-freezing, working late hours instead of going on dates, constantly explaining to others why she did not have a boyfriend or husband, and enduring the painful question "Do you even want kids?" While this was DX's chosen and empowered reality, enacted through many years of questioning, processing, wondering, then deciding, the loss, confusion, and doubt were still present. In treatment, we worked on her goals while addressing her sense of grief, particularly the perception of disappointing her parents, not continuing a legacy through childbirth, not introducing suitors to her parents, and insecurity about who would help her take care of her disabled sibling once her parents died.

Our goals included fully processing how and why she made the decision to create a legacy of work versus family; developing responses to uncomfortable and intrusive questions; healing from the struggles, sacrifices, and emotional scars that resulted from her educational and career journey; and finding ways to enjoy and live a full life that included all her dreams, not just a few. DX decided to change careers and focus on an occupation that would provide lifelong fulfillment, which would keep her engaged and motivated, resulting in the possible result of increased money, status, and connections that would allow her to excel and take care of her impaired sibling. In therapy and with this decision, DX constructed ways to talk to her family about this decision, build buffers in case she did not receive full support, and move in a direction that was inspiring, accepting, and one that she made for herself. It was her own freedom.

Years have passed since the therapeutic relationship ended; however, DX continues to check in and give updates on her career. She is doing an amazing job. She completed her newest degree, is creating a name for herself within her industry, is earning a salary that makes her feel secure in the present and for the future, and is inspiring others. She continues to delay marriage and having children and is perfectly clear and fine that she wants her legacy to be rooted in her work. While it took years of deconstructing, processing, and reconstructing, she is living the life she created for herself.

THERAPIST'S TIP: Bloom's Taxonomy

The taxonomy of educational objectives, familiarly known as Bloom's taxonomy, is a collaboratively created framework that was created to allow educators to track and support educational goals for their students. The six-level framework was created as a pyramid image, demonstrating that once one concept or skill is mastered, the student can move up and gain the next skill. The skills are knowledge, understanding, application, analysis, synthesis, and evaluation.

While Bloom's taxonomy is primarily used in the education setting, it is also a helpful resource when developing therapeutic questions for clients, especially when there is a therapeutic need to deconstruct and reconstruct cognitions and thoughts.

In using the pyramid-style steps to develop questions, therapists can move from basic open-ended questions that are centered on facts and perception to deeper questions that allow for a robust exploration of thoughts, feelings, behaviors, and goals. For the purpose of therapy, Bloom's taxonomy is used to deepen a client's knowledge and understanding of themselves and their experiences, while adding skills that will aid in the application, analysis, synthesis, and evaluation of their own lives. It is used to deepen, solidify, and empower the clients.

Including Bloom's taxonomy in this chapter is meant to ensure you have a skill-based framework when developing questions for your client, not just related to their legacy with work but for all aspects of their lives.

Catalyst Questions: Bloom's Taxonomy

When considering questions that can be asked to deepen the therapeutic process and treatment, consider questions that center on:

Knowledge: Facts, observable details, outlining, repeating, concrete, easily accessible and in agreement.

> Starter question: What do you recall seeing and hearing?

> Starter question: What details were present when _____ happened?

Understanding: Perception, summarizing, paraphrasing, interpreting, categorizing, making connections.

> Starter question: As you consider the facts that you have identified, what stands out to you? What is your summary and interpretation of the experience?

> Starter question: When you think about this experience, what do you connect it to in your present life? What are the parallels between that experience and some of the reasons you have decided to participate in therapy?

Application: Preparing for a decision, examining, weighing options, comparing/contrasting, determining, deciding.

> Starter question: Now that you have made connections and have a deeper understanding of _____, what do you want to do? What would you like to see happen next in this situation?

> Starter question: When we consider all the options for the future, especially as they relate to this topic, let us frame them in if/then statements. If _____ happens, then _____ will happen. Let us start positively: If _____ (what you want to occur) happens, then what will it mean for _____ (another area of your life)? If _____ (opposite of what you want to occur) happens, then what does it mean for _____ (another area of your life)?

> Starter question: For your homework, consider doing _____ to determine how you feel and if you can move closer toward the goal that you want.

Analysis and synthesis: After a decision has been made deducing, comparing/contrasting, appraising.

> Starter question: In thinking about this decision, where, when, or with whom do you anticipate a barrier? How can you plan for that barrier now so you can reduce the likelihood of a negative impact or a dissuading action?

> Starter question: In understanding that this decision may go against societal norms, your own norms, or the expectations that others have of you, how do you want to prepare for it now? What are some seeds that need to be planted with a few influential people in your life? What are some minor changes you need to make now so you slowly and easily enact this decision?

The following questions would be posed during later sessions, not in the same session in which you would be guiding the client through knowledge, understanding, or application.

Evaluation: Judging, considering, measuring, choosing the best options.

> Starter question: A few weeks ago, you experimented with your decision. What were the three pros and two cons to your decision? What would you do differently now?

> Starter question: In understanding the rationale of your decision and results of your decision, what will you do differently? What will you keep and maintain? What will you reduce or eliminate?

Creating: Proposing, planning, determining, deciding.

> Starter question: Now that you have increased your knowledge, added more understanding, prepared for a decision, decided, and analyzed and evaluated your decision, what are you determined to do? What is the result? What is the change in you or your situation that you are determined to see?

> Starter question: With the decision that you have made, what else do you want to or need to do to maintain this decision for the long run?

Note that this series of questions can be used repetitively for all decisions and processes that a client may need to make. The structure of the process creates predictability that can be learned by the client, which will allow her to go through this process outside of therapy and continue to make healthy and well-informed decisions based on her processing. This is a good thing because we do not want clients to be dependent on us as therapists. We want them to gain structures, skills, and resources that will allow them to maintain a healthy mental health. Therapy is the springboard. Not the result.

HAVING MORE MONEY THAN PREVIOUS GENERATIONS

The American dream is centered on democracy, liberty, equality, capital, individuality, and consumerism (Churchwell, 2021). Historically, Black Americans were without access to and legal support for many of these options, including democracy and the right or access to vote; equality. They faced obstacles to diversity in the workplace; lacked access to capital and suffered the redlining of businesses, homes, and schools; and they felt social pressure against individuality, resulting in a lack of authenticity in hairstyles, speaking patterns, and cultural nuances. As a result, many Black Americans centered their experiences on community and survival, which did not include a lot of money, discretionary or excess money, or access to money (Conley, 1999). Black Americans were socialized to the American dream by proximity and integration into the larger social norms but also socialized to community and social investment. However, as they continue to pursue education and careers, they are often confronted with a dual reality because they have more access to money than the previous generations and need to balance this new reality with a historical sense of community and expectation.

While it is true that there is wealth and prosperity in some Black families, it is not general, universal, or as common as with white families. The U.S. Census Bureau reported that in 2022, the median household income for Black Americans was $52,860 compared to the median household income for white

Americans at $81,060 (U.S. Census, 2023). There is a difference between household income and family wealth. Household income refers to earnings from a job, investment dividends, or social support programs. Wealth is the value of assets built over a lifetime including but not limited to homes, vehicles, and savings accounts minus debt related to mortgages, student loans, and so on. Family wealth refers to the total accumulation of each family member's individual wealth combined. Generational wealth refers to the value of accumulated assets passed down from the family's elders to the succeeding generation (Atske, 2024).

In the most recent report from the Federal Reserve 2019 Survey of Consumer Finances, Black family wealth is a mere $24,100 compared to white family wealth at $188,200 (Bhutta et al., 2020). The data is clear. There is a difference of $164,100 in the wealth gap between white families and Black families. Many Black women are closing the gap due to educational and career advancement, the ability to move to cities that have more career-based opportunities, and the results of the Civil Rights and Women's Liberation movements such as more access and sustainability in high-salary jobs and the diversification of high-income opportunities. Your Black woman client may be the first person in her family to reach middle-class or upper-middle-class status, have access to discretionary funds, and build wealth.

In a 2022 article titled "Money Attitudes, Financial Capabilities, and Impulsiveness as Predictors of Wealth Accumulation," the authors explain that money is retained and wealth is obtained through a set of learned skills (Fenton-O'Creevy & Furnham). Often, these skills are taught at home, either through direct conversation or role modeling (Lusardi & Mitchell, 2014). If raised in a family that lacks wealth and money management skills, the children often enter adulthood without the skills necessary to obtain or maintain wealth. This reality may be a factor for a Black woman who is the first in her family to earn a high salary, create a foundation for wealth, and have access to more resources and knowledge than the previous generations in her family. In understanding this phenomenon, we must consider the insecurities that arise when a client realizes that they do not know something or have not learned the skills to master an experience like wealth but are expected to know how. It may be difficult to acknowledge gaps in knowledge about key concepts while also wanting to know more about such concepts. Additionally, it may also be difficult to learn skills while continuing to make mistakes, especially when those mistakes may have significant consequences such as a loss of savings or an extreme reduction in financial security. It may also be difficult to learn skills and make mistakes while being expected to teach other members in the family or community. These issues will arise with your Black women clients who are the first generation to have significant money or access to money.

As clinicians we can address these challenges through a number of avenues such as political advocacy, social teaching, public scholarship, and direct questioning of our clients. Our ethical codes encourage us to be advocates for our clients, not only related to explicit mental health issues but also to the social and environmental issues that create or exacerbate mental illness. Separately, as mental health is being normalized in media, many clinicians are asked and encouraged to contribute to articles and news segments. These are opportunities for you as a clinician to educate our society on these issues while providing solutions, suggestions, and thought-provoking questions and statements. Lastly, and equally important, clinicians can address these issues during our sessions with clients. We can use Bloom's taxonomy, motivational interviewing, or various therapeutic modalities and ask questions: Ask questions that require the client to think about the implications of systems on their livelihood. Ask questions that require the client to consider how they have operated in and outside systems and social norms. Ask questions that require clients to consider how they manage their finances and feelings. Ask questions that require clients to create and compose a new identity that will enable the financial outcomes they want to have for themselves and the succeeding generations.

TALENTED TENTH: EXPECTATION AND/OR PRESSURE TO OPEN DOORS FOR OTHERS

The *talented tenth* is a term that was originally coined in the 19th century to define the 10% of the Black population who have the ability to lead the Black community due to their acquisition of a college education and thus impact social change. It was generally believed that this talented tenth should subsequently sacrifice their personal interests and use their skills, intellect, and resources to lead and build the Black community (Battle & Wright, 2002). According to King (2013), the term was originally introduced in 1898 by the American Baptist Mission Home Society but adopted and credited to W. E. B. Du Bois in 1903 as part of the essay "The Study of Negro Problem." Within today's Black community, though far more than 10% of the population now acquires a college education, the term talented tenth is still often used to refer to the 10% of the Black population that are most educated, resourceful, connected with other leaders, visible, and professionally skilled. The expectation of some Black peoples is that the talented tenth can and will learn information and teach it to other Black people. The belief is that in learning, teaching, and applying information within the Black community, the gap of knowledge and skills between Black and white populations will decrease because more Black people will have access to knowledge and skills that will allow them to succeed within the systems that are present in the United States. Controversially, this approach has been taught at universities and within homes and churches, and is a source of debate among Black people. Some Black people believe that, if they are in the talented tenth, they are responsible for helping their community, while others believe that their only and prime responsibility is to help themselves and possibly serve as a role model.

Whatever position one takes, it is likely that your Black woman client will feel and experience an expectation to help another Black person, either through a career, a civic organization, a social and personal setting, or even in their partner and spouse, because the root of the talented tenth is to identify who can help and expect them to open doors for others.

While this seems admirable, it can also be daunting if one is climbing the proverbial ladder while being expected to lift someone to the next rung, too. The question your Black woman client may be asking herself is: When should I focus on me and when should I focus on helping someone else? This question and its answer may seem easy and less complex when the Black Woman client acknowledges the intersection of race and gender and the subsequent socialization of her life. It is clear that Black women may feel at a crossroad in choosing themselves versus choosing someone else and determining when there is harmony and when there is incongruence. As therapists, our role is to ask the questions and provide the space for Black women clients to explore ideas of being within the talented tenth and helping them decide how to create harmony between self-preservation and helping others.

INSIGHT FROM A CLIENT: FR

FR came to therapy to understand her family dynamics, the role she played in them, ways to break negative generational cycles, and whether she was in the right career. At 28, she was willing and ready to explore areas of her life that she perceived as dysfunctional or stagnant. Through the therapeutic process, we identified that there was an overlap between her family dynamics and her career as a social worker. Oftentimes, her family members wanted therapeutic engagement without understanding that her job was to help others and there were clear boundaries around work hours, style, theory, and ethics that were preventing her from consistently being able and willing to help her family. In diving deeper into the family dynamics, we noted that she was expected to be the savior: to save others from repeating mistakes and perpetuating maladaptive patterns of behavior, from financial despair or mismanagement, from mental illness, from bad relationships, and even from poor academic grades.

FR had a lot of expectation placed on her and most of it was communicated nonverbally, through implicit messages, body language, avoidance of conversations, and statements creating guilt. Over 4 years, she was able to resolve her initial concerns, address her presenting issue, gain skills in boundary setting, communication, problem solving, and releasing things out of her control. She remained in the mental health field and had less countertransference due to her boundaries on work and personal life.

BEING "THE ONLY" AT WORK

Many Americans are familiar with the polarity of personality and politics manifested through Malcolm X and Martin Luther King Jr. And while they were men, they also became representations of modes of being within the Black community: Malcolm X came to embody a style that was clear, radical, confrontational, and bold while King was seen as compliant, strategic, passive, and collaborative. Many Black women heard stories about these exemplars from their elders, perspectives from their educators, and opinions from their peers, while creating opinions, options, and their own personal stances. And while these men and their passions, perspectives, and actions seem generations removed, their polarities may still manifest in the lives and workplaces of Black women.

Some Black women may enter the workplace with a goal of being bold and confrontational of improper policies and workplace culture, following Malcolm X's approach. Others may align with reasoned compliance and measured resistance while acquiescing to the norm until it is unbearable, represented by the strategic approach of Martin Luther King Jr. Despite whatever perspective, stance, and approach she chooses, a Black woman may feel disconnected and invisible at work whether she attempts to be bold and seen or quiet and yielding. This may be especially true if she is the only Black person, the only woman, or the only Black woman in her workplace, on her team, or in leadership. In short, despite how a Black woman shows up, she is likely to feel isolated in the workplace system and lonely.

Prior to the COVID-19 pandemic, researchers had begun studying loneliness as a precursor to mental illness and disease, specifically related to generalized anxiety disorder and major depressive disorder (Yanguas et al., 2018). During and after the pandemic, several researchers noted the impact of the pandemic on loneliness and general life satisfaction (Lim et al., 2023). The World Health Organization identified loneliness as a social epidemic rooted in social isolation (World Health Organization, 2023). The U.S. surgeon general, Vivek H. Murthy, noted that people across the country "felt isolated, invisible, and insignificant" (U.S. Surgeon General Advisory, 2023). In a 2020 study, it was noted that one in six Black Americans feels socially isolated, thus increasing the risk of depressive symptoms and serious psychological distress (Taylor et al., 2020). In a 2021 *Harvard Business Review* article, Constance Noonan noted that employees have been far lonelier in the past 3 years than they were in the previous decades. The coordination of the international, national, workplace, and race-specific qualitative data demonstrates that Black women may feel the most loneliness in the workplace, due to the intersection of their culturally conditioned interdependency and teamwork, compassion, and empathy contrasted with the experiences of social isolation, marginalization, and racial and gender rarity. When a Black woman is the only Black person, woman, or Black woman at work, she is likely to feel lonely and disconnected, affecting her work performance, interpersonal engagement with team members, and responses to supervisors. At the same time, she is also dealing with the negative impacts on her psyche, decline in emotional health, memory loss due to gray brain matter reduction caused by stress, and a general compromise to her sense of self, sense of safety, and workplace worth. It sounds like a lot because it is a lot. And she may not be able to articulate all these factors while living through them.

THERAPIST'S TIP: Research on Black Women at Work

It is important to stay current on articles, books, and other publications related to topics that affect your clients. As more research is emerging on topics related to loneliness, consider finding articles that highlight interventions and tips. To find these articles and ensure they are credible, consider:

> Opening your search engine.

> Typing in: Black women at work peer review or Black women at work professional journal article

> Selecting sites that end with .org, .edu, or .gov. Articles that end with .com should only be used for specific journal article sites like Sage Journal or Wiley Online Library. Selecting these types of sites indicates that the articles have likely been written by or reviewed by scholars according to accepted research principles.

> Reading the articles and write/type your comments, thoughts, and questions in a notebook.

> Looking at the references at the end of the article and select one or two additional articles to read.

> Reading no fewer than four articles.

> Reviewing your comments, thoughts, and questions from all the articles.

> Composing two or three questions that you plan to ask your Black women clients.

Lastly, when working with a Black woman client, be sure to ask her about her feelings of community or her feelings of isolation at work.

INSECURITY AND IMPOSTER SYNDROME:
NAVIGATING LACK OF WORKPLACE KNOWLEDGE

While your client may not be the only Black woman at work, she could still feel insecure or unstable. In 1978, psychologists Pauline Clance and Suzanne Imes coined and defined *imposter syndrome* as:

> an internal experience of intellectual phoniness, which is particularly prevalent and intense among a select sample of high achieving women. . . . Despite outstanding academic and professional accomplishments, women who experience the imposter phenomenon persist in believing that they are not bright and have fooled anyone who thinks otherwise. Numerous achievements, which one might expect to provide ample object evidence of superior intellectual functioning, do not appear to affect the impostor belief.

When intersected with the experiences of navigating race and gender in the workplace, Maura Cheeks (2018) noted that Black women often feel judged, compared, devalued, misunderstood, and undersupported, which aligns with the historical research and perspective of Clance and Imes but is coupled with the sense of powerlessness that accompanies a marginalized identity. This phenomenon serves as reality when one considers the brief amount of time that Black people have been integrated in the professional office workplace.

The U.S. Equal Employment Opportunity Commission (EEOC), which enforces federal laws that prohibit workplace discrimination, specifically highlights four federal laws that describe the illegality of discrimination based on one's race and gender. However, the most senior of these laws was established 62 years ago, in 1963, which indicates that your client's parents may not have been in a professional office role during your client's childhood. Consequently, your client may not have had a role model to teach her the skills necessary for office success or career success, thus creating the foundation for insecurity and imposter syndrome.

The Organization for Economic Cooperation and Development (OECD; 2017) reports that many professional office employees must engage work skills, mindsets, and actions to fully acclimate to the culture of workplace dynamics. There is an implicit expectation that employees, including the Black woman client, bring skills and mindsets to the workplace that enable them to learn how to navigate workplace dynamics, some of which skills and mindsets may have been learned from parents and elders. Such learning may occur through the conversations that the client has engaged in with her parents, the statements and questions she overheard as a child, the explicit advice that is given throughout the client's career, and the observations that the client makes in watching their parents navigate their work life. While these may not be the only ways that the Black woman client learns how to navigate workplace dynamics, it likely gives her a foundation but not a direct role model or mentor. The lack of a role model and direct access to mentorship could create a mindset and skills gap for the client. A Black woman's insecurity at work may be a response to a lack of role modeling and a lack of understanding how to navigate workplace culture. Thus, the insecurity of imposter syndrome is more than a cognitive distortion and may be a factual reality.

Catalyst Questions: Imposter Syndrome

When working with your Black women clients, be sure to ask them questions specifically about imposter syndrome and navigating workplace culture.

> What is the culture of your workplace? What are the phrases that are explicitly stated?
>
> What are experiences that are implicitly communicated? What are the cultural elements that you believe you are missing?
>
> If there are things that you believe you are missing in the workplace culture, list them. What are three things that you are missing in your acculturation to the workplace culture?
>
> Have you experienced imposter syndrome? If so, what does it mean to you? When did you experience it?
>
> How is imposter syndrome showing up in your life now? Which thoughts is it connected to and how do you want to resolve it?
>
> If imposter syndrome is a series of cognitive distortions, which distortions do you believe are present when you are at work? (Be sure to show a list of the distortions and explain them to the client.)

Imposter syndrome is a new concept. It is only two generations old. When growing up, did you hear your parents and elders talk of ways they experienced imposter syndrome and the ways they addressed it? Keep in mind, they may not have used the term imposter syndrome, yet they could have still felt, thought, and experienced it.

Currently, how do you protect yourself from imposter syndrome? Would you like to add more protective mechanisms?

Currently, how do you cope when you are feeling imposter syndrome? Would you like to add more coping mechanisms?

MICROAGGRESSIONS AND SEXUAL HARASSMENT

The emergence of the Me Too movement (coined in 2006 by Tarana Burke and popularized in 2017) coupled with the research of Derald Sue et al. (2007) centered on microaggressions have made the workplace reality for Black women abundantly clear: Black women are experiencing microaggressions and macro-aggressions in staggering numbers.

Lloyd (2023) cites 24% of Black women experience microaggressions in the workplace and Black women who earn more than $90,000 experience more microaggressions than Black women who earn less than $90,000. Black people who are younger than 40 years old are twice as likely to experience microaggressions than Black people who are more established in their careers. Seventy-five percent of Black people experience workplace discrimination compared to 42% of white people. Microaggressions are hidden and subtle messages delivered through verbal, nonverbal, and everyday slights that communicate negative messages based on one's marginalized group identity (Sue et al., 2007). However, discriminatory actions are not limited to microaggressions but include actions centered on wage gaps, promotion denials, lack of credit for project completion and success, improper citation of ideas and intellectual property, dismissal of claims of harassment unfair treatment, and unwarranted termination. While reviewing and thinking about this data, please note that it is likely to be underreported, thus indicating that there are many more Black women who experience microaggressions in the workplace. The underreporting is likely to happen due to a concern about a lack of anonymity, a fear of retaliation, a numbness to the experiences, a notion that it is too common and unaddressed, or a passive acceptance of microaggressions as a consequence to their success and perceived intimidation from supervisors or coworkers to the Black woman in the workplace.

The EEOC (2022) notes that 9,000 sexual harassment claims are reported annually. One third of all sexual harassment claims are reported by Black women (National Women's Law Center, 2018). One third of sexual harassment claims are reported by women who believe they experienced the harassment due to workplace retaliation.

Mosley et al. (2021) noted that while reported rates of gender-based harassment are similar between Black women and white women (24% of both populations), Black women are more likely to experience posttraumatic stress after they have experienced harassment. The fear that many Black women experience becomes their daunting reality while attempting to manage their workplace roles and responsibilities. The pressure on these Black women can be debilitating. In carrying the identity as a double minority, Black women are especially vulnerable in the workplace due to the combination of microaggressions, harassment, and psychologically unsafe environments that contribute to mental illness onset.

THERAPIST'S TIP: Microaggression and Sexual Harassment

When working with your Black women clients, be sure to ask questions specifically around microaggressions and sexual harassment. While it may be tempting to avoid these questions because they are uncomfortable to ask and equally uncomfortable to answer, remember that clients enter therapy so they can uncover root issues, address present challenges, and construct a future of their desire. When composing the questions, consider using a 5 Ws (Who, What, When, Where, Why) chart that will allow the questions to remain objective for you and subjective for your client.

Understand that sometimes Black women have been raised to be numb to these experiences because of the frequency of exposure. However, therapists know that while a client may report feeling numb, sensitivity to these adverse experiences is still often present; the client simply lacks a space where it is safe to process these experiences. Your office can be that safe space.

CRABS IN A BARREL

Many marginalized communities have systems, actions, and cultural expectations to support community development, financial stability, and career advancement. Consider that in many cultures worldwide, one of their business practices is to establish a community-style savings plan that allows individuals to draw from community funds in order to open an individual business and then repay funds to their community so another person can later open a business. While this is a well-known and intricate process that has traveled from West Africa to many countries in the continents of Africa and the Caribbean, known there as a *susu* or *sou-sou*, it is not a common practice within the Black American community (Mtshali, 2020). Instead, the historical foundation of a lack of Black American community support can be traced to the history of enslaved people and the introduction of Black overseers, also known as *drivers*, who were of the Black enslaved elite, due to their higher ranked position compared to other enslaved Black people (Van Deburg, 1977). The Black enslaved driver's role was to monitor enslaved people's work performance, drive work productivity, report noncompliance to the enslaved people's owners, and at times, enforce consequences and discipline as a community correction. The latter included beatings, rape, and death. As a result, Black enslaved drivers were rewarded with more resources, such as food, housing, and a sense of safety rendered by the enslaved people's owners; however, they were unwelcome amid their fellow enslaved communities.

While formal slavery in the United States has ended, the history of Black enslaved drivers creates a minor and unfortunate legacy of Black people who actively work against the advancement of other Black people. Similar to the metaphor of "crabs in a barrel," in which crabs that are trapped in a barrel could get out of the barrel and escape if the other crabs didn't grab the one that is trying to escape and keep that crab in. This phenomenon reflects an anecdotal message in which people, laden with fear, insecurity, jealousy, envy, or competitiveness actively seek to ensure that another person does not advance further than they do or take their position or station in life (Miller, 2015). Aligned with enslaved Black drivers and crabs in a barrel, there may be Black women who have an internalized oppression mindset that works against other Black women such as your client and actively hinders individual progress and community unification.

The crabs in the barrel toxic mentality and behaviors can be found by many Black women in the workplace. Examples include but are not limited to one Black woman holding back information that could allow another Black woman to successfully complete a project, one Black woman speaking negatively about another Black woman with the intent of undermining her character or work ethic, or one Black woman choosing not to hire another Black woman because she does not want to compete with or be compared to another Black woman.

Crabs in a barrel may be part of your client's lived experiences or fear profile. Yet, she may be hesitant to talk about it due to the prohibition against airing one's dirty laundry. In Black culture, this idiom refers to people being conditioned to not tattle, report, and share experiences that occur within the community, in fear that other communities may use this information against the Black community or against the person who shared the information. With the reality of both experiences and perspectives, it is likely that your client has experienced a crab in a barrel moment while also responding to the conditioned action of not talking about it. It is worth exploring with your client and assuring her that she is safe to talk about these experiences with you.

INSIGHT FROM A CLIENT: IW

IW comes from a family of entrepreneurs and scientists. I met her at a conference centered on Black women and our lived experiences. A bit of time passed, and she reached out to see if she could begin therapy. During intake, she mentioned several factors in her life that were causing distress and a complicated mental well-being. These factors included a romantic relationship, a complicated relationship with one of her parents, and some challenges at work. When we dove into the work challenges, it became clear that IW did not feel seen, heard, or appreciated at work, which caused her to be less productive, less engaged, and less motivated. As she described these feelings and experiences, I noticed a thread in her life. When she is seen, she gives more. When she is appreciated, she tries harder. When she is supported, her productivity and products exceed the standard. Over the following months, we explored several topics that are specifically related to Black women at work, such as being "the only" in the decision-making process and the crabs in a bucket unsupportive mindset that existed among the rest of the Black staff. About 5 months into this therapeutic goal process, she asked for a letter to support a modified schedule. She was overwhelmed with everything she was learning about herself in therapy, discovering how she chose this career and this specific job, and also thinking of ways she could change so she could be healthier, happier, and centered on self and peace. I wrote the letter, increased our therapy sessions, and encouraged her to add more positive experiences to her life that were not centered on work. Toward the end of her leave, she became anxious about going back to that specific job. She put in her resignation, searched for another job, interviewed the interviewers to make sure it was a good fit, and landed a new job that she loves and still has. Without understanding workplace experiences and dynamics for Black women, I might have missed asking a few exploratory questions that eventually led to her feeling more secure and stable in a job that she loves.

CONCLUSION

Many of your Black women clients will have experiences related to their workplaces and work identities that need to be addressed in therapy. While they may not present these experiences and thoughts as their primary presenting issue, work issues will take up enough psychological space to warrant several processing conversations. These could include discussion of choosing work as their legacy, trailblazing in their families and communities, identifying with the talented tenth, addressing workplace microaggressions and harassment, dealing with crabs in a barrel, or experiencing imposter syndrome. The therapeutic space is the perfect setting for your client to process, explore, share, and make decisions about how their work life affects them.

Therapist's Introspection

Personal	Professional
Before reading this chapter, what did you think about Black women and their engagement with work?	Which clients came to mind while you read this chapter?
What were you taught or did you assume about Black women and their engagement with work?	If you had an opportunity to redo a previous session with a Black woman client, what would you do differently, based on the information you learned in this session?
All of us have biases. What are two biases that arose for you while reading this chapter?	Whom do you need to talk to about this chapter's content? What do you want to say to them? How will you say it?

After reading this chapter, what did you learn and how will you apply that information, both personally and professionally?	In thinking about your client's treatment plans, what new goals, objectives, and interventions need to be added?
What else did this chapter bring up for you?	

Therapeutic Guide

Therapy	Clinical Focus	Sample Therapeutic SMART Goal	Technique or Intervention
Reality Therapy	Humans have five basic needs that must be met: survival, love and belonging, power, freedom, fun All behaviors are a choice; thus mental illness is a manifestation of choice, and choices and decisions have to be addressed	Client will identify which of the five basic needs are being met by choosing to create a legacy through work, to be addressed and achieved within 6 months. Client will identify which of the five basic needs are not being met and will create a plan to address the missing needs, to be addressed and achieved within 6 months. Client will make two correlations between current choices and the development of her ideal self, to be addressed and achieved within 6 months.	Development of supportive relationships, specifically related to work and career industry Therapeutic contract Creation of plan to meet missing needs List and review weekly choices Make a correlation between choices and mental health Review which choices need to be reassessed Assess control and determine where and how control can be met and where it should be released

Therapy	Clinical Focus	Sample Therapeutic SMART Goal	Technique or Intervention
Existential Therapy	Finding life meaning Everyone has free will and is responsible for their own choices Everyone is constantly being reborn and recreated by each experience and choice in their life Life is a personal phenomenon	Client will explore her life meaning through the correlation of the four worlds: the physical, social, personal, and spiritual worlds, to be addressed and achieved within 6 months. Client will identify three values that influence her decision to make her legacy through work to be addressed and achieved within 6 months.	Identifying and considering personal and professional values Assessing the intersection between the client's life meaning and choice to make a legacy through work Visualization activity: ideal life Increasing understanding of the client's worldview and the development of perspectives Explore the four worlds: the physical, social, personal, and spiritual worlds and the relation to the choice of work as a legacy
Individual Psychology	Focus on individual experiences, personal growth, and goal-oriented experiences Social connections shape behaviors and personality Each individual is unique and indivisible Individuals strive for superiority, purpose, and free choice	Client will create a year-long goal-oriented plan for herself to include two goals, four objectives, and eight interventions, to be achieved within 12 months. Client will explore the three ways that her personality influences her work and three different ways her work influences her personality, to be achieved within 12 months.	Create goals that align with purpose, to include but not limited to work Map out client's lifestyle and determine where the client may want to increase experiences to align with purpose Identify how social and work connections shape the client's behavior Identify how the client's personality aligns with or contradicts the presenting issue or challenging experience Encourage the client to identify when, where, how, and why superiority is important Identify the correlation between purpose and free choice

Journal Prompts

In your own words, define work.

What does work entail and what does it exclude?

What is the purpose of work? List four things and prioritize them.

What are the pros and cons of working?

What are the pros and cons of how you work?

What is your ideal work environment? List details and be willing to dream big.

Under what circumstances are you most encouraged to be authentic at work?

Under what circumstances do you feel silenced at work?

When considering your upbringing, what were the messages that you received about work?

When thinking about the messages you saw or heard about work, what were the messages from:

- Your mother?
- Your father?
- Your grandparents?
- Two of your teachers?
- Your school counselor?
- Your first boss?

When have you felt like an imposter at work? Think of one or two specific examples and dive deep from there.

- Under what circumstances do you feel like an imposter?
- How does it affect your relationship with work?
- How does it affect your relationship with your colleagues?

What do you need to feel appreciated at work?

- When you are appreciated, which feeling words do you experience?
- What do you do when you feel appreciated? How do you reinforce this experience with your supervisor, colleagues, or staff?

When you are not appreciated, which feeling words do you experience?

- What do you do?

Do you have a mentor? If so, what qualities do you appreciate in your mentor?

- What made you choose this person to be your mentor?
- What do they have that you would like to add to your professional repertoire?

What are three major lessons you have learned about yourself within your career to date?

- What are three lessons you have learned about yourself at your current job?

When you dream and think about your future, how does work fit into your vision?

- What do you want to be doing (actions and thoughts) in the next year?
- Next 5 years?
- Next 10 years?

How do you want to see yourself in your career in the next few years?

- What changes need to be made today to become the person you want to be in the next few years?

When thinking about work and your career, what are five things you are grateful for having and experiencing?

- What can you do to improve your work and career so there are 10 things you are grateful for having and experiencing?

3

Breaking Generational Cycles

I have learned over the years that when one's mind is made up, this diminishes fear; knowing what must be done does away with fear.

—Rosa Parks

There's so much creativity in brokenness. Brokenness will have you making it work.

—Issa Rae

Trust yourself. Think for yourself. Act for yourself. Speak for yourself. Be yourself. Imitation is suicide.

—Marva Collins

In therapy, I often use the analogy of a grandmother teaching her granddaughter how to ride a bike. The grandmother may work hard to teach the young girl the proper balance techniques, stopping and swerving skills, the importance of using both feet, the vigilance of paying attention to one's surroundings, and more. The grandmother often has additional thoughts related to pride, understanding that the granddaughter can escape many environments with this skill set of riding a bike. The grandmother may be experiencing humility in knowing that she is passing one of her learned skills to another generation and beyond. For the grandmother, riding a bike may represent access to a certain sort of freedom and independence.

The granddaughter walks away feeling connected to her grandmother, proud, empowered, and secure. Yet, the moment the granddaughter gets into a car and tries to use those same bike skills, she will feel ignorant, discouraged, mishandled, and unprepared. In some situations, she may blame her grandmother for not teaching her how to drive a car, when the reality is, the grandmother may have only known and been taught to ride a bike. The grandmother did her best to teach the granddaughter everything she knew. But she did not know that cars would be made, that women would be allowed to drive cars, and that bikes would not be used with the same frequency in the next generation as they were used in her generation. Lastly, the grandmother did not know that the future would offer a different kind of access to independence than she was able to experience.

In this analogy and many aligned examples, the grandmother did her best, based on what she knew and predicted. The granddaughter in her childhood was open, positive, and happy; yet in her adulthood she feels unprepared, ignorant, and cheated of what she assumes others know but she does not. The granddaughter (who is often your client) still walks away feeling slighted and may feel there is the need to break a cycle. But it is not a cycle that has to be broken. Instead, what your client likely needs is an understanding that each generation had its own pinnacle of knowledge, success, and application. With the advancement of culture, understanding, and technology, things change, and new skills are needed.

On the other hand, some clients may come to you with the burden of generational cycles and curses that truly do need to be broken. This may look like creating new cycles such as leaving toxic marriages, being fiscally disciplined, obtaining a college degree, escaping poverty, raising children with an authoritative rather than authoritarian parenting style, not creating trauma, addressing and treating mental health disorders, preventing or treating addictions, remaining physically healthy and fit, utilizing healthy communication and problem-solving skills, and engaging in self-love and self-care.

Your Black women clients may need your guidance in differentiating between the two legacies. Sometimes there is a need to break a generational cycle of harm and dysfunction; other times, there is simply the need to learn new information in order to adapt to an era that differs from the one in which your clients' elders were raised.

In understanding that bikes are still a very common mode of transportation, the use of this particular analogy within this context can help your clients understand the difference between being ill-prepared for their life because of the limits of the previous generations and the need to break generational cycles and curses. While it is true that some generational cycles must be broken—such as domestic violence, abuse, neglect, insecure attachment styles, and so on—it is also true that many Black women are in a position to learn new information and apply new skills simply as a way of being and not as a matter of breaking generational cycles.

There are skills that previous generations did not have access to because of the other challenges they had to face and trails they had to blaze. This chapter will discuss how a therapist can help clients develop skills to be learned to continue a family's legacy or to create a new legacy. It addresses core beliefs, behaviors, and boundary setting.

CHILDHOOD MESSAGES AND CORE BELIEFS THAT NO LONGER APPLY

Through the cognitive behavioral therapy (CBT) model that was created by Aaron Beck (1964), therapists can explore *core beliefs* with their clients, with the expected outcome of exploration, cognitive restructuring, and behavioral shifts. The CBT model is based on the concept that core beliefs are formed in childhood as a reflection of events and actions and cemented over time to form the core essence of our thoughts (Fenn & Byrne, 2013). The model continues with the notion that our thoughts, as core beliefs, will influence more thoughts and subsequent behaviors. In this model, Beck states there is a process: Core beliefs lead to intermediate beliefs (rules, attitudes, assumptions) that lead to coping strategies (Batmaz & Altınöz, 2023).

Core beliefs can be adaptive and positive, such as believing that one is lovable, worthy, and effective, or they can be negative, such as believing that one is unlovable, helpless, or worthless (Otani et al., 2017). As you read this section, please keep in mind that core beliefs are based in childhood experiences and that others' reactions created these beliefs of love and worth or the lack thereof. Children receive explicit and implicit messages about their worthiness that they learned to believe, and these beliefs continue to their adolescence and adulthood. Each situation that occurred over the course of your client's development either reinforced or challenged her core beliefs, intermediate beliefs, and coping strategies. One of these factors may have led her to your office.

In these situations, we hear clients say, "I can't do this anymore," "I do not know what to do," "This is who I have always been," or "This isn't working for me anymore." Often, this is a layperson's language for: My beliefs, thoughts, coping strategies, and actions are no longer aligned with who I currently am or who I want to be.

While there are hundreds of websites, organizations, and books dedicated to positive messages, affirmations, and mantras for young Black girls, one must note that oftentimes, these statements were created as a counter-effort, to combat the negative messages that young Black girls receive over the course of their development (Liao et al., 2019). While not always intended to hurt the psyche of a young Black girl, some of these negative messages come through the media, educators, family members, and even friends.

Media messages include but are not limited to beauty standards that have been centered on whiteness, straight hair, slim bodies, narrow facial phenotypes, and daintiness. Educators have created negative messages around intellect, intelligence, and ability centered on girls in helping professions versus scientific, technological, or mathematical careers. Family members have created negative messages around how one shows up in the world, often disapproving of loudness, boldness, and quick thinking and speaking while encouraging submission to men and perceived authority and simply being seen but not heard. Friends, who are often receiving similar messaging through media, educators, and family members, become the most consistent reinforcers of these messages because they are peers who spend the most time with them in the various settings of the young Black girl's life. While there are many more messages that are formed, either verbally or nonverbally, these main areas tend to be the root of the development of core beliefs.

Many of the creators or enforcers of these messages did not intend to hurt, harm, limit, or create negative core beliefs in the young Black girl. However, intention and impact are not always aligned. Core beliefs were formed and reinforced over the course of development. As time passes and generations continue to give birth to the next generation, the core beliefs of elders often become the core beliefs of our clients. They now seek therapy to address, correct, or end these generationally taught and reinforced core beliefs or generational cycles. The cycle starts with an internal core belief that becomes an observable action, which is viewed and mirrored by the young Black girl who is watching, learning, and internalizing in each situation that she experiences. And then she comes to you for therapy.

THERAPIST'S TIP: Creating Harmony Within Generational Cycles

When addressing generational cycles, you must be careful to create harmony between the respect of elders, authority figures, and friends who initiated the core beliefs and the strategic and therapeutic way to support the client's desire for change.

It is critical to keep in mind that not all messages delivered to the client by these people in her life were negative. These people, the elders, authority figures, and friends, may have created positive core beliefs in various situations, too. Your client may believe that she is phenomenal at work, sports, or boundaries because of certain core beliefs, but may believe that she is worthless in romantic relationships, finances, or maintaining physical health because of a different set of core beliefs. And one person in her life may have been the source of multiple beliefs, both positive and negative.

Depending on how you as the therapist approach the situation, you may cause harm if you demonize that creator of certain positive core beliefs in a misplaced attempt to side with or understand the client. Be sure to ask the client how she sees this person and their role in her life, rather than voicing your own assumptions.

Catalyst Questions: Addressing Core Beliefs

Consider asking:

> I notice that this thought is a core belief.
>
> Who taught you that belief?
>
> What do you think about this belief? (This is a matter of metacognition: thinking about your thoughts.)
>
> What do you think about the person who taught you this belief?
>
> Did the person explicitly say _____ (repeat the belief), or did they teach you through their actions or the ways they engaged with you?
>
> Is this belief still true for you now? Does it have relevancy in your current life, or should it be discarded and replaced with another thought?
>
> What were some of the other things that this person taught you?
>
> How shall we address those thoughts on this therapeutic journey?

Core beliefs are often formed due to recurrence, which make sense for the creator of the belief but not necessarily for the young Black girl who was a witness. A core belief may be adaptive for a certain period of the young Black girl's life, but as she continues to grow and develop, the same core belief may become misplaced and thus unproductive for who she is now as a Black woman. Equally important, the core belief may be misaligned with who she wants to be.

Core beliefs can also be formed by repeated messages via media and behavioral reinforcers by friends, family, and strangers. An example may be related to hair. Media-based beauty standards may have told the young Black girl that to be beautiful, she had to have straight and flowing hair that reaches her shoulders or beyond. She may have created a core belief that she is only beautiful and acceptable if her hair looks that way. In showing up to the world with straight and flowing hair, she may have heard messages from her teachers, classmates, friends, family, and strangers about how pretty she looks so she continues to straighten her hair throughout her childhood, adolescence, and even adulthood. When it is not straightened, she may believe she is less beautiful and attractive. These core beliefs may have made sense at the time, to prevent her from standing out, being different, being bullied, or not being taken seriously because she looks different from the beauty standard. However, as she grows older, she may challenge her core belief around beauty and attractiveness. She may want to become a woman who does not straighten her hair or to not see herself as beautiful because of straight hair. She may want to see, embrace, and love her coils and show that off to the world.

While it may seem easy to change her mind and thus her decisions, it may challenge her self-perception. She may struggle and form a dissonance between what she once believed and what she wants to believe. The challenge of this core belief creating dissonance may be why she is in the office with you but she may not know how to say, "I think I am changing my core beliefs and how I see myself." Instead, she may say, "I don't know what's happening with me, but I feel that I am changing and that scares me."

THERAPIST'S TIP: Utilizing Workbooks and Worksheets

In addressing core beliefs, consider using workbooks and worksheets as a guide.

Some therapists are opposed to using intervention tools, but therapy is about meeting the client where she is and providing her with pathways to get what she needs. In this case, the use of workbooks and worksheets may guide her to meet her therapeutic goals with more eagerness, application, and sustainability.

You can also search for workbooks via your preferred search engine or local library.

During the search process, put in keywords like, but not limited to:

Workbooks for Black women

Mental health workbooks for Black women

Counseling workbooks for diverse clients

_____ (insert therapeutic modality, such as cognitive behavioral therapy [CBT]) workbooks for Black women

---

Core beliefs may have made sense at one period in life as a matter of social, emotional, or physical survival, but they do not make sense to the client in the current period of her life or for who she wants to be in the future. As therapists, we must be willing to dive deep into a client's conscious and subconscious core beliefs of who she is and probe to determine if it is who she still wants to be.

LEARNING NEW SKILLS

When a parent or grandparent realizes a baby has been conceived and will be carried to term, they dream of the life the baby will lead. Sometimes there is fear, but most often there is hope (Noroozi et al., 2020). There is hope that the baby will be like the parents, especially if the parents enjoy who they are and the general experiences they have had in life. Sometimes they dream that the baby will be different from the parents, avoiding certain experiences, limitations, fears, and actions.

These dreams turn into hope, which is a key factor in raising children. Several studies, such as the National Survey of Children's Health, conducted 7 times, and the National Health Interview Survey, starting in 1957, have reported on the role of hope when addressing the rearing and development of children (Child and Adolescent Health Measurement Initiative, 2022; National Center for Health Statistics, 2022). It's been found that parents' hope is a key factor in the development of the child.

As a state of mind, hope is a longer-lasting emotion than many other fleeting emotions such as joy, irritation, sadness, confusion, and excitement. Its power to remain more consistent over time helps the parents remain focused on the optimistic and positive outcomes of who their child will be. While most parents and grandparents do not lose hope in the process of raising their child, they may accidently lean into their daily activities, personal coping strategies, and negative internal thoughts, all of which may dull the hope given to the child. When this occurs, it may overshadow the intention of creating new skills and mindsets that would allow the young Black girl to shift the generational cycles of the family, thus accidently promoting unhealthy behaviors and skills that have been passed down from generation to generation.

It is important to note that to break a cycle, awareness, intention, and consistency must be present (London et al., 2022). Yet, the rote activities of daily life may dull the ability to see and change a cycle. Most young children are far more observant than verbally expressive. While they can use some language through a string of 1 to 3 words by age 3, most are unable to fully align their thoughts with words to be expressed in full sentences until after age 3. Therefore, most children observe the world before they are able to verbally express themselves. On average, they spend their first 3 years in observation and listening versus using words and speaking (McLean et al., 2023). They are watching how adults manage their lives and handle conflicts and obstacles, rather than asking clarifying questions or expressing concern. They learn cycles before they can ask questions to clarify or correct the cycles. Familial and age-based hierarchies may prevent a child from asking questions, even after they have learned to use language, thus allowing their cycle to continue out of fear of confrontation or perceived disrespect.

In the *Frames of Mind: The Theory of Multiple Intelligences* (2011), Howard Gardner suggested that humans generally learn through eight different kinds of intelligence: linguistic intelligence, logical-mathematical intelligence, spatial intelligence, bodily-kinesthetic intelligence, musical intelligence, interpersonal intelligence, intrapersonal intelligence, and naturalist intelligence. Gardner created the multiple intelligence theory to counter academic psychologists and promote the understanding that humans can learn in a variety of ways.

As many Black women clients are entering counseling to address and break generational cycles, it is important for the therapist and client to be aware of not only *what* the client has learned but also *how* the client tends to learn new information. It is also important for the therapist and client to know what the client wants to retain from the lessons she has learned and to decide what she needs to release, unlearn, or replace from her lessons. The ultimate goal is for the client to retain or release lessons in order to align with who she wants to be.

Through this awareness, intentionality, and consistency, the Black woman client will be able to determine which aspects of her childhood rearing and adult reinforcement shall remain active elements of her life, and which elements should be discarded and replaced with new and healthy skills.

It is important to note that skills are more than a manifestation of hope but rather an active and intentional outcome of learning, practicing, reinforcing, evaluating, relearning, repracticing, reinforcement, and reevaluation, and the continuation of this process until the skill set matches the desired intention of the client.

In the book *Nobody Knows the Trouble I've Seen: The Emotional Lives of Black Women* (2021), clinical psychologist Inger Burnett-Zeigler notes that eight out of ten Black women have experienced some form of trauma and have learned to bury that trauma under the guise of the *strong Black woman* persona. This assumption of a false persona results in Black women having recurring discomfort in their interpersonal and intrapersonal relationships. These learned discomforts may look like accepting mistreatment; being gaslit and accepting unnecessary blame; being physically, emotionally, or financially abused; or isolating oneself in fear of misunderstanding or judgment. In other words, some of the core beliefs and coping strategies they learned as children are resulting in dissatisfaction in how they engage with themselves and others. Oftentimes, this may be a root issue that causes a Black woman client to engage in therapy. She simply wants to learn new and healthy coping strategies to deal with her life, as a double-marginalized Black woman.

In these situations, it is important to determine which skills the client may be lacking to reach the alignment of her current self, perceived self, and desired self.

THERAPIST'S TIP: Skills—Communication, Problem Solving, and Restorative Conversations

Skills deficits are related to communication, problem solving, emotional expression, boundaries, and a lack of restorative conversations. Each skill set deficit may not have been intentionally created by a parent or caregiver but implicitly learned through observation and the lack of a follow-up conversation or change in behavior. A therapist must be careful to not demonize the teacher of these unhealthy skills but rather approach the client and situation through the intervention of psychoeducation.

Below are some ways you can educate and practice skills with your client.

Communication Process
- Step 1. Person A begins the process, using the problem-solving process (focused on the problem, emotion acknowledgment, and solutions).
- Step 2. Person B summarizes what they heard (only summarizes but does not respond until Step 4).
- Step 3. Person A confirms or clarifies what Person B said.
- Step 4. Person B responds (cannot enter a new topic or grievance at this point; only responding to the original problem and acknowledgment of feelings).
- Step 5. Person A summarizes what they heard (only summarizes but does not respond).
- Step 6. Person B confirms or clarifies what Person A said.

Steps can be repeated once a solution has been identified and a plan of action has been made. If a new grievance is emerging, both parties (mutually; not one over the other) can decide if they have the emotional and logical capacity to address the new grievance at this time or if it should be delayed. If it is determined to delay, the new conversation should occur within 24 hours and the same process should be followed.

Problem-Solving Process
- Step 1. Identify the problem. Try to be concise with one or two sentences and one example (if needed).
- Step 2. Label and acknowledge the feeling. (Be honest. Be vulnerable. Use feeling words.)
- Step 3. Propose one or two solutions.
- Step 4. Implement one solution and determine the time frame for expectation/completion.
- Step 5. Schedule a check-in within 1 week. Add those dates/time frames to the conversation.

Remember, this is one problem at a time, not a tennis volley of problem after problem.

Restorative Conversations
1. Get Permission for Time and Place
   - Restorative conversations should always be voluntary for everyone involved. If you spring an important conversation on someone at a bad time or in an uncomfortable place, you decrease the likelihood that they will be ready to listen and connect. Understand that some people need time to process and time to gather their thoughts. Respect their time even if it makes you feel uncomfortable.

2. Appreciate the Relationship
   - Before you dive into what is bothering you, offer genuine appreciation for the person or relationship. Do not do this if it is not authentic.
3. What Happened?
   - It is time to bring up what has gone wrong. In very clear and direct terms, describe what you believe has happened or is happening that is causing harm to you or to the community. Avoid assigning motivations or blame at this point. Stick to the facts, and to how *you* perceive the facts. Keep it brief, so that it does not turn into a lecture before the other person gets to speak.
4. Who Is Impacted and How?
   - A restorative conversation always focuses on the harm that needs to be addressed—not an abstract conversation about right and wrong.
5. What Can Be Done to Repair the Harm?
   - Restorative conversations are solution focused. They usually culminate in a formal or informal restorative agreement. If the agreement is formal, it will be written down so that each person is clear on the solution, desired outcomes, time frames, and elements of measurement. Additionally, there should be two or three solutions, mutually offered, and one or two to be implemented. At the time of review, different solutions can be offered/implemented.
6. Offer Gratitude
   - It can be difficult to be on either end of a restorative conversation. Thank your partner for listening and for having a conversation with you. Express gratitude for a relationship that can survive the ups and downs in a kind and honest way.

INSIGHT FROM A CLIENT: TTT

TTT entered therapy because she simply wanted to "be different." Throughout her childhood, she watched the way her mother, grandmother, and aunts engaged in their marriages and romantic relationships. While there was genuine love, care, and consistency, there was also a lack of healthy modeling for emotional expression and problem solving. TTT watched the women in her family remain quiet when issues of miscommunication, misunderstanding, and disrespect arose in the households. She was explicitly and implicitly taught that men have difficult lives, and it was important for women to be the safe, loving, affirming, peaceful, and quiet space for men. The characteristic response of these women was to remain quiet on issues until the weight of the issue was unbearable, resulting in emotional and expressive outbursts. In these situations, the women would behave uncharacteristically, with a lot of yelling, throwing things, overspending, fighting, and threats of departure from the relationship.

They would use language and actions that mirrored the hurt they felt. Later, they would lament and engage in self-deprecating statements and actions as a punishment for behaving differently from how they wanted to behave.

As a learned response, the men in their lives would respond to the emotional outbursts rather than the root issues, which would serve as a temporary salve but never a true change for the issue that was present.

The learned cycle of silence, outbursts, and self-deprecation continued and eventually became the learned cycle for TTT too. However, in her most recent relationship, her boyfriend told her that she was toxic. He used this term to explain that she did not communicate well, causing their relationship problems to persist. He noted that he would patiently wait for her to figure it out but that she had to attend counseling and make efforts to communicate differently and trust that he wanted to work on their issues and have a lifelong commitment with her. But she had to do the work to address what we later referred to as her generational cycle.

Through the intake and case conceptualization process, I assessed that TTT was lacking skills in healthy communication and problem solving. I created a therapeutic goal that focused on skills development along with objectives that addressed her unproductive foundational learning. Homework allowed TTT to practice her new skills, which in turn allowed for reinforcement, corrections, and the measurement and evaluation of her progress. At various suggested times, she invited her partner to her therapeutic sessions, to allow him to express his perception of the skills development and application, while also allowing her to hear how he felt about her, their life, and their future.

The homework I assigned TTT included thought tracking; emotional expression in a journal, with the use of sentence starters and prompts; and scheduled emotional expression times with her partner. These scheduled expressions included a six-step communication process and a five-step problem-solving process. The scheduled times allowed her to prepare what she wanted to express, and the structure of the processes allowed her to remain focused on outcomes and resolution.

These two processes, communication and problem solving, allowed her to correct a skill set that she had learned through observation in her childhood while also breaking a cycle for herself, her family, and her relationship. The restorative conversations created the opportunity for both TTT and her partner to emotionally reconnect after an incident occurred, which decreased the time of tension, allowed safety to occur through consistency, and created security to be present in both. The learned skills allowed her to address and break generational cycles while creating a pathway for a successful future.

A year after TTT started therapy, her partner proposed marriage to her. Today, they are happily married and schedule maintenance therapeutic sessions that allow them to have skill-based reminders, reinforcement, practice, and success.

ENGAGING IN PARENTING IN A HEALTHY WAY

In the 2014 article, "Racial Differences in Parenting Style Typologies and Heavy Episodic Drinking Trajectories," researchers Trenette Clark et al. reported on their study of racial differences in parenting and parenting style, with a research question centered on the mental health outcomes of each group's children. In this study, over 9,000 adolescents' responses were tracked and analyzed to determine the impacts of parenting approaches and styles on the mental health of their children.

The four identified styles were: balanced, authoritarian, permissive, and uninvolved/neglectful. The results of the study, and many similar studies, note that Black parents who have an authoritarian parental style are likely to have children with compromised mental health issues (Clark et al., 2014). Additionally, children who experience authoritarian parenting styles are more likely to experience social exclusion by peers and expulsion by teachers, which impacts their academic, social, and emotional functioning along with creating a negatively skewed perception of themselves and others. Additional studies have been conducted to determine how racism complicates Black parenting styles, to include how parents see themselves and self-identify within the four common parenting styles. King (2015) cited the American Sociological Association study researching 302 Black adolescents and their mothers, which resulted in a clearer understanding of the common authoritarian parental approach as related to religion, social class, values, gender, and race. It was noted that most parental and caretaking responsibilities were placed on mothers, as a standard general norm and expectation. However, the intersection of factors such as religion, social class, values, gender, and race indicated that most Black mothers felt misunderstood in their approach, which, for them, was prioritized by fear that others would mistreat and abuse their children, resulting in the physical, emotional, or spiritual death of their children. Nurturance was secondary to sternness and fear because Black mothers were concerned more about their children's survival than the perceived luxury of nurture. This fear is valid, especially when Black children and youth have disproportionate infant mortality rates, childhood accidents, death by murder, and rates of depression, anxiety, and trauma.

Saleem et al. (2016) noted that many Black parents take an authoritarian style as a response to slavery and the inability to protect their children from harm rendered by the overseer and slave master. The concept implies that Black parents took an authoritarian approach to establish rules, boundaries, expectations, and fear, which was rooted in love but also a sense of preparation for and prevention of the harm that could be rendered by those with the authority to cause harm. Through this approach, Black parents used the only control they felt they had, which was to love their child through fear and prevention rather than the comfort of nurturance. The idea is: There is no love and nurturance if the child is dead. Survival trumps nurture and fear is stronger than comfort. In these situations, the nuances of right and wrong or good and bad are muddled in the reality of surviving versus thriving.

In relation to generational cycles, Black parents may continue the cyclical use of authoritarian parenting style because it is all they know. Remember, many people learn first through observation and then by Gardner's multiple intelligences. Yet, studies show that the skills used with the authoritarian parental approach may have made sense during slavery and the decades and centuries since slavery ended, but may not be necessary as society has begun to shift and change. This is indicated through the study results that note that most Black children who experience an authoritarian parenting approach are more likely to struggle or deal with a mental health disorder in their adolescence and adulthood. In my work, I associate this authoritarian approach with a lack of freedom and with silencing for the child, which later gets internalized and forms a core belief related to worthlessness and confusion, especially when the parental approach is void of context and conversation.

As Black women, who are often charged with child-rearing due to socialized gender norms, engage in counseling, they are likely to address and talk about their parenting styles and experiences within the safety of their therapeutic sessions. Their goal may be to share information, have a safe space to discuss their insecurities, or find a guided process to break a generational cycle. However, learning new skills and taking a stance against old parental approaches comes with a risk and the fear of doing it wrong or without familial and cultural support. In these situations, practice in taking a new approach and the counselor's support of a new approach are important if Black women's desire to change their parenting style is to have an impact on the life of the child and the generations that may follow.

THERAPIST'S TIP: Creating Space for a New Parenting Style

It is important to guide your client through the positive challenges of learning while applying a new approach and keenness to avoid comparison of other parental styles or racial identification.

Consider that your Black woman client may not want her parenting style to be comparable to another racialized or cultural approach to parenting, but she may not want to be authoritarian and potentially negatively impact their children either. While the correct approach to parenting may not have been created yet, be sure to address your own thoughts, biases, and countertransference in parenting so you do not project or displace your thoughts on your client.

CREATING NEW SKILLS

Learning new skills is a process that requires awareness, intentionality, and consistency. However, one may ponder the question of: How you can learn what has yet to be created? While the four parental approaches are clear and research bound, they are rooted in implicit biases that are void of the consideration of politicized race, incorporation of socioeconomic status, the changes of location and proximity of support due to educational pursuits or economic growth, or simply knowing and trying to heal for a parent's adverse childhood experiences (ACE) and personal traumas. Therefore, Black mothers may need to create an approach that is unique to them and each of their individual children. This approach can be time-consuming, stressful, and frustrating while riddled with insecurity, confusion, and a sense of defeat. To complicate the experience, some mothers may wonder if their efforts will lead to their desired outcomes, especially because they will not know if their changed approach was effective until their children become adults.

In the therapeutic setting, the therapist's role is to create a safe space for the Black mother to ponder, consider, question, prepare, express, vent, and become empowered to continue to try to break the parental cycles that she has identified within her family.

INSIGHT FROM A CLIENT: BR

BR is in a same-gender loving relationship with her long-term partner, SD. BR entered therapy in turmoil about her identity as a lesbian who considers herself masculine but who wants to carry and raise a child. While she noted that her presenting issue was around anxiety in her identity and parenting, she later discovered that it intersected with the ways that her mother responds to her identity and her choice to live a life of authenticity even amid religious condemnation and familial rejection.

Throughout the therapeutic journey, BR made several comments that she later expressed were Freudian slips or subconscious expressions related to the existential meaning of motherhood. Her familial cycle of motherhood consisted of women who birthed children, then used ridicule for correction and comparison as a matter of goal achievement. BR grew up questioning many aspects of her life and existence, until she made the determination to cease communication with her mother for 5 years. During this time, she entered therapy and restructured many of her cognitions of herself, familial and intimate relationships, and motherhood.

One of the techniques that was used during this process was the *miracle question*, which will be discussed in detail later in this chapter but, in summary, involves asking a client to fabricate a miracle after recounting a memory or scenario. While this technique is aligned with solution-focused therapy (SFT), it applied to this work because BR wanted to create something new (Miller & De Shazer, 1998). However, before she was able to create something new, she needed to explicitly identify what she wanted to create.

Through the repeated use of the miracle question, BR began to dream big and create a vision for herself through the lens of being a mother. She explored the ways she would confront her mother and the responses she would provide her. She imagined the obstacles that would occur and created a plan to overcome them. She dreamt of what her family would look like with her partner and began to invite her to sessions so they could dream and plan together. And she began to see herself as a mother in training who was empowered to break cycles and create new ones. To date, she is the mother of two children.

Additionally, for these types of sessions and topics with my Black women clients that are mothers or mothers to be, I check in on how they are feeling and what they are thinking about their engagement as a mother. I know that many women have been conditioned to talk about the beauty of parenting but are silenced in talking about the woes of raising the next generation, and this can be more complicated for Black mothers. Therefore, I ask miracle questions and provide a space for processing in each session.

THERAPIST'S TIP: Utilizing the Miracle Question— Solution-Focused Brief Therapy

(MILLER & DE SHAZER, 1998)

While there are several ways to create the miracle question, the format consists of:

- Recalling or summarizing a scenario that the client mentioned
- Making a statement at the end of the scenario: " . . . and a miracle occurred."
- Asking the client: "What was the miracle?"
- Deconstructing the miracle to uncover
  - The explicit problem or obstacle
  - The subtle problem or obstacle
  - The ideas of possible solutions
- Creating the miracle through
  - Identifying the locus of control
  - Empowering the client to become the locus of control
  - Forming a step-by-step, observable, and action-based approach to creating the miracle
- Serving as the client's accountability partner

TAKING A STAND AGAINST
OUTDATED PARENTAL WAYS

Trauma psychologist Elena Cherepanov (2020) notes that when parents live under oppressive circumstances, they create or reinforce survival messages, which can be transformed into resilience but also an emotional wall that may be hard to penetrate even for their own children. The result is a well-intended parent who may be emotionally unavailable. When that parent's child grows up and becomes a parent herself, she is likely to reflect on her own childhood; determine which lessons, observations, and beliefs were healthy; and which experiences, lessons, and approaches she would like to correct with her own children. At times, the way she parents her child or questions her mother's approach may be perceived as an affront to a mother who did her best under the circumstances of her own generation, socialized roles, and oppressive experiences. In these situations, we see that Black mothers become defensive when questioned by their Black adult daughters.

When considering the topic of breaking generational cycles in Black parenting, it is quite likely that many Black grandmothers lean into these three defense mechanisms, of the 12 identified by Sigmund Freud: identification (attach to something positive), rationalization (excuse and justify mistakes), or sublimation (divert negative into acceptable). When these defense mechanisms are used, the Black mother's child, who is likely your client, must be prepared to understand the placement of the defense without internalizing her mother's reaction when her mother is questioned about her parental approach or informed that her daughter will use a different approach when raising her own children. The preparation of this engagement can be processed in the therapeutic setting with the *empty chair* technique (from gestalt therapy, an imaginary conversation with a person in the client's life), reflection, sentence starters, question prompts, setting time limits on the conversation between the mother and adult daughter, or even scheduling the next session after the conversation occurs. The preparation of the conversations and defense mechanisms is to prevent your client, the Black adult daughter, from internalizing her mother's defenses or seeing them in a subjective manner.

When breaking generational cycles, one must consider the role of intergenerational trauma and how both addressed and unaddressed trauma are transmitted to the next generation, along with the defense mechanisms that are used to cope with this trauma. Intergenerational trauma is defined as "a discrete form of trauma which occurs when traumatic effects are passed across generations without exposure to the original event" (Isobel et al., 2020). In the article "Addressing Intergenerational Trauma in Black Families: Trauma-Informed Sociocultural Attuned Family Therapy" (2023), researchers Aiesha Lee et al. note the effects that historical trauma, race-based trauma, and intergenerational trauma have on the parenting style and approaches of Black families. They suggest that the combination of all three traumas creates a parenting style that is rooted in deep-set fear, a surviving-versus-thriving mentality, and seemingly impulsive reactions and overreactions. The additional complication may be that the mother and foremothers may lack complete consciousness of their behaviors, thus actively passing down trauma through their unconscious and subconscious motivations. Therefore, when a Black mother questions her Black mother (or Black father) on her parental approach, there must be preparation and prevention strategies in place that allow your Black woman client to process her own thoughts and feelings while also being able to utilize the six-step communication process. With respect to the relationship between an adult child and their parent, the therapist must also encourage the client to consider the context of her own childhood and her parents' approaches and the rationalization and practice of breaking any cycles that were unhealthy.

Due to the respect and deference that is given to elders in the Black community, the therapist must tread lightly in the preparation and boundary-setting process for the Black woman client. While she can question, confront, and express the ways she wants to be different, she must also consider the cultural context in which she was raised and the manner in which she can address or correct her mother without causing irreparable damage to their relationship while breaking generational cycles.

Additionally, Elizabeth Dixon (2021) noted that when choosing to break generational cycles, one should:

> Open up a conversation with their parents, notice any embedded patterns, attitudes, or narrative from one's family that one continues to portray, talk through these areas with a trusted friend, family member or therapist and consider an alternative way of coping or communication, culture a sense of empathy and compassion for one's family and the struggles they endured, and recreate a new narrative that one wants their children to embody and believe about their family, themselves, and the world (core beliefs).

Through this process, one must also be prepared to set boundaries with parents and family members who disrespect the ways your client wants to parent. When creating boundaries, clients should be encouraged to be clear in their semantics and tone, explain the boundary and provide an example that is centered on an "I" message, set a positive standard through if/then statements, and thank the family member for listening and respecting the boundary. The client must be sure not to cross her own boundaries because that will demonstrate to the family member that her boundaries are flexible instead of fixed, and therefore it is appropriate to cross the boundary.

Coparenting Relationships

In a study conducted by Elizabeth Riina and Mark Feinberg (2018), they note that the success of a coparenting relationship is determined by the support that they render to each other and the ways they manage conflict. The implications of coparenting for the family are centered on the child(ren) within the coparenting relationship, but also the mental health of each parent and the community that supports them. Feinberg's Internal Structure and Ecological Context of Coparenting model addresses a range of factors that influence the coparenting relationship, to include the context in which the union ended, financial strains, work characteristics, community cohesion, and differences between the two parents (Feinberg, 2003). Each factor is measured in satisfaction scales with ranges and descriptions for each variable. It is important that clients process their feelings and emotions in the therapeutic setting, but that they engage with their coparent in a manner that is more reflective of a collegial relationship than a former romantic relationship. This approach, especially when trying to break generational cycles across two different households, allows the conversations and engagement to be centered on logic, plans, and outcomes and less about emotions and feelings. This is especially important when contextualized with the fact that 38% of Black children live in the home with their parents that are married to each other, while 62% of Black children live between coparent homes or single-parent homes (Adeshay, 2024). In short, there are more Black children and thus more Black parents that experience coparenting relationships than traditional parenting relationships therefore Feinberg's research has specific application in the experiences of Black women, either as children of coparenting relationships or as parents within a coparenting relationship.

Remember, when breaking cycles, one must have awareness, intentionality, and consistency, which may be complicated when the time with the child is shared, and the child may have different experiences at the different parents' homes.

THERAPIST'S TIP: Coparents

Consider encouraging your client and her coparent(s) to have weekly coparenting meetings to discuss thoughts and changes.

While parenting is not a business, it is important that people can plan and predict a time during which ideas should be discussed, problems addressed, solutions created, and implementation strategies addressed and reformatted. The structured approach, which should include the use of communication process skills, problem-solving process skills, and restorative conversations, can serve as a barrier to intense and explosive emotions that are often accompanied by negative and impulsive statements.

Many people do not choose to be coparents. Upon conception, most parents dream of a traditional family unit. While working with clients who are in coparenting relationships, be sure to ask questions around grief within the relationship and the loss of a dream.

CONCLUSION

The process of breaking generational cycles is a harmonious effort between feelings and logic, reflection and introspection, and conversations and problem solving while remaining hopeful, aware, intentional, and consistent. It is possible for your Black woman client to break a generational cycle and create a future that is void of the challenges from the previous generations. However, she will need her therapeutic environment to be safe and void of judgment, projection, displacement, countertransference, and advice. She will need a space to dream big, create action plans, experience positive reinforcement, and be validated for her efforts.

Therapist's Introspection

Personal	Professional
Before reading this chapter, what did you think about Black women and their engagement with breaking generational cycles?	Which clients came to mind while you read this chapter?
What were you taught or did you assume about Black women and their engagement with breaking generational cycles?	If you had an opportunity to redo a previous session with a Black woman client, what would you do differently, based on the information you learned in this session?
All of us have biases. What are two biases that arose for you while reading this chapter?	Whom do you need to talk to about this chapter's content? What do you want to say to them? How will you say it?
After reading this chapter, what did you learn and how will you put that information into application, both personally and professionally?	In thinking about your client's treatment plans, what new goals, objectives, and interventions need to be added?
What else did this chapter bring up for you?	

Therapeutic Guide

Therapy	Clinical Focus	Sample Therapeutic SMART Goal	Technique or Intervention
Analytical Psychology Therapy	Humans are connected ancestrally Three parts of the brain: conscious, personal unconscious, collective unconscious. Collective unconscious is inherited from one's ancestors Lifelong development includes spirit Humans model life on archetypes, as primitive mental images from the collective unconscious	Client will analyze her archetype selection in relation to the insight on the collective consciousness to be done by review of two selected elders and two selected ancestors, to be completed within 12 months. Client will engage in two cathartic expressive moments per month, to last no less than 10 minutes each, initiated by words connected to family, individual family members, and elders.	Creation of genograms Creation of communal ecomaps Review of elders' and ancestors' personality and behavioral patterns Archetype analysis Dream (nocturnal and daydream) analysis Cathartic expression
Strategic Family Therapy	Families are a system; if one family member changes, the family will need to change or the sole member will be excluded or forced into regression Difficulties with one family member have an impact on the full family unit Development of a healthy family hierarchical system is available especially with the development of subsystems, acknowledgment of limitations, and acceptance of healthy boundaries	Client will understand her role within her family by identifying three roles that were assigned or accepted by the client, to be achieved within 6 months. Client will address three current or past familial rifts that may contribute to the continuation of unhealthy generational cycles, to be addressed and achieved within 12 months.	Empowering and strengthening the family through the lens of the family's current strengths and current collective goals Assessing and improving rifts in the parent/child bond through skill development in emotional access and availability Invite singular family members to the session and assess the sense of family cohesion as a unit Identify challenges within the family unit and create solutions for each individual challenge Prepare individual client for invited family member sessions through the use of the empty chair technique, role modeling, practicing statements, and creating responses

| Behavioral Therapy | Behavior is a result of the environment

Behaviors are taught, learned, and reinforced

Behaviors are present and can be corrected and changed with intentional effort

Related to mental health, behaviors are the issues and the reduction of maladaptive behaviors create a solution in mental health and processing | Client will break generational cycles through the identification of two behaviors that contribute to undesired outcomes, to be addressed and achieved within 18 months.

Client will adjust two parts of her environment to allow for positive role modeling and positive reinforcement as a replacement of broken cycle pattern to be achieved within 18 months. | Systematic desensitization

Behavioral modeling

Contingency management (contract)

Extinction

Behavioral Interviews

Mindfulness

Antecedent, Behavior, Consequences (ABC) Chart

Self-monitoring |

Journal Prompts

Some generational cycles are helpful and positive, such as supporting a positive cultural identity or extending behaviors that lead to financial and social abundance. However, there are some generational cycles that are outdated and need to be broken.

- When considering the generational cycles within your family that need to be broken, what are three messages, observations, or behaviors that no longer serve you or the generations that will come behind you?
- Honestly, is it your purpose or intention to break these cycles?
- If so, what are the three actions that you will take to correct these cycles within yourself?
- If so, what are the three actions you will take to break these cycles for the generations that will follow you?

In observation of our families, we tend to notice behaviors that impact the intimate relationships of our elders. Some marriages have lasted long because they are healthy while others have lasted long because of social and cultural pressure to remain married.

- What are the generational messages you have heard or observed that were helpful to the previous generations but no longer apply to you or the generations that come behind you?

- Which generational messages need to be broken for you to excel in your long-term relationships?
- Which messages do you need to create and state so the generations that come behind you can excel in their long-term intimate relationships?

When considering skill enhancement, which of the identified three skills (communication, problem solving, restorative conversations) do you need to improve?

- What is your three-step plan to improve these skills? What is your ideal outcome?
- Which barriers will you encounter? How will you address each encounter to ensure you can and will break the cycle?

When reflecting on parenting skills and experiences, we recognize that many of our parents did the best that they could do given the experiences, knowledge, environment, and understanding that they had. We understand and appreciate their knowledge and efforts. Currently, we may know more information and can do things differently.

- What are three parenting skills and experiences that need to be addressed and broken for the next generation to thrive?
- Which messages need to be erased?
- Which limitations do not serve the next generation?
- Which three repetitive and consistent messages need to be composed and stated for the next generation to thrive?

What parenting style did each of your caregivers use? What were the benefits to you? What were the consequences to you? Consider:

- The parenting style of your mother
- The parenting style of your father
- The parenting style of your maternal grandparents
- The parenting style of your paternal grandparents
- The parental style of other family members who influenced your childhood

When thinking about how you want to influence the next generation via parenting, what changes do you need to make to ensure the next generation does not experience the challenges, trauma, or obstacles that you experienced?

When breaking generational cycles in parenting, people may feel misunderstood and judged by their elders and by their peers. What do you fill your cup with so you can continue the work of breaking generational cycles?

- Who is in your corner and how will you express gratitude?
- Which statements do you need to compose so you are readily able to respond to those who may judge you?
- What statements do you need to compose so you can explain the rationale of your decisions?

Coparenting is tough for several reasons. Like most relationships, it is one that has intersecting emotions and experiences and even some moments of grief and loss, especially as one acknowledges the end of a relationship.

- If you have a coparenting relationship, what is the hardest part?
- What protective factors need to be put in place to ensure that you can engage with your coparent from a place of fullness instead of sadness and anger?
- Where and when do you experience gratitude to your coparent?
- How can you share those moments of gratitude with your coparent?
- What do you want your children to see and experience when they witness or recall their moments with you and their other parent?
- What can you begin to do today to ensure that your children's experiences are positive and solid?

4

Understanding Friendships

Anytime you get more than a couple of Black women together, you're creating this powerful mechanism for change.

—Kimberly Bryant

It means everything to be able to have support and hopefully be open enough to talk about things that another sister has gone through so that she can help me out. I think it is all about trusting. If you can trust a sister to be open and speak your truth, she can possibly come right back to you with something that can help you through the scenario.

—MC Lyte

I am my sister's keeper.

—Maya Angelou

ATTACHMENT FORMATION

During adolescence, our primary attachment figures shift from our parents and caretakers to our friends and social groups. Under the theories of attachment and object relations, the security of connection, emotional intimacy, moral alignment, and identity formation extends beyond the walls of our homes and into the spaces of schools, neighborhoods, and civic organizations. As we continue to grow older and mature, we tend to keep the same patterns of connections with friend groups even as the friends themselves shift. This simply means that the ways we interacted with our family will show up in our interactions with friends, either causing us to mirror or reverse the roles we play in our families, and nothing in between, unless we have done the work to identify, address, and change what we want to amplify or leave behind in these relationships.

With the understanding that many Black parents raised their children for survival and the tenacity to break generational cycles or break glass ceilings, there were times in which nurturing was less a priority, because who shall one nurture if one does not survive (Berrey, 2009)? Therefore, nurture was an afterthought, and when it was present it often showed up as tough love, strict rules, or a special day of care such as a birthday, a vacation day, or the making of one's favorite food item.

In thinking about *The 5 Love Languages* by Gary Chapman (2015), it is likely that most Black children experience all aspects of love but not the fullness of love languages. For example, one may have experienced physical touch but not daily, or one may have experienced words of affirmation but only when they did something spectacular. The lack of the fullness of that love or the fullness of understanding the complexities of that love expression is internalized in the lives of many Black children, and they are left to seek this affirmation in their friend groups. It is likely that many Black children establish friendships based on what is missing in their lives at home. However, the challenge is that they can know or feel what is missing and not know how to get what they need or what their role is in fulfilling the need.

As adults, people move through friendships based on what was present in their childhood and what was missing. This is a strength if awareness is present, because it means that one can choose the people that are in one's life. There is power in choice. While this may be true for all people, it may be especially true and heightened in the case of Black people, especially when conceptualized with history, marginalization, oppression, and choice.

This chapter will address the importance of friendship for Black women and the skills that are needed for them to remain consistently invested in their friendships (despite potentially insecure attachment styles) and aware of their expectations, triggers, and boundaries in these unique engagements.

While this chapter may seem straightforward, the connection to the historical implications of friends and one's village and the biological and chemical development for girls, integrated with theoretical orientations such as attachment theory and object relations theory create a nuanced position that many Black women feel and experience. However, some of these Black women, who might be your clients, may have a hard time labeling their friendship-based emotions and experiences, thus making it more difficult to address, both within and outside the therapeutic environment.

Emotions related to friendship (or its lack) can include loneliness, confusion, frustration, abandonment, disconnection, and more. While we acknowledge that healthy friendships yield primarily positive feelings, we must also note that maintaining friendships can be challenging too. The implications for both positive and challenging friendships can and do arise in the therapeutic setting; therefore, it is important that you as the therapist are aware of the intersections and overlaps that can and will affect your Black woman client.

History

In Ghanian Akan Adinkra history and symbolism, the Sankofa represents the concept of looking back while moving forward. As we consider history, the Sankofa reminds us that we must know and accept our past, so we know when and how to look ahead and be better (Stanley & Chukwuorji, 2024).

With this in mind, we must consider the historical significance of friendships among Black women. Rooted in the traditional African elements of the village, a Black girl's parents were the primary caregivers but the neighborhood, consisting of friends, was equally responsible for the child's emotional, mental, and physical survival too (Reupert et al., 2022). With the shared and equal investment in raising a child, this collectivist cultural mindset both aligned with and was opposed to attachment theory. The privilege to provide all emotional needs was not just placed on one or two individuals who were the birth parents, but rather it was placed on the entire community. The individual was attached to the entire community, including the parents, the grandparents, the elders, the ancestors, the siblings, cousins, and peers, and their friends.

During slavery, friendships were much more important. Indeed, there was slavery prior to European colonization in the Americas; however, in those situations, warriors and families who were enslaved were kept together (*Lowcountry Digital History Initiative*, n.d.). They were able to maintain family bonds and community-centric socialization, which allowed for the continuation of values and of stories and parables that aligned with courage, resilience, emotional awareness, and psychological stability. However, when the transatlantic slave trade began, families were separated, cultural communities were violated, and values, religion, and language were divided (Williams, 2012).

However, one of the main concepts that remained was village. This concept and practice of the connected village crossed the Atlantic Ocean and was extremely important to the physical, emotional, and psychological survival of our African ancestors, especially in the face of separation, as children were removed from their mothers and the plantations of their birth and sold to other slave masters and given to other enslaved people to care for (Field, 2014). It was during this time that Black people's connections to friendships and nonfamilial relations became just as important, if not more important, than family ties. These fictive kinships allowed for the development of interdependence that resembled traditional kinship and community ties like a village.

THERAPIST'S TIP: Imagination Exercise—Separation From a Child

Imagine being a mother who just gave birth to a child. Engorged with milk, swollen from pregnancy, exhausted from natural birth sans any epidural or pain medicine while experiencing hormonal and emotional shifts oscillating between happiness, gratitude, fear, and pain. Imagine bleeding from the birth, but being required to tend to the plantation the next day, despite the temperature, weather, or healing delays. Imagine the possibility of this baby being fathered by your master and you still loving the child as if she were conceived in love as opposed to rape and possession.

In all of this, imagine your newborn infant being forcibly removed from you before you can nurse, bathe, pray over, and bless your baby.

Imagine your baby being taken to an unknown place, given to unknown people, to experience the pain and destruction of what is known: enslavement without care, identity annihilation with no traceable kinship and legacy, and the lack of a mother's love.

Imagine being taken to a new plantation while still swollen from childbirth and needing people, complete strangers, to still take care of you in your postpartum state that is ridden with anxiety as you struggle to imagine how your newly born child is doing. Imagine the thoughts and feelings that flow through your mind while your body is trying to regain strength, and knowing that within days, you will have to labor day and night for a slave master who does not know you but has placed financial value on your strength and abilities.

Imagine all these things and consider how much you must rely on the fellow enslaved people on the plantation with you and the fellow enslaved people who are on the other plantation, raising your child, whom you may never meet or see again.

Then imagine being the child who was forcibly separated from your mother, and being raised by nonfamilial members of the plantation. In this imagined scenario, consider how it would be to be physically and emotionally dependent on people who do not have to take care of you but choose to take care of you. That element of choice would not replace the mother's love and care, but it demonstrates that you are still seen, heard, and valued, even within the confines of slavery.

This is a gentle imagining of the real experiences that enslaved Black women faced with regular cadence. And because of these experiences, Black women, and their separated babies, learned that chosen family, fictive kinships, and friends were likely to be more long-lasting than familial relationships.

Catalyst Questions: Fictive Relationships

When working with your Black women clients, ask them about the roots and reasons for their deepest fictive kinship relationships and the roles that each of these friendships have on the impact of their physical, emotional, and spiritual survival.

- When thinking of fictive kinship and close friendships, who are your two closest friends? Why?

- What characteristics and personality types distinguish them from your other friends?
- When thinking of these fictive kinships, name three examples when they have aided in your survival, physically, emotionally, and spiritually.
- How would your life be different without these fictive kinships?

Development

In the textbook *Exploring Lifespan Development*, Laura E. Berk (2017) notes that there are at least seven theories that are specifically related to human development, including Piaget's cognitive development theory, Vygotsky's sociocultural theory, and Erikson's psychosocial theory. There are many other human development theories that are woven into some of the other traditional theories too, such as behaviorism and social learning, ecological systems theory, and attachment theory. Most of these human development theories were written by white men and a few white women, such as Urie Bronfenbrenner, Erik Erikson, and Mary Ainsworth.

While we know and understand that mental health and psychological theories were developing across the world at the same time, our collective learning is centered on just a few theories of human development and nature that were written by white people, who are only 9–12% of the world's population (Leahey, 2017). The influence of white European culture on Black development is based on misguided theories created by white people—who are a universal minority in the world. Yet, these theories have dictated the ways Black children are measured in development and curved normalization.

Most traditional and published theories of psychology and mental health were developed by men who, according to the Pew Research Center, are only 2% higher in worldwide gender representation than women (Blazina, 2024). Most of the human development theories that were developed were created by a worldwide racial minority group and a bare majority gender group yet drive perception of normality for all other racial and gender groups land specifically Black women.

In most human development theories, there is a common theme that girls' social development occurs before boys' social development while boys' physical development occurs before girls' physical development (Papalia & Martorell, 2021). This perception is supported by the advanced frontal cortex development that occurs in girls before it occurs in boys, which tends to result in early speech and vocabulary coupled with the perceived nature of care and nurturing (Papalia & Martorell, 2021). Consequently, it creates a gender stereotype that girls are more inclined to have healthy social relationships in childhood before boys have similar experiences (Papalia & Martorell, 2021). Furthermore, stereotyping creates gendered behaviors that girls will have friends and sustainable interpersonal interactions before boys. This theoretical perspective creates expectations of friendship development and the influence that friends who are girls have on the social development of their other friends who are also girls. In short, there is a skewed perception, supported by research, that women make and keep friends longer than men and that these friends can and should influence each others' lives.

However, another realistic perspective is centered on the fact that, early frontal cortex brain development aside, girls are often socialized to sit and talk, especially with their dolls and siblings, while boys are socialized to move and show strength through their bodies. Therefore, when we look at friendships, primarily for girls, we must intersect gender, natural development, and nurture-based socialization. Women-based friendships tend to contain a lot of words because language development occurs in girls quicker than boys, a lot of expressed emotions because language acquisition allows for increased emotional expression and acknowledgment, and a lot of intimacy and bonding because women release the bonding hormone oxytocin at a rate that is four times more frequent than men (Adani & Cepanec, 2019; Lindquist et al., 2015; Marazziti et al., 2019).

When these biological and chemical factors are conjoined, it can create an environment in which women form friendships quickly and with ease. When these factors intersect with race, specifically for Black women, who have a historical connection with and need for consistent community, we can recognize the paramount role of friendships in their lives. The need for friendships surpasses the historical yet still present need of fictive families but extends to the establishment of safe havens in different areas of their lives. These safe havens that allow for authenticity, vulnerability, full emotional expression range, and general companionship can serve as salve to women who are in emotional pain or in the healing process. Modern day safe havens can be formed as *sister circles*, book clubs, neighborhood groups, mother-based organizations like Jack and Jill of America and Mocha Moms, sororities like Delta Sigma Theta or Alpha Kappa Alpha, or business collaborations such as The BOW Collective or The Links. Other safe havens can form as 1:1 friendships, small groups, or shared experience commonalities. The goal of these safe havens is to provide a sense of safety, security, and most importantly friendship.

INSIGHT FROM A CLIENT: KJJ

KJJ is in therapy to address her family lineage of depression. It is likely that her grandmother and mother lived and suffered with depression. However, without access to services or the opportunity to overcome the stigma associated with receiving therapeutic services, neither woman was able to address, treat, and heal from her depression. They developed coping skills that created distance in their families, whether it was an emotional wall that did not allow for vulnerability, transparency, or connection or whether it was the development of a substance use disorder to self-medicate. KJJ was predisposed to major depressive disorder and learned how to live and suffer within the diagnosis.

With months of contemplation, she decided to engage in therapy. There was much to address, including grief, core beliefs, fighting against gender norms, and accepting that her life might not be how she thought it would be, but she could create a new version that aligned with her hopes, dreams, skills, and abilities.

While in therapy, she realized that she did not have a lot of friends because she did not know how to be a friend. She lacked the skills, self-awareness, personal operational definition of friendship, and the trust to be vulnerable, transparent, and secure. In one simple statement, this reality became clear, and she began to understand that she had to learn, work, and trust in friendship as a matter of combating the loneliness she was experiencing. Equally, she understood that she had to communicate this awareness and deficit to the people in her life with whom she wanted a closer relationship, so everyone could understand, agree, and accept to walk on the treatment and healing journey with her.

FROM THE FIRST FRIEND TO THE CURRENT FRIEND

Oftentimes, when we use the term *relationships*, we are referring to intimate partnerships, collegial interactions, or friendships. However, the first relationship we often experience and the one that tends to be most long lasting is the relationship we have with ourselves. This unique yet unavoidable relationship should resemble a friendship.

In all friendships, especially the friendship that we have with ourselves, we should speak kindly, be encouraging, hold ourselves accountable for growth and evolution, learn from our experiences, and apply wisdom. When creating a friendship with ourselves, we must consider the role of communication and the outcomes on our self-concept, self-esteem, and self-regulation (Racy & Morin, 2024). While each of these impressions is centered on ourself and our friendship with ourselves, it is important to note that these skills and concepts are transferable to our friendships with others and our engagement in and out of their presence.

Communication with ourself, referred to as self-talk, is constant, consistent, and inevitable. How we speak to ourselves is connected to our thoughts about ourselves, which reflects our core beliefs.

The demonstration of core beliefs, either by self-talk or reaction formation is transferrable to the external friendships that we form. Using the common assumption that people tend to create friendships with people who are like them, we can understand that our clients may be friends with people who have similar beliefs, self-talk expressions, and demonstrations of reactions to experiences. A 2023 study conducted by Schwyck et al. suggested that most people form friendships with others who are like them and can create predictability and reciprocity within the friendship. In other words, people tend to be friends with people who will treat them the way they treat themselves.

From a therapeutic perspective, we must consider what our clients' friendships are with themselves, because that will determine what types of friendships they have with others. Therefore, we must take an approach of exploring our clients' self-talk, self-concept, ways they manage internal and external conflict, and ways they find hope and joy. These concepts will be likely be reflected in the friendships they form and the friendships they maintain.

We must prepare our clients that as they shift and change due to exploration, healing, and transformation, there will be an effect on their closest friendships. Since friendships have formed on similarities, reflections of beliefs and behaviors, and reciprocity, when our clients transform, they will need and want different experiences and demonstrations in their friendship. For some friendships, the shift may be welcomed, and the friend will choose to shift and match their friend. In some friendships, there may be loss coupled with grief. The therapeutic space can serve as a safe haven for processing, decision-making, and sustainability within their chosen transformation.

The first friendship is with the self and that friendship becomes the blueprint of how the client will interact with other people. To be a good friend and have good friends, the client must know herself, the type of person she is, the type of person she wants to be, the friendships she wants to have, and the boundaries she will have with herself and with others. Therapy is useful in this process because it allows a client to explore, understand, gain vocabulary, add labels, engage in behavioral rehearsals, and have a safe space to process growth, hurt feelings, and the implications of relational evolution.

SELF-AWARENESS

In our society, education and experience are held in high esteem. Those who have formal and informal education are deemed experts, wise ones, leaders, and guides. To gain this sense of esteem, many people will spend decades and thousands of dollars to study, to learn, to be educated, and to create awareness on a specific topic or within a particular industry. Yet it is likely that most people will study anything and everything except themselves. They will know all the jargon of their occupation and industry; they will read books on how to lead and learn; and they will study magazines on fitness, home décor, gardening, and more. They will engage in couples counseling to learn about their partner and will observe their supervisors to learn how to excel at work. In a 2022 Gallup study, it was noted that 31% of Americans have a bachelor's degree or higher, thus demonstrating the importance that is placed on higher education and occupational expertise (Gallup & Lumina Foundation, 2022). However, in Tasha Eurich's 2018 book, *Insight*, she notes that only 10–15% of people are quantitively self-aware. Eurich explained that most people who believe themselves to be self-aware do not actually meet the standard for self-awareness. Most people will think and assume that they know themselves based on their preferences, hobbies, occupation, personality, and behavioral tendencies; however, very few have explored the depths of their being, the nuances that create their personality expression, the foundation of their core beliefs, or the root of their behaviors.

The quantitative difference between occupational or educational knowledge and awareness versus self-knowledge and awareness is nearly 20%; thus most people will study everything besides themselves. This equates to nearly 90% of the population that will not spend an equal amount of time studying themselves. They will not sit in silence, read self-exploration books, use writing prompts, journal, or even go to dinner alone. They are experts on everything and everyone except themselves.

This phenomenon carries over into their friendships because people who do not know themselves through the lens of self-study, emotional intimacy, and transparency are not likely to fully know how to be reflective, emotionally intimate, and transparent in a friendship.

One of our roles as clinicians is to help clients increase their awareness. We use a range of therapeutic modalities that derive from our theoretical orientations. Sometimes we ask questions and encourage answers. Sometimes we make statements and assess responses. Sometimes we request a particular yoga move and guide them in releasing tension through their thoughts and breaths. Using a range of modalities, our goal is to help clients increase their awareness. The same is true for concepts and ideas related to friendships. We want our clients to understand who they attract and are attracted to in friendship, how this connects or disconnects from their attachment styles, how these friends make them feel or think, and which skills they should use to engage, extend, or end the friendship. Yet, most clients are not thinking about these elements and factors because they do not consider the awareness and work that must be put into the sustainability or termination of friendships. This tends to occur because most people began having friendships before they were conscious of it.

Some of our first friends were our siblings, cousins, neighbors, or children of our parents' friends. Thus, many of our friendships were with people we have been around since before we were aware of what a friend is, was, or could be. We did not learn to consider what it means to be a friend, how we should act or assess in a friendship, or what we need from others; it seemed as if friendships were natural rather than learned.

However, as we get older and engage with more people who have unique thoughts, feelings, actions, and needs, we become more aware of what we need and what others need. Yet, we do not call it that. Instead, we just stay in a friendship because of the convenience or longevity, or we end it because it fizzes out or we do not have the awareness, skills, or insight to fix it.

Many of our clients have been or will be in situations in which they grieve a friendship and haven't identified or can't identify what they did to influence the end or what they could have done to make the friendship more robust or sustainable—or even what they can take or leave as they prepare for their next friendship or next season of friendships. Part of our therapeutic practice is to help them increase their awareness and understanding so they can create healthy thoughts and actions for the future so that awareness may yield outcomes they want in their friendships.

Catalyst Questions: Self-Awareness

When exploring self-awareness through a friendship lens, consider asking your client these starter questions. Remember, these questions do not have to be asked in order and can be explored as various topics arise in the sessions.

> On a scale of 1–10, with 1 being the lowest and 10 being the highest, how well do you know yourself?
>
> How can you move the scale by one point? For example, if you scored yourself at a five, how can you move the scale to a six, to increase your self-awareness?
>
> Which factors do you know about yourself?
>
> What do you believe is missing?
>
> In relationship to friends, on a scale of 1–10, with 1 being the lowest and 10 being the highest, how well do you know your friends?
>
> If your scale numbers are different, what do you think is the cause for the difference? For example, if you scored yourself at a six but your friends at an eight, what factors contribute to the difference?
>
> In understanding that you may know your friends better than you know yourself, how have you created a standard for how your friends should treat you if you do not fully know yourself?
>
> How can you determine how friends should speak to you unless you know how to speak to yourself?
>
> How can you trust others if you do not trust yourself?

THERAPIST'S TIP: Self-Awareness Assessments

When working with your clients, consider giving them a self-awareness assessment so you will have quantitative data to measure their self-awareness. You can use this data to build the treatment plan goals and objectives.

Reflection Rumination Questionnaire (Trapnell & Campbell, 1999)

Self-Awareness Outcomes Questionnaire (Sutton et al., 2015)

The Mindful Attention Awareness Scale (Brown & Ryan, 2003)

The Self-Reflection and Insight Scale (Grant et al., 2002)

WHAT THE BLACK WOMAN BRINGS TO A FRIENDSHIP

Considering TV portrayals as the mammy, the angry Black woman, the single and sad woman, the career-driven woman, or the promiscuous woman, it is difficult for many Black women to see a healthy representative of themselves in media. Fürsich (2010) notes the importance of healthy representation in media, especially related to the personal identity development of marginalized communities. However, the advancement of reality television shows that create models of friendship through aggression, negativity, pettiness, and disloyalty permeate the beliefs and behaviors of many people, including Black women.

It is important to note that without a strong model for friendship development and sustainability, some people will develop friendships based on unhealthy behaviors. They may question their own role and contribution to friendships. They may mischaracterize themselves negatively if they are positive, decent, and loving, When asked about their contribution to friendships, they may stall on an answer. This would not occur because they lack a dynamic nature, spirit, and energy but because it may be hard to identify what they do not see. Therapy serves as a place of identity development and friendship refinement too.

Catalyst Questions: Exploring Contributions to Friendships

While there have been a few examples of healthy friendships between Black women in media, many of the portrayals are negative, compromising, and unhealthy. When exploring friendships with your Black woman client, consider asking:

What role models have you seen demonstrating healthy friendships between Black women?

How have these role models supported your identity development within your own friendships?

What have you avoided in friendships that you have seen in media portrayals?

What are your contributions to your friendships?

How do you want to show up in your friendships? What do you want to continue to do? What do you want to end?

INSIGHT FROM A CLIENT: JST

JST is an amazing person who is challenged about seeing the fullness of herself. She compares herself to media portrayals and believes she falls short in being a friend because she does not have discretionary money to loan or vacation funds to travel the world and is slow to give advice but quick to give a hug. She does not like to watch TV shows and movies with others because she enjoys getting into the script and acting, and she does not attend concerts because she would rather hear the music in the comfort of her own home. Her time with others is not traditional and thus is hard to cultivate. Yet, because she is aware, she does not put herself in situations that would make her uncomfortable even though she still questions her worth in friendships and what she brings to the table. In counseling, we have discussed her other attributes such as integrity and loyalty and simply being willing to sit quietly with a friend, grab a wad of tissue, and say, "It's going to be okay." She has yet to define herself as a friend. She acknowledges that she is not the "party friend" "social friend," "ride-or-die friend," or "travel friend." And while she has not identified the type of friend she is, she at least knows and acknowledges that she is a friend.

PHILOSOPHY OF FRIENDSHIPS— REASON, SEASON, LIFETIME

There may be some truth to the cliché "a person is in your life for a reason, season, or lifetime." Based on the history of nonfamilial relationships and the intersectionality of Black women, one can suspect that many Black women would prefer the stability of a lifetime friendship. However, the very nature of humans coupled with trauma that comes with friends who lack self-awareness, may result in friendships that end up being lessons learned (reason) or phases in life (season). The challenging element is knowing when to let go. Many people hold on to friendships far longer than they should for several reasons. These reasons can include lack of emotional awareness, fear of loneliness, concerns of the negative implications on other areas of their lives, lack of courage, or other debilitating causes. It becomes our responsibility as therapists to encourage our clients to explore the friendships that may need to end and their thoughts or behaviors about continuing the relationships beyond the moment of healthiness.

Once we have created the path toward awareness, we can trust that they can make their own informed decisions, which includes ending a friendship, rebuilding a friendship, challenging a friendship, or accepting the friendship as it is.

Many people are comfortable in friendships when there is a healthy harmony between similarities and differences. Most people want to be understood and to not have to explain every detail of their experience, while also being challenged to consider things from a different perspective and to grow. A client may choose a friend based on her own strengths but also based on her own challenges. She may choose a friend based on her own challenges because she wants to be friends with someone who thinks differently than she does, is willing to challenge her norm, and can expose her to a new way of being. Friends can fill gaps in the client's life while allowing her to grow. It is important to explore your client's emotional and psychological attraction to each of her friends. That will assist in self-awareness and the determination of how to continue the friendship—and when it may need to end.

Deal-Breakers

Oftentimes when the term deal-breakers is used, people are referring to the extreme boundaries that are seemingly and expressively present in an intimate romantic relationship. This makes sense because people should have boundaries around acceptable behaviors, safe environments, and emotionally vulnerable spaces, especially when dating and in a relationship. However, many people in friendships do not use terms like deal-breakers.

Most clients have not identified deal-breakers within their friendships because it makes them uncomfortable; they do not want to think of the possibility that their friend would do something egregious, hurtful, or intentionally harmful. In not wanting to consider the worst-case scenarios with friends, the client may avoid formulating a deal-breaker within the friendship. This avoidance leads to an unprotected space of vulnerability that can be very dangerous for anyone, but especially for Black women, who are always in a state of unprotected vulnerability due to their dual identity in marginalized spaces of being both Black and a woman. Addressing this topic directly in sessions can be a powerful move toward protection, awareness, and mental stability.

Additionally, many clients may not want to think of deal-breakers because they assume that people know how to be friends, since they have been in proximity of others for their entire lives.

Junge et al. (2020) note that babies and toddlers make friend-based connections, choosing to be around a selected individual, participating in side-by-side play, experiencing conflict, and finding some ways to create resolution, all before they can fully form words and sentences that reflect their thoughts. Most people remember, know, or witness this when watching others; they stick with the assumption that friendships are natural, self-learned, and reflective of what one wants to experience. However, the skills that are necessary for healthy friendships are taught and learned.

People must teach others how to interact with them. What may be acceptable in one friendship between two people may not be acceptable in another friendship between other people. What they need in one friendship may not be what they need in a different friendship. What they needed at one point in their life may not be what they need at a different point in their life. The awareness of these needs and the acknowledgment of their personal evolution often comes with boundaries that must be expressed to their friends. This expression serves as a protection of the friendship, the respect to allow their friend to know what they are thinking and needing, the respect to allow their friend to make an informed decision regarding what they can and will do and what they will not do. It also serves as a model to the friend, who may not have been thinking about boundaries and deal-breakers in friendships, either. Most people create boundaries as a coping mechanism, after they have already been hurt and do not want to be hurt again.

THERAPIST'S TIP: Skills for Maintaining Healthy Friendships

As with other relationships, friendships must include skills for success. These skills include communication, problem solving, and restorative conversations.

See Therapist's Tip: Skills-Communication, Problem Solving, and Restorative Conversations in Chapter 3 and apply those skills and techniques to your clients and their friendships.

NAVIGATING THE OVERLAP OF FRIENDS

Some of our first friends are in our lives from a young age. Consider a kindergartener. It is likely that she already has friends in siblings, cousins, neighbors, or classmates at preschool. How we make friends does not change much as we grow older and mature. Yes, there are apps and planned meet-ups to introduce people to each other, in hopes that they will have similarities and choose friendship. However, most friendships occur organically, based on environment and circumstances. It is quite likely that you client will have some situations in which one part of her life, like her job, intersects with other part of her life, like friendships, thus creating the work *bestie* persona. Another possibility of overlapping occurs when one person interweaves friends from different areas of her life. She may introduce her elementary school friend to her exercise buddy and those two become friends, too, resulting in the elementary school friend and exercise buddy becoming close. When things are going well with the client and each of her friends, the new friendship between the elementary school friend and exercise friend may be a bonus to her life. However, when things are not going well in her life or there is a rift or conflict between her and one of her friends, or between the friends, it may feel upsetting, distressing, or simply uncomfortable, or it may be seen as a form of betrayal. Things may be even more complicated if the overlap of experience and friendship occurs at work, in a beloved civic organization, in one's neighborhood, or any place that she usually feels safe and secure.

The rift or conflict does not only affect the client and her one friend, but also it will have a ripple effect in other areas of her life or with other friends she has in her circle or pseudo-village.

As clinicians, one element of our job is to guide the client to awareness, realization, and acceptance of these overlaps. Another area of our job is to give the client space to process the overlaps, how she feels, and what she wants to do. This may occur quickly and briefly; however, if any challenges, conflicts, or traumas from her past are involved, the rifts that occur and the repercussions due to the overlaps may take much longer to resolve.

INSIGHT FROM A CLIENT: KT

KT entered therapy at the urging of her friends. They noticed that she was complaining about things far more than she had in the past. Yes, her life was tough and not how she envisioned it would be, but during that time, she was hypersensitive to any misstep, misunderstanding, and miscommunication as well as simple elements of conflict in life such as traffic, the wrong food being delivered, or someone stepping on her toe. During the intake and case-conceptualization process, I asked about her relationships with her friends and her functioning in her social circles. She broke down in tears. She said she had not taken time to really think about it because she was just trying to stay afloat in her life. Once hearing the question, she was hit with the feeling of loneliness. She felt lonely even though she was speaking with her friends each day. She felt lonely because there had been a conflict a few months prior. Two other friends had a misunderstanding, and the rest of the friend group tried to help them resolve their issues but it did not work. Everyone chose sides and the group became smaller. While she was going through her personal issues, she felt that she did not have the support of all her friends, and each time she mentioned anything everyone got upset again. So, she made the choice to stop trying to address it and to just focus on her life. She was grieving because she missed her friends. Through therapy, we addressed these elements and more. She acknowledged her feelings, identified which behaviors and decisions she made that were positive and healthy and which ones were counterproductive and unnecessary. As we wrapped up this issue over several months, she eventually had a conversation with everyone, mended some of the friendships, and accepted that some of the other friendships were irresolvable. She grieved and she healed.

CONCLUSION

Friendships are integral parts of our mental health. Knowing that there are people who love and care about us is important when navigating our lives and our identity development, and when addressing solutions to some of life's hardest problems. However, as with any relationship, friendships must be healthy so that our clients can be healthy. In understanding the history of friendship development in the lives of many Black people, approach the topic with sensitivity, cultural care, and a desire to create awareness with our clients. While all friendships may not last a lifetime, they can create lessons and memories that help our clients be who they want to be. We can help our clients get to that place of awareness.

Therapist's Introspection

Personal	Professional
Before reading this chapter, what did you think about Black women and their engagement with friendships and social relationships?	Which clients came to mind while you read this chapter?
What were you taught or did you assume about Black women and their engagement friendships and social relationships?	If you had an opportunity to redo a previous session with a Black woman client, what would you do differently, based on the information you learned in this session?
All of us have biases. What are two biases that arose for you while reading this chapter?	Whom do you need to talk to about this chapter's content? What do you want to say to them? How will you say it?
After reading this chapter, what did you learn and how will you put that information into application, both personally and professionally?	In thinking about your client's treatment plans, what new goals, objectives, and interventions need to be added?
What else did this chapter bring up for you?	

Therapeutic Guide

Therapy	Clinical Focus	Sample Therapeutic SMART Goal	Technique or Intervention
Multicultural Counseling and Therapy	Culture based Problems may be external and a result of culture Culture is embedded in all identities, not just race and gender	Client will identify three cultural factors that influenced the way she chooses to engage with her friends, to be addressed and achieved in 6 months. Client will identify her culture-based role models and have three conversations with them to learn about how they engage with their friends, to be accomplished and achieved with 12 months.	Exploration of cultural influence Identification and cultural intersections Examination of cultural differences Exploration of cultural values and norms Identify cultural jargon that can be helpful or harmful in interpersonal communication
Narrative Therapy	Clients define themselves through stories All stories have meaning, thus one must determine the meaning for the stories they tell and the stories they do not tell Clients construct their identities and perceptions of others through the stories they tell themselves and tell others In unhealthy stories, narrative therapy helps to separate the person from the story	Client will describe three stories that she believes defines her in friendships while identifying three personal strengths and three personal growth points, to be addressed and achieved within 12 months. Client will recall three stories, with friends, that emphasize the choices she makes in friendships, to be addressed and achieved within 12 months. Client will create two stories from a different perspective to analyze her role within friendships, to be addressed and achieved within 6 months.	Externalizing the problem Deconstructing stories into manageable parts that allow for choice identification Emphasis on healthy collaborative relationships Reconstructing new stories Increasing identification and choices Unique outcomes technique

Psychoanalytic Psychotherapy	Personality is developmental across seven stages	Client will explore her unconsciousness as it relates to five patterns of behaviors, specifically in her desire to development and maintain friendships to be achieved within 12 months.	Free association
	Exploration of the unconsciousness to understand the influence on behavior is vital for growth		Identification and analysis and defense mechanisms
			Management of defense mechanisms
	Necessity to analyze deep rooted emotional patterns	Client will identify two of her most common defense mechanisms and the onset of use for each mechanism, to be addressed within 6 months.	Exploration of the unconsciousness and correlation to present behaviors
	Defense mechanisms are psychological strategies to protect the ego from stress and anxiety. Overused defense mechanisms create neurosis that can interfere with a client's life functioning		Analysis of emotions, emotional expression, and emotional alignment to experiences and thoughts
			Exploration and determination of fixation in any of the seven developmental stages

Journal Prompts

How did you see your mother in friendships?

What were the explicit and implicit statements that she made about friendships?

What did you internalize about who your friendships should be?

How did you determine who you would be in friendships?

Through introspection, what are your strengths in friendship? What are your challenges? What do you want to change?

What type of friend are you? List three things that define who you are as a friend, for example, the prayer warrior friend, the fashionista friend that will style your friends, or the friend that follows and supports.

Where do you have friendship overlaps in your current life? Do you have a work bestie? A gym friend? A book club? Or a sister circle? What would you do if you and your friend got into an argument, and you did not want to see her at work or with any other mutual friends? How would you feel and how would you address it?

In thinking proactively, what conversations need to happen now to be preventative of any issues that may have a ripple effect?

Think over the past 5 years; which friendships are you grieving? You may still be in each other's lives, but things have changed, and you miss what once was. Acknowledge the shift. What was your role and their role? Acknowledge the feeling. Is it grief (loss), frustration, confusion, betrayal, or abandonment? Acknowledge the outcomes. Have you all changed? Is there still a friendship? Can it be resolved? Do you want to end it? What are your next steps?

5

Embracing Newfound Freedom

The biggest adventure you can ever take
is to live the life of your dreams.

—Oprah Winfrey

It is not about supplication, it's about power. It is not
about asking, it's about demanding. It is not about
convincing those who are currently in power, it's
about changing the very face of power itself.

—Kimberlé Williams Crenshaw

Freeing yourself was one thing; claiming
ownership of that freed self was another.

—Toni Morrison

Freedom: *The power or right to act, speak, or think as one wants without hindrance or restraint*

Freedom: *The state of not being imprisoned or enslaved*

Freedom: *The state of not being subject to or affected by (a particular undesirable thing)* (Merriam-Webster Dictionary, 2024)

THE EMANCIPATION PROCLAMATION

On September 22, 1862, President Abraham Lincoln signed the Emancipation Proclamation into law, determining that the enslavement of Black people was both illegal and an improper pursuit of economic and lifestyle gains. While the Emancipation Proclamation was drafted and signed as a war measure for suppressing rebellion in the Civil War, to openly welcome free slaves into the armed forces, and to cease the enslavement of Black people across the United States, it only and specifically addressed the freedom from forced confinement and violence from one person to another person (Library of Congress, n.d.). It did not address the freedom from structures, systems, and institutions that caused and still causes a Black person to be marginalized, hindered, restrained, or adversely affected by undesirable actions that would not allow for and support comprehensive economic equality or complete physical, mental, and emotional safety (Kretz, 2022).

We have already explored the intersection of race and gender, particularly as a strength for Black women but also a rationale to explain the unique elements of their engagement in counseling. However, when a person enters counseling, rarely do they consider that their own community, neighborhood, and families can be a source of restraint or hindrance for their dreams, goals, and even their purpose, especially considering the history of enslavement. Sadly, although many Black women may be prepared for the marginalization and oppression by non-Black Americans due to the history of enslavement and racism in the United States, they may not be prepared for the oppression that comes from within their own racial and gender communities. The lack of preparedness may cause shock, confusion, and other emotions and adjoined thoughts that lead to their engagement in counseling.

LIMITATIONS: FROM BLACK PEOPLE TO BLACK PEOPLE

For 200 years, community-based structures such as self-selected segregation, race-based organizations, religion, education, and Black-owned businesses have created a small sense of safety to Black persons' physical, emotional, and mental well-being. In these spaces, a Black woman may not have to explain who she is, why she behaves a certain way, what nuances reflect her cultural upbringing, or when she has certain unexplainable fears. This may occur because she is around people who look like her, were raised like her, are invested in her, and believe in her. It is a sense of being at home.

However, while well-intended, these community-based structures may limit Black women from exploring different elements of opportunity, senses of self, and in some cases, freedom from proximity. In these cases, a Black woman may feel determined to be different from those in her community, at her church, or even in her home, but the risk and fear of being unsafe may be greater than her personal desires, dreams, or goals (Burnett-Zeigler, 2022). Yet, we see that more Black women are addressing and overcoming their fears and deciding to lean in on their newfound freedom by leaving their birth states, moving abroad, dating outside their race, and accepting the peace that comes with autonomy.

There is a precedent for this. While the data is unclear on the start date of the Great Migration, largely due to the undocumented records for many formerly enslaved Black people, the U.S. Census estimates that between 1910 and 1920, nearly 1 million Black people left their birth states in pursuit of a safer environment, free of the risk of lynching, targeting, and unemployment. Between 1940 and 1970, the second Great Migration ensued, with the motivation for Black people to pursue formal education, homeownership, and the opportunity to create a different life for themselves (Collins, 2020).

One part of the Great Migration was centered on fear for safety while another part of the Great Migration was centered on freedom, choice, and hope. The timely intersection of the Women's Liberation movement and the Civil Rights movement in the 1960s allowed Black women to begin visualizing and creating opportunities for themselves. However, many were still limited to expectations from their communities and families. While some Black women moved away from home for college or work, many Black women stayed within their home state or within a local proximity that was easily accessible to their family. In the 1980s, more Black women began to identify as career women and were eager to move to places that allowed them to pursue work in offices and industries that aligned with their dreams and goals not just the expectations that were placed on them as due to their race and gender (Bell, 1990).

These women, and many other women, became the mothers of your current Black women clients. It is likely that your Black woman client was told that her possibilities were limitless while also facing the undeniable implications of oppressive structures such as patriarchy and racism. The contradiction of what was told versus what was experienced oftentimes produced dissonance for Black women who were trying to create the version of themselves they were eager to be.

Many Black women are challenging their fears, leaning in on their hope, and creating the lives they want to have despite the barriers and structures that are in front of them. They are accepting that freedom is their right and that restraint can be broken. We see more Black women moving away from their home-base communities, moving outside of the United States, dating outside of their race, dating within their gender group, and doing things that they may have never or rarely seen, done, or supported before (Girma, 2023; Davidson & Hannaford, 2022).

It is important to recognize that these same Black women may have different emotional needs than people who have not compromised their sense of safety. In other words, Black women who engage in their newfound freedom may feel empowered to explore themselves but less grounded in who they were told they should be. Therefore, when they enter therapy, it is often less about anxiety, depression, or a mental health diagnosis and more about creating something new and all the thoughts that come with that process. These clients tend to have more existential needs and question things like purpose, meaning, direction, spirit, alignment, and wanting the safe space.

In this chapter, we will discuss the various experiences that catalyze internal exploration and existential alignment with goal setting and the acceptance of peace.

MOVING AWAY FROM THE HOME STATE

To make a new life for themselves, some Black women will have to make new friendships, heal from traumas, break generational cycles, or address stereotypes. For some Black women, this may mean that they create physical space and distance from the life they once knew to the life they want to have in the future.

When I was a young child, I always felt out of place. I was a nerdy Black girl in a neighborhood set and centered on survival. I escaped in my books, read stories about life around the nation and world, and felt more included in those stories than in the reality of my dwellings. And I was not the only one to see it. My family saw it. They never teased me but often told me that there was something different about me. My teachers saw it. They gave me the award of "Most Likely to Succeed." My athletic coaches saw it. They steered me toward team management versus athleticism (I cannot really hit a softball). My friends saw and consistently encouraged me to continue to move in the direction of my dreams.

In high school, I realized I would have to leave my home state to be free enough to create the version of me that was most authentic and not bound by the communal expectations of my neighborhood, church, family, or childhood friends. I had to leave my physical home to create a new home in me. And I did. I vowed that I would return home, not to live but to give new opportunities to my younger family members. To date, several of my cousins have felt encouraged and empowered to leave home and now live across the nation, pursuing their own dreams and creating lives for themselves.

While my story is familiar to many Black people, especially within the context of the two Great Migrations, it is still unfamiliar to those who do not personally know someone who has decided to leave their home state in pursuit of a new freedom. In these situations, the Black woman who decides to leave is utilizing emotions such as courage and thoughts such as determination that have never been activated by aligned actions. She is stepping into new territory and blazing a trail. Trailblazers are praised after the trail is created. They are noted for creating paths for others to follow and celebrated for using emotions and skills that are uncommon for others. However, when they are in the process of blazing the trail, they will likely get scraped and bruised by trees and bushes, fall into unexpected ditches, get bitten by insects or wild animals, and have to mend themselves alone and keep moving until the path behind them is clear and the goal is accomplished. The analogy is a close comparison to the challenges and emotions that your Black woman client who is creating a new life for herself will experience. There may be emotional bruising, dips in success, fear of failure, hurts and discomfort, and yet the need and desire to continue pushing forward.

These Black women may be your clients. When they come to your thera-peutic session, it is likely that they will need to process all the emotions and thoughts they had to create and sift through in order to leave home and create a path for themselves. This process includes acknowledging the risks and other factors that come with being different, creating plans for how to sustain the newfound freedom and life they want for themselves, and processing any grief that has accompanied them on the chosen loss of leaving all that they knew.

MOVING ABROAD

While there is little research on the migration of single Black women across the United States, there is a lot more data that addresses Black women moving inter-nationally. The pattern is rooted in minimizing marginalization and increasing a sense of connection and belonging, specifically to escape the woes of racism in the United States. Most of the data points back to the research of Schlossberg et al. (1989). This study focused on a sense of belonging in academic and edu-cational settings, and many scholars and womanists have used it to explain why Black women are leaving the United States and moving to various nations across the world. They want to feel that they are seen for who they are, which is more than their race and gender. And they want to be valued and appreciated for the essence of their being. They want to matter.

Schlossberg et al.'s (1989) five-dimensional framework of mattering includes the factors of: attention, importance, dependence, ego-extension, and appre-ciation. Attention is rooted in commanding and receiving attention from another person. Importance is about the perception that another person cares about what one thinks, wants, and does. Dependence is related to two or more people working together to have an experience or reach a goal. Ego-extension is the belief that others take pride in one's success and are concerned about one's failure. Appreciation is when one feels thankful for who they are and what they do.

As one can imagine, these factors are difficult to achieve in a society in which one's race and gender are systemically used against them as a weapon. Based on the historical and reinforced structures in the United States, many Black women wonder if they matter to their fellow citizens. Their experiences through travel, books, online groups, and shared stories from friends push them to believe that they can live a life in which they do feel that they matter to the masses; how-ever, it may have to be outside the confines of the United States. Many Black women are utilizing their newfound freedom to leave the country of their birth to escape the feelings and experiences of marginalization and exclusion.

According to the Association of Americans Residents Overseas (Speer, 2024), 5.5 million Americans have chosen to live outside of the United States, with a steady incline of a 2% increase per year. Of these numbers, Black women are creating a great exodus too. They are most often immigrating independent of spouses, children, or families. Therefore, they are taking different risks in making the choice to leave without a natural support system.

INSIGHT FROM A CLIENT: JRS

JRS came to therapy in 2015 at the suggestion of her eldest son. A professional in the medical field, he was worried about her mental health and decline due to recurring physical health issues. As a survivor of cancer, she had lived a portion of her life worried about death and making decisions that were cognitively distorted and simply extreme. Everything was black or white, good or bad, right or wrong. There was no room for shades of gray, nuanced experiences, and even hope for change. This thought process was affecting her relationship with her family, the ways she interacted with her children, and even the way she perceived herself.

While she had suicidal thoughts in her youth, her adulthood produced various thoughts of escaping the life she was currently experiencing but without clear direction or action steps.

In therapy, using the miracle question, she began to explore what her ideal life could be like as a Black woman in her late 50s. She explored ideas of dating and partnership, creating gray scales in her thought process, being free of systemic oppression, and living in a society where physical health was not a costly endeavor but rather a simple way of being.

As an active participant in therapy, she began to increase her feelings of hope, explore possibilities, and take micro-actions toward creating the life she wanted. She had difficult conversations with her children, acknowledged her mistakes and extreme behaviors, released feelings of exclusion from her childhood, and addressed many of her negative core beliefs. As she freed up some of her mental space, she began to consider life outside of the United States and reignited her love for travel. Every quarter, she would go to a different country and stay for a short amount of time. She chose to stay in areas that were less touristy. She wanted to experience the culture in manner that was not centered on tourism to determine if it were a place where she could live.

In 2021, she made the decision to leave the country and move to Western Europe. She chose a country that was low cost, had a respectable and valued health care system, boasted a culture that focused on lifestyle instead of work, and had a strong and interconnected expatriate community. While her children were concerned about the distance in travel, they agreed that the move was the best decision for her mental health and the subsequent impact it would have on her self-perception and relationship with her family.

Due to the laws connected to international teletherapy, I had to reduce her sessions; I only see her when she is in the United States to visit her children or friends. In these sessions, we discuss her thoughts, feelings, and actions. Oftentimes, she explains the fears she had about leaving the United States because it was her known home. However, she addressed it by using a range of thera-peutic techniques such as cognitive restructuring, acceptance of her decisions, and journaling. Additionally, the concept of *mattering* became clearer to her, as she interacted with people within the expatriate community and became a mentor to newer cohorts of Americans that were choosing to live in the same country as her. She has created a life for herself that includes being involved in her local neighborhood, taking leadership responsibilities in her civic organiza-tions, investing in hobbies, walking daily, getting a pet, sleeping regularly, and feeling free of oppressive systems.

MARRYING OR DATING OUTSIDE OF ONE'S RACE

When I was in high school, I dated a young man who was fun, adventurous, eager to experience life, and a bit nerdy, like me. He was an ideal boyfriend, but I had to keep our relationship private because he was white. When one of my neighbors informed my dad that she saw me with him, my dad confronted me, and I confirmed that I was dating a white guy.

His response was "What a horrible disrespect to your ancestors who have been raped and killed by white men, and yet you openly give your love and attention to this young man." My father is neither racist nor a bigot. Many of his loves have been white women who have cared for him, and he has shown the same reciprocal energy. But, when I dove deeper into this response with my dad, he noted that he felt that a woman chooses her love interest based on how she sees her father. Since he was a Black man, he assumed I would choose to love and marry a Black man. His initial response was based off his insecurity that I did not fully see or appreciate him and that I marked him worthless.

None of these statements were true for me. They were self-centered thoughts he had, based on how he perceived himself, how he wanted me to perceive him, what he dreamt my relationship and family would look like in the future, and his own fears of how others would treat me in an interracial relationship.

Even as a young girl, I believed in the power of direct and effective commu-nication, centered on emotional expression and solutions. Therefore, my dad and I explored his rationale, were able to ask each other tough questions, and experienced a shared vulnerability.

With his support, I continued to date my boyfriend for a couple more months and then we broke up for normal adolescent reasons.

There are many Black people who have experienced the same recoiled response when people, including friends and family members, see Black woman dating outside her race. For various historical, personal, and legal rea-sons, family members may struggle with accepting that Black women may fall in love with a non-Black person. While that may be their issue, it will affect her, emotionally, financially, or even physically. Additionally, she will have to contend with statements about self-hatred, being afraid of her race, or not loving the Black men in her family. While none of these may be true statements for herself, they may be statements she needs to address while she is exploring her newfound freedom.

In 1924, the General Assembly of Virginia passed the Racial Integrity Act, which legally banned interracial marriages. This law was like other state laws across the country that forbade marriage between people of different races and termed them miscegenation (Wolfe, 2020). At the time, the largest racial populations were white people and Black people; the laws were strictly upheld between these two groups.

Until 1967, it was illegal in certain states, mostly in the South, to marry a person from a different race. While the laws have changed now, there are still many elders who were raised and indoctrinated in the belief that people should marry within their race only. This is not strictly a reflection of racism or prejudice but also a response to years of socialization via internal and external conversations, media portrayal, stories of violence toward interracial couples, and more. While it seems unfair and unjust, many people are only one generation removed from the time in which interracial laws were legal and upheld.

According to the Pew Research Center, in 1967, 3% of marriages in the United States were between partners of different races (Mitchell & Mitchell, 2024a). In 2019, 19% of marriages in the United States were between partners of different races. While the 16% difference appears to be remarkable and an indication of acceptance, the U.S. Census notes that this percentage difference includes interracial marriages between Asian Americans and white Americans and Latino Americans and white Americans, accounting for 57% of the increase (U.S. Census Bureau, 2024). Eighteen percent of all interracial marriages include a Black person (U.S. Census Bureau, 2024). When factoring in gender and interracial marriages, 24% of Black men marry outside of their race while 9% of Black women marry outside of their race (Pew Research Center, 2024). In other words, while Mildred Loving fought to ensure that her marriage was legally recognized in the United States, many Black women do not marry outside of their race.

Some factors that may influence this phenomenon are concerns and reception from in-laws, safe places to live without discrimination, racial identity confusion for their children, acceptance by members of the community, and being able to live an authentic life without assimilation into another culture.

Yet, there are Black women who are choosing to engage in interracial dating and marriages, thus challenging the conservative and oppressive expectations that are placed on them. When making this choice, they may have to use discernment to determine if their partner is interested in them for the essence of who they are or for the fetish of being perceived as exotic; to determine if their partner sees them as a whole person or through the media-promoted lens of a sexual Jezebel; to risk exposure to ignorance about what it means to be Black while correcting and justifying common cultural responses; to face overt and microaggressions while being out with their partners; and to simply ensure that they are using their newfound freedom to explore themselves as opposed to suppressing or losing themselves.

Additionally, Black women who date outside their race may have to address their own biases and prejudices about people outside their races and any messages that may have been introduced to their core beliefs about people who are different from them.

THERAPIST'S TIP: Creating and Processing Possibilities

While the abovementioned list is not exhaustive, it can be used as a catalyst for conversations with your Black women clients who are curious about dating outside their race but may not feel or believe they have a safe space to initiate the conversation or even process their thoughts and feelings.

When you engage your Black woman client in the discussion, be mindful to lead the conversation through a lens of possibility and freedom and encourage her to use the journal prompts to process independently too.

Using the journal prompts, she will be able to explore thoughts, feelings, and ideas related to:

The existential meaning of dating outside her race

The labeling of her feelings about dating outside her race

Ways she will protect herself when she receives disparaging messages from others

Ways that she will keep her relationship healthy and comfortable in the face of discrimination and ignorance

These concepts and prompts, can be used as a catalyst for exploratory conversations or given to clients for therapeutic homework.

CONCLUSION

For many, freedom is a matter of right and justice, something that has been given and earned by the labor of the generations before them. However, for many Black women, the sense of freedom is less about lack of physical restraint and enslavement but the alignment between possibilities and mindset. In stepping outside the norm, there are risks and challenges that come with being free and exploratory. In this chapter, I hope you have received a greater understanding of how to support your Black women clients as they explore what freedom means to them. It may be different from living outside of their home state, moving internationally, or marrying outside their race. It may be a matter of how they choose to spend their money, where they spend their time, or what they do to express the fantasies and realities of who they are. In all cases, freedom can be self-defined, but they may need you, their therapist, to create the same space to explore, process, challenge, and encourage action in the direction that they want to go.

Therapist's Introspection

Personal	Professional
Before reading this chapter, what did you think about Black women and their engagement with freedom?	Which clients came to mind while you read this chapter?
What were you taught or did you assume about Black women and their opportunities or decisions about breaking the norms and creating their own freedom?	If you had an opportunity to redo a previous session with a Black woman client, what would you do differently, based on the information you learned in this session?
All of us have biases. What are two biases that arose for you while reading this chapter?	Whom do you need to talk to about this chapter's content? What do you want to say to them? How will you say it?
After reading this chapter, what did you learn and how will you put that information into application, both personally and professionally?	In thinking about your client's treatment plans, what new goals, objectives, and interventions need to be added?
What else did this chapter bring up for you?	

Therapeutic Guide

Therapy	Clinical Focus	Sample Therapeutic SMART Goal	Technique or Intervention
Feminist Therapy	Examine oppressive systems that contribute to mental and emotional distress Acknowledge societal norms and psychosocial factors that influence gender-based decision-making	Client will reclaim personal power through the identification of three experiences in which her personal power and vision were compromised, to be addressed and achieved in 12 months. Client will increase protective mechanisms by creating five counterstatements to be expressed to naysayers, to be developed and expressed within 12 months.	Creating and promoting self-compassion Development and demonstration of empowerment Reframing societal messages Externalization in separating one's personal identity from how the world perceives them Intersectionality identification; temporary separation of identities to address root issues, when possible or when needed

Solution-Focused Brief Therapy	Change occurs in a brief amount of time Future oriented Client has a vision of what she wants to change Very specific change model Measurable goal-based	Client will create two SMART goals related to creating and maintaining newfound freedom, to be achieved and accomplished in 2 weeks. Client will create a habit of identification of micro-change by documenting two change moments each day, to be established in 4 weeks.	Miracle question Scaling question Goal development Identification of micro change
Strength-Based Therapy	Client resourceful and resilient Client has experiences and traits that can be used for goal achievement Discovery of hidden strengths through the resilience from adversity	Client will identify three strengths that can be matched with one current obstacle, to be achieved within 6 months. Client will complete three strength-based assessments and determine how each strength can be used to create or maintain a newfound freedom, to be completed within 6 months.	Strength assessments Matching of current strengths to cope with current obstacles Evaluation of communal and environmental resources to combat obstacles Creative thinking and alternative methods

Journal Prompts

In your own words, define freedom.

What does freedom look like to you?

What does freedom look like for you?

How will you know when you are experiencing freedom?

It is possible that we have freedom in one area of our life but feel in bondage or oppressed in another area of our life.

- Where do you feel free?
- Where do you feel in bondage?
- How are the two different?
- How can you leverage your experiences with freedom in one area to create freedom in another area?

Who is managing your freedom or your bondage?

- How can you increase your power to gain your freedom?
- If you are the person keeping yourself in bondage, what is the deep-seated reason?
- Do you find comfort in the predictability of your bondage?
- Do you really want to change?
- How can you change?
- Whom do you need to help you or hold you accountable for creating freedom?
- What are three to five sentences you can say to that person, to let them know that you need their help?

Many of us are aware of the concept of crabs in a barrel and how it is related to marginalized communities.

- How have Black people or a Black person kept you in bondage?
- How has that affected the ways your see and experience Black people?
- How have other women or a woman kept you in bondage?
- How has that affected the ways you see and experience women?
- If noting these experiences as trauma or a loss, what did you lose?
- How do you restore the loss?

Moving away can be liberating. Sure, there are moments when it is scary, as you are experiencing newness, getting acclimated to the people and environments and how you want to show up in the new space. But it can be quite exhilarating, too.

- Have you ever moved away from your hometown?
- How did you feel?
- What did you learn about yourself?
- Did you create a new version of yourself?
- How do you like the new you?

There are times when dating and marrying outside one's race can be scary but revolutionary.

- Have you ever dated outside your race?
- What were you most afraid of when you began to date that person?
- What were you looking forward to when you began to date that person?
- Did you experience any type of loss?
- How did you grieve that loss?
- How are you restored?

- If you are not restored yet, what three thoughts do you need to create to be restored?
- If you are not restored yet, what three feelings do you need to create to be restored?
- If you are not restored yet, what three actions do you need to create to be restored?

6

Moving Beyond Stereotypes

I will not have my life narrowed down. I will not bow down to somebody else's whim or to someone else's ignorance.

—bell hooks

I don't have any time to stay up all night worrying about what someone who doesn't love me has to say about me.

—Viola Davis

Sometimes, I feel discriminated against, but it does not make me angry. It merely astonishes me. How can any deny themselves the pleasure of my company? It's beyond me.

—Zora Neale Hurston

STEREOTYPES AND SCHEMAS

Contrary to popular opinion, stereotypes are not always bad. Social Darwinism posits that social stereotypes were a matter of grouping to understand those who were similar and different from oneself as a matter of distinction, natural selection, and survival (Rudman & Saud, 2020). It can be argued that, overall, stereotypes increase knowledge and understanding more than they promote generalization and marginalization. But, in all aspects of learning, the filter that one applies to the content will create the layer of context. When knowledge and information are placed in the hands of an individual with distorted thoughts, the content can be skewed and result in harm.

Consider the generalizations from your graduate school program core multicultural competencies and diversity course. It is likely that the information was taught to create a generalization of different cultures so that you could understand the racial, gender, economic, and sexual orientation groups that are similar to and different from your own. The course curriculum is well intended, but if the professor was ill-equipped to properly diversify the text content, it is likely some students left with a sense of confusion or a confirmation of bigoted thoughts. Yet, authors such as William H. Frey (2018) contend that information centered on diversity can provide a standard for understanding that is positively dynamic and culturally vibrant and inclusive, especially when considering one's engagement with those who are different from them.

This is how the world works, too. We notice differences, first through a sensory experience and then from an emotional processing and cognitive forming perspective. When something is unknown or people want to fill in the blanks of their own understanding and knowledge, they rely on generalizations. It is a survival mechanism. We ask natural and normal questions like: Is this safe? Is this thing the same as the other thing? What are the similarities and differences?

In 1952, Piaget coined the term *schema*. It is a reference to building more knowledge based on what we already know. And, when one lives outside of the identity of another, oftentimes, they do not know much about that differing identity and thus they may not have much knowledge to build on. This occurs because our society has been built on differences and those differences have been labeled to create a sense of hierarchy. To simplify this concept, when one person is different from another person, they tend to rely on generalizations and stereotypes before they get to know an individual person and form individualized thoughts, opinions, and interactions about that different person. This occurs in animal-based nature, too, not just in human-based society. However, the challenge is that we are not in the wild and our sense of survival has shifted to collectivism versus individualism, especially in relation to emotional engagement, healing, and transformation.

When a Black woman client works with a non-Black woman clinician, there will be a lack of understanding of lived experiences, processing, protective factors, coping mechanisms, identity formation, and more. And most clinicians will fill in the holes or the deficits of understanding with stereotypes and academics-based generalizations.

As clinicians, we would like to believe that we are exempt from stereotyping and generalizations, particularly because we took a multicultural class and had a couple of professors talk about our own biases and possible countertransference. The reality is we were human before we were counselors, and stereotyping and generalizations have been part of our survival. They are counterproductive in the therapeutic setting and yet they are real and present. The nuances are clear, and our professionalism encourages us to continuously challenge our stereotypes so we have the open mind space to see our clients as they are and as they want to be.

As this chapter unfolds, please understand that many Black women face stereotypes that are unfair and unfounded. They are breaking cycles and stereotypes and facing backlash for that and then they are going to therapeutic settings and facing more stereotypes from their clinicians. This chapter will center on stereotypes that are both external and internal for Black women, but I challenge you to challenge yourself as you read this chapter too.

Catalyst Questions: Exploring Stereotypes

Consider this: Stereotypes are normal but the way they are applied can be counterproductive.

> Think: When was the last time you used a stereotype to justify a statement you made? Maybe you were completely alone or with a trusted friend.
>
> How did you use the stereotype? Did you feel safe saying it because nobody heard you? Would you feel ashamed if someone of that stereotypical group heard you?
>
> What is the root of your stereotype? Does it make you a bad person because you have a stereotype?
>
> Action: Reflect on these questions and pose them to one person in your personal life and one of your clients. Do not ask them about you. Ask them about them.

History tracks that most humans can survive when we are in a community or part of a collective. Championships are won by teams, neighborhoods survive disasters by leaning in on each other, and traditional survival occurs when multiple people are together and can move as one. There are many pros to this realization; however, a major con occurs when one is part of the collective but has a new and unique purpose, resulting in the experience of standing out. They may still be part of the community but do not fit into some of the cultural norms or may be breaking cycles, trailblazing, or doing something new, which is neither understood by the community nor can be fit into the stereotypes that community nonmembers may have formed.

In the case of Black women, history has created many stereotypes for them to lean into such as the mammy, the angry Black woman, the coon, the loud ghetto girl, and more. History has also proven that it is not always safe to stand out, as witness the assassinations of Malcolm X, Martin Luther King Jr., or the difficulties of any Black trans woman in any city in the United States. That being so, many Black women who have been divinely destined, designed, and purposed to stand in spaces that are new are not safe.

Many Black women, as a matter of survival—emotional, physical, spiritual, economic, relationally, role-wise, etc.—lean into certain stereotypes, despite knowing and feeling that they can and should stand out. The dissonance created in the moments between authenticity and stereotyping often leads Black women to counseling. In this chapter, we will explore the various ways stereotyping affects Black women and the ways that their clinicians can support and guide them to authenticity and purpose without compromising their realities around safety.

DUAL MASKS

In 1903, W. E. B. Du Bois coined the term *double consciousness* in his book, *The Souls of Black Folk*. In 1952, French philosopher Frantz Fanon wrote his book, *Black Skin, White Masks* (first published in French as *Peau noire, masques blancs*), which crossed the concept of double consciousnesses. Two Black men, in two different countries, nearly 50 years apart, wrote about a similar topic in two different languages, centered on the reality that Black people must split themselves in two halves to survive as a minority around white people.

For many Black people survival is associated with their ability to be authentic to themselves and among their Black families and friends and yet wear a mask and hide significant parts of themselves when they are in white spaces. Examples of this include code switching, relaxing one's natural hair or wearing unwanted weaves or wigs, bleaching skin, not talking about their personal lives at work, having to contend with intrusive questions like the number of fathers their children have or the type of education they received, or even hiding aspects of their religious and spiritual practices. These elements of double consciousnesses or dual masks are emotionally debilitating factors that weigh heavy on many Black women, even if and when they can predict that an occurrence will arise or a question will be asked (Davies, 1992).

Even more troubling is the increasing number of incidents in which a Black woman faces stereotypes by other Black people. As Black women increase their status and positions at work, according to Melissa Harris-Perry (2011), they get referred to as sellouts. If they move to different neighborhoods across the country, then they are leaving their people behind. Even having experiences not commonly afforded to Black Americans such as international travel, luxurious experiences, and self-care is criticized as "forgetting about the little people." A Black woman cannot win. She will be stereotyped and scrutinized by white and non-Black people who do not understand her because of her race and gender and by Black people who may not understand her because of her education and social positioning. This may lead a Black woman to therapy in hopes of understanding how to navigate these unique stereotypes while developing ways to address them with the people in her life. More importantly, she may need to be in therapy to understand what authenticity looks like to her in different environments.

Oftentimes, I remind my clients that a chameleon is still a chameleon even if it changes its colors. The true form and essence of what a chameleon is does not change, but the external presentation may change. For some clients, this reminder is helpful because it gives the client permission to be dual or double. For other clients, it is not helpful because they believe their purpose is in the authenticity and solidarity of one's representation. In both cases, we explore their thoughts, beliefs, pros and cons, and desired outcomes and behaviors of being of double consciousness or not, especially when considering and comparing their double consciousnesses to their emotional, economic, social, and physical survival.

Catalyst Questions: Stereotypes

When one is raised to uphold certain stereotypes, as a matter of emotional or communal survival, she can find herself in a position of suppressing who she naturally is or who she is supposed to be. In some situations, a Black woman client may even state that she does not know who she is but only knows who her parents told her to be.

As you embark on this delicate balance with your Black woman client, consider asking a few questions that can invoke thoughts, feelings, and actions leading to your client's own self-awareness in the face of stereotypes.

> Under what circumstances do you feel like you must code switch or be less authentic and original?
>
> After these circumstances pass, do you feel empowered, whole, and complete, or tired, worn down, and depleted?
>
> If you feel depleted after these circumstances, how do you restore yourself and how long does it take?
>
> What are some things that you would do or say if it were safe to fully express yourself?

While these probing questions may be helpful to your clients, continue to consider that many Black women have been conditioned from birth to behave one way around Black people and a totally different way around non-Black people.

Continue to consider that this is rooted in slavery in the United States, when it was unsafe to be seen as more than property, or in the Jim Crow era, when it was unsafe to be seen as more than a lesser human being, or even currently, when Black skin is perceived as a threat to many law enforcers, bank lenders, human resource leaders, colleagues, and even classroom teachers.

Lastly, while you ask these questions, consider that the Black woman client may need time to deeply explore these concepts, even when she is living them each day.

REJECTING RACIST STEREOTYPES

The CROWN (Creating a Respectful and Open World for Natural Hair) Act was passed by the U.S. Congress in 2020, to ensure protection from discrimination as related to race-based hairstyles, to include but not limited to braids, locs, twists, and knots. While it is absurd to consider that Black women had to fight to protect themselves from discrimination as recently as 2020, the reality is that the fight was and continues to be necessary to counter stereotypical discrimination.

THERAPIST'S TIP: The Clinician's Role in Advocacy

Imagine being a highly talented professional, with several degrees, several years of training and experience, remarkable evaluations from customers and colleagues, and yet uninvited to high-order sales meetings because your hair does not look like your colleagues'. Imagine your hair being neat, clean, healthy, but coiled instead of straight, braided instead of loose curls, or wrapped instead of low hanging. Imagine your access to information is solely blocked by your hairstyle.

What would you do? How would you feel? What would you say? How would this affect your work performance? How would this affect your engagement with your team?

As a clinician, how will you use your own thoughts, feelings, actions, and statements to advocate for your Black woman client in this society?

Some suggestions include: learning and leading workplace trainings on the obliteration of workplace biases and stereotypes, writing peer-reviewed and public scholarship journal articles around workplace discrimination, speaking on podcasts and panels about your position on supporting Black women in therapy, having casual conversations with your family and friends around their perception and engagement with Black women at work, and continuing to read this book to learn about other ways you can use your privilege, whatever privileges you have, to create space and open doors for Black women who may be discriminated against based on things they cannot control.

The term *dreadlocked* was coined by white missionaries when visiting the continent of Africa. These missionaries noticed that the civilians of the region had hair that was tightly coiled in several individual masses, which was either free flowing or styled in culturally specific ways. The foreigners to that region said the hair looked dreadful and passed judgment on the hairstyle and the people who culturally embraced it. (Byrd & Tharps, 2001) This judgment was centered on a certain group of people who had hair texture, cultural connections, and generalized but real commonalities that were different from those of the missionaries. However, the statements, sentiments, and actions of the missionaries resulted in a transformation from a perception and conversation to a one-sided standard of appropriateness and professionalism. This standard carried into the workforce for decades and centuries predating the CROWN Act.

According to the 2023 study conducted by McKinsey and Company on the beauty market, the beauty business—consisting of skin care, fragrance, makeup, and hair care—in the United States is worth $430 billion. Eleven percent is exclusively targeted on marketing and sales to Black consumers whose hair texture does not mirror the majority group in the United States but who want to assimilate for success. There is a general sense of beauty that reflects hair that flows and flips. It is considered both sexy and professional. Therefore, many of the products that are marketed to Black women are straightening chemicals or devices, designed to straighten their hair and extend how long it is straight so their hair aligns with sexy, professional, and beauty standards.

Black women reinforce this experience among themselves too. It is a form of self-confusion, self-hatred, and a specific social and career survival strategy that is demonstrated when mothers "press" their daughters' hair, and then call them pretty; when curls are big and loose and people give that young Black girl more attention with her modified hair versus her natural hair; or how straightened hair is a treat for special events like school pictures, proms and dances, church events, or weddings. These experiences and expectations are carried into adulthood when a Black woman straightens her hair for interviews, when she buys a new wig for dates, when she suffers through weave installments for vacations, or when she simply says negative and derogatory things about herself and her hair on a daily or frequent basis.

While Black women should and do have the autonomy to choose hairstyles of their preference, as a matter of economic and social survival there remains an implicit sense of a need for assimilation when the workforce and work environment are factored into the preference. They do not have complete autonomy when the risk of increased marginalization is a factor in decision-making.

All of this is rooted in racial discrimination because this hair type and texture is represented in a particular racial group, Black women, whose hair was once and continues to be referred to as dreadful.

Changes are emerging, especially with the CROWN Act and an adjoining rejection of stereotypes such as dreadful hair, unkempt hygiene, unrefined professionalism, and more. As therapists, we are charged with asking questions that other people cannot or do not ask. When working with Black women, the conversation about rejected stereotypes and the connections to one's mental health may start with their past, present, and future thoughts about their hair and what it means to their identity.

INSIGHT FROM A CLIENT: MP

MP is a 32-year-old woman who graduated from a prestigious, historically Black college or university (HBCU). When younger, she and her mother participated in historically Black-centered organizations such as Jack and Jill of America and the National Pan-Hellenic Council. They watched TV reruns of shows that uplifted the Black community, such as *The Cosby Show* and *A Different World*. MP was heavily rooted and influenced by the beauty of Black identity.

Over several months, she interviewed for job openings for which she was highly qualified and had wonderful references and a stellar work portfolio. Yet, each time she was denied the position. When following up with the human resources director for each position, she received ambiguous messages about the interview, so it was difficult for her to create a pattern to determine what she could and should change for the next interview.

In speaking with a few friends, they suggested that she straighten or braid her small afro to create a straight hairstyle or one that allowed for more flow. Reluctantly, she modified her hair for the next set of interviews and received the opportunity for follow-up interviews. As a result, she received two different job offers. To challenge the notion that the opportunities were awarded because she modified her hair, she went to work for the first quarter with straightened hair and attempted to go to work during the second quarter with her modified hair. One month within the second quarter, or 4 months into her work experience, she was required to attend a meeting with human resources. She was informed that she had made some changes that made customers and management uncomfortable and that she would need to correct the changes before she could meet with customers again. The only change she had made was her hairstyle. Reluctantly, she resumed straightening her hair and was able to resume her work with customers.

Emotionally devastated, she entered therapy to process her thoughts and feelings of being forced to modify her natural hair for a style that was more comfortable for her customers and colleagues.

During therapy, she asked herself questions such as:

Am I only as worthy as the way I look?

Will I always have to straighten my hair to be valued at work?

Which customers and colleagues are uncomfortable with my hair?

Are they uncomfortable because they do not value my hair or do not value me?

Are they uncomfortable because they have unaddressed biases?

Is the pay and status worth the modification of my hair and consequent look?

Since I am in places and roles that my elders never had a chance to experience, do I change in gratitude for their sacrifices or do advocate for myself instead?

What am I willing to lose while advocating for social justice?

In taking a cultural stance, I assessed her statements and behaviors in comparison to diagnostic specifiers in the *Diagnostical and Statistical Manual* (DSM) to discover that she met the criteria for posttraumatic stress disorder (PTSD) based on her workplace experiences strictly connected to her hair. With this knowledge, I begin to treat her for PTSD, using trauma-focused cognitive behavior therapy (TF-CBT) interventions and carefully guiding her to revisit the trauma while encouraging empowerment along the way.

Two years later, she made the decision to leave her job. Additionally, she sued the company for workplace discrimination and found another employer who hired her while interviewing with her naturally coiled afro.

HISTORICAL STEREOTYPES
AND CORE BELIEFS

Not all stereotypes are rooted in bad intentions. In fact, many stereotypes are created for general understanding, application of knowledge, and survival. Yet, even with positive intentions, stereotypes may result in negative outcomes. People generalize as a form of quick assessment, which leads to behavioral shifts, actions, or a sense of safety. These generalizations and stereotypes can serve as a matter of awareness, protection, safety, or ease. However, stereotypes become problematic when a person cannot move past the specific stereotypes and limits placed on them. Another example is when a person chooses to cause implicit or explicit harm to another person based on an upheld stereotypical thought. During clinical supervision, therapists are encouraged to bring forth the stereotypes they have about people, races, gender, locations, and even themselves. This process, associated with countertransference and bias awareness, creates a more aware therapist, especially if they are willing to make changes such as allowing a person to be more than the stereotype or box in which they are placed.

Since Black women entered the United States first as enslaved people and later as immigrants or world travelers, certain stereotypes were placed on them. These stereotypes include but are not limited to being uneducated, ignorant, opportunistic, scammers, social services exploiters, bad mothers, unhealthy, poor, and only capable of being blue-collar workers as well as having low time management skills and low financial management skills. Most of the stereotypes were unwarranted, untrue, or assumed without historical acknowledgment and contextual understanding.

INSIGHT FROM A CLIENT: SRJ

SRJ has three children, all of whom she loves deeply, equally but differently. When growing up, SRJ often heard stories and comments about women who loved many men over their lifetimes and demonstrated their love by birthing their children. The birth of each child was a public display of their love for that person. While that sounds beautiful, it was often criticized in society as reckless, irresponsible, and nasty. This public reckoning was based in patriarchal views around women including fidelity to one man, sexual purity and modesty, and religion. While men were able and even encouraged to have multiple partners, women, who carry the children and who cannot physically hide the display of love through their physical pregnancies, were shamed for it.

As SRJ enters the therapeutic space, she is proud of each relationship she had, each lesson she learned, each way she evolved, and each child that resulted from that relationship, and yet she is ashamed that she has willingly walked into the space of "baby mama." This label follows her when people ask her about her children, who do not resemble each other but all belong to her; when she fills out forms and each child has a different last name but are very close as siblings; or simply when events and holidays come, and one child goes to one father and another child goes to another father. Again, she is proud of the extended families that she has created because of her unions but ashamed that society sees her in a negative way and will openly express it, via media, movies, books, commercials, and standard socialization.

The core beliefs that formed in her childhood were:

> Women are valuable when they are coupled.
>
> Women are valuable when they birth a child and more valuable when they birth multiple children.

So, when given an opportunity to love at different times in her life, she leaned into it. When given the opportunity multiple times to have children, she leaned into that too. Only through therapy did she start to explore a few other core beliefs that she has formed based on additional messages that she received. Some of the other addressed and processed core beliefs were:

> Women are dirty when they have children by more than one person.
>
> Women are sluts when they have children outside of marriage.
>
> Women are horrible partners if a man chooses to leave a relationship.
>
> Women do not deserve love if they cannot keep their partners happy.

These powerful core beliefs emerged when we started to explore the complex statements of shame that arose from the statements of pride. A therapist may inadvertently and inappropriately skip over subtle signs and statements of shame. While this is not explicitly neglectful or harmful, it does not lead to deeper processing and healing.

In our sessions, we addressed them head-on, primarily because these core beliefs are rooted in gender-based socialization but more complicated for Black women, who are often labeled as "baby mamas" instead of ex-girlfriends or ex-wives or who are labeled as "welfare queens" instead of being seen as powerful and informed women who made direct and significant choices for their lives.

Using common worksheets like Venn diagrams, counterposed visual activities, and compared guided questions, SRJ was able to see the complexity of pride and shame, healthy versus unhealthy internalizations, and core beliefs that created distortions. To extend the cognitive restructuring and create action, I composed scenarios of behavioral rehearsals (formally known as role-plays) in which she could practice the ways she would respond to negative, inappropriately curious, or intrusive statements while also restructuring the ways that she would enter conversations about her children through the use of strategic vulnerability and clear boundary setting.

She was able to use her increased self-awareness, clear thoughts, and rehearsed behaviors to address people within her family, within the children's families, at the children's schools and extracurricular activities, and on her dates with new suitors.

The case of SRJ demonstrates the impact of stereotypes, even in the midst of moments of positivity. Aside from the joy and grief that comes with each relationship, each union, and each birth, Black women must contend with the perception that people have of them and the choices they make. While women in other groups may feel free and liberated in their choices in this century, Black women still often consider how their actions are going to be seen, either in alignment with or opposing the stereotypes that people will have about them.

Another problematic stereotype that tends to be detrimental to a Black woman's mental health is the persona of strong Black woman. This persona has been transmitted from one generation to the next through a sense of cultural learning via modeling, explicit statements, and implicit observation. The root of this persona and consequent stereotype is the idea that Black women have a limitless capacity to endure repetitive and harmful obstacles as manifested through their constant survival, lower comparative suicide rates, longer lifespans, and ability to continue to be productive even in times when others would stagnate, regress, or simply opt out of the situation.

This historical stereotype formed when enslaved Black women continued to work and be productive in the fields and owner's home even while having endured rape, birthing a child that wouldn't belong to them, lack of autonomy to legitimately marry a partner of their choice, inability to live in places and among communities that inspired them, prohibition against practicing a religion that aligned with their beliefs and ancestors, destructive embargos against reading, writing, creativity, peace, and so much more. It is through this endurance that a foundation of a detrimental historical stereotype formed and continues through reinforcement. This stereotype implies that the Black woman is a superhuman who can endure beyond the realities of mental health, emotional health, physical health, and spiritual alignment (Reynolds-Dobbs et al., 2008). The ongoing challenge is that this message is continued, supported, and reinforced by other Black women and then by the Black woman client herself.

Since some stereotypes are rooted and strengthened in years, decades, and centuries of reinforcement, it is possible that the Black woman herself lacks the awareness of the core beliefs that she has formed, either in alignment with the stereotype or in confrontation with it. In the therapeutic setting, a therapist can probe, guide, and explore the role of stereotypes and the ways they have influenced the Black woman client's life, both positively and negatively.

Catalyst Questions:
Reforming Counterproductive Statements

When working with a Black woman client, begin to track how many times you say, "Wow, that is impressive" or how many times you say, "That is amazing. How do you do it all?"

Consider that while your intentions are to be supportive, it can also reinforce the stereotype that a Black woman can and should do more than average. Even popular movement terms like *Black Girl Magic* can be counterproductive, especially when considering the sacrifices and losses that one has experienced to create magic.

As a replacement, ask your clients:

How does it make you feel to have many things on your plate and the expectation to manage each area to precision?

If you could remove one thing from your plate, even temporarily, what would it be and why?

When you accomplish much more than the average person in 1 day or 1 week, do you feel extraordinary or exhausted?

If the client indicates both, ask her to choose one over the other to discuss.

Remember to ask open-ended questions that allow for exploration, long-term processing, and a continuation of homework activities so the client can

address imbedded cultural thoughts and core beliefs in and out of the therapeutic setting.

STEREOTYPES AND SOCIAL INCLUSION

Not all stereotypes are bad. Some are helpful when one wants to be seen for
aspects of who they are without having to explain who they are. Think about
the success of Historically Black Colleges and Universities and the stories that
students tell when they describe being in a classroom, getting to focus on being
a student and learning content rather than having to explain their piece of the
Black experience or how the content aligns with or challenges their existence.
Think about the rise in Black-led therapy practices when clients come in and
use cultural language like "protective hairstyles" and the need to not be "ashy"
(having dry and unmoisturized skin) without having to explain why either is
important to them. Or consider the home-based shared experiences when Black
youth describe their Saturday mornings, filled with gospel music or the blues,
bleach smells, and vacuum cleaner sounds. In these examples, leaning into the
stereotype may bring a sense of comfort, like donning a favorite pair of worn-
down sweatpants.

As you openly ask your Black woman client about the role of stereotypes in
her life and how she embraces or rejects them, be sure to address your own relationships with stereotypes too.

CONCLUSION

Most stereotypes predate our existence. While they are upheld and reinforced by
people within our generation and younger, the development of most stereotypes
originated during a time prior to our birth and our opportunities to counter the
stereotypes. Yet, these stereotypes continue to impact the daily internal and
external lives of many people. For marginalized and double marginalized communities, the adherence to or denial of stereotypes may be a matter of survival.
That survival may be physical, emotional, psychological, or spiritual. In some
cases, that survival may be a compound of all four of the previously mentioned
experiences. That being so, there is power in exploring stereotypes with your
clients, to allow them the safety of discovery, understanding, self-synthesis, and
empowerment. While our own biases may attempt to paralyze us as humans,
we must lean into our professional training to be objective and create a space for
our clients to explore, address, and heal themselves. Now is the time to confront
stereotypes and allow our clients to do the same thing.

Therapist's Introspection

Personal	Professional
Before reading this chapter, what did you think about Black women?	Which clients came to mind while you read this chapter?
What were you taught or did you assume about Black women and their most common stereotypes?	If you had an opportunity to redo a previous session with a Black woman client, what would you do differently, based on the information you learned in this session?
All of us have biases. What are two biases that arose for you while reading this chapter?	Whom do you need to talk to about this chapter's content? What do you want to say to them? How will you say it?
After reading this chapter, what did you learn and how will you put that information into application, both personally and professionally?	In thinking about your client's treatment plans, what new goals, objectives, and interventions need to be added?
What else did this chapter bring up for you?	

Therapeutic Guide

Therapy	Clinical Focus	Sample Therapeutic SMART Goal	Technique or Intervention
Person-Centered Therapy	Congruence is a matter of accepting oneself (and another) without judgment and being self-aware Suffering/problems occur when one is incongruent. Problems occur when we lack awareness, acceptance, and judge ourselves	Client will increase self-awareness by identifying two incongruencies between desired stereotypical identities and undesirable stereotypical identities, to be addressed and reassessed in 12 months. Client will increase self-awareness through the humanistic approach to therapy, to include completing one introspective journal activity after each session. The activity should include introspection of concurrency, triggers, annoyances, and insightful moments.	Enhance the client's understanding of themselves Eliminate or mitigate feelings of distress Identify where and in which conditions the client may feel judged Identify where and in which conditions the client may self-judge Identify and set clear boundaries Accept all elements about self; then decide what can and should be adjusted Utilize sand tray table to address the onset of incongruence

Therapy	Clinical Focus	Sample Therapeutic SMART Goal	Technique or Intervention
Gestalt Therapy	The present is most important. The past and future are less of a priority Humans strive for congruence and self-actualization While humans are individuals, they are part of a social network Humans can learn more about themselves in relation to their interactions with others and their social networks People are capable of solving their own problems if given a chance to be authentic One shall not avoid emotions but rather walk into them, experience them, confront them, understand one's motivations and behaviors	Client will increase self-awareness related to stereotypes by identifying three stereotypes that she internalized and determine maintenance or release of the internalization, to be addressed and achieved in 6 months. Client will assess three aspects of her stereotypical nature in relation to three (family member, friends, work, school, authority, etc.) relationships, to be addressed and achieved in 6 months. Client will practice four confrontational response statements to be used in moments of external projections from others, to be learned achieved within 12 months.	Remain in the present. Do not veer to the past or future for more than 5 minutes Empty chair Increase awareness through confrontation of incongruences Two chairs Identify three problems and self-directed solutions Assess body language Use feeling wheel to increase emotional awareness around choosing to live a nontraditional life Daily, assess one's engagement with the five senses (smell, sight, taste, touch, hearing) as a protective mechanism and a coping strategy
Behavioral Therapy	Behavior is a result of the environment Behaviors are taught, learned, and reinforced Behaviors are present and can be corrected and changed with intentional effort Related to mental health, behaviors are the issues and the reduction of maladaptive behaviors and create a solution in mental health and processing	Client will use two mindfulness techniques when confronted with external stereotypical projections to be practiced and achieved as needed. Client will identify two stereotypical behaviors that she would like to extinguish within 12 months. Client will identify two behavioral models that she would like to emulate through the integration of stereotypes to be identified within 12 months.	Systematic desensitization Behavioral modeling Contingency management (contract Extinction Behavioral interviews Mindfulness Antecedent, behavior, consequences (ABC) chart Self-monitoring

Journal Prompts

Stereotypes may include race and gender but may also be related to education, dating, work capabilities, and more. What are your first memories of being stereotyped?

- How did this experience impact how you began to see yourself?
- Did you accept it, or did you reject it? How did that decision of acceptance or rejection affect your following thoughts of yourself and your actions?

Schemas are often built on patterns. What are the patterned stereotypes of Black women that you see around you?

- What stereotypes of Black women did you see around you?
- How do those impact how you see yourself?

In each area of our life, we may have received messages that we were too much or did not show up enough. We may find ourselves in positions where we put on a mask to become who we think someone wants us to be.

- What is the mask you choose to wear?
- Under which circumstances do you don that mask?
- Under what circumstances do you feel that you must code switch or be less authentic and original?
- After these circumstances pass, do you feel empowered, whole, and complete, or tired, worn down, and depleted?
- If you feel depleted after these circumstances, how do you restore yourself and how long does it take?

What are some things that you would do or say if it were safe to fully express yourself? Which masks do you wear but wish you can permanently take off?

- If you were to permanently take this mask off, which vulnerabilities would be exposed?
- With whom would you like to share those vulnerabilities and how would you like them to respond?
- How would you manage your own exposed vulnerabilities if nobody else were available to share them with you?

How many hairstyles have you had over the last 10 years?

- Which hairstyle did you love the most?
- Which hairstyle made you feel most empowered?

How has your hair affected your dating life?

- Who is attracted to you?
- How do those types of people make you feel?
- Do they see themselves the way you see you?
- When have you changed your hair to please a partner?

How has your hair affected your career?

- When have you changed your hair to appease a supervisor or work colleague?
- How have your hair and hairstyles affected your relationship with your supervisor or work colleague?
- How has your hair or the way your hair is perceived affected projects that you worked, experiences you had, or desires you lost?

Which stereotypes have you yielded to in order to fit in socially?

- Fit in at work?
- Fit in at home?
- Fit in at college?
- Fit in at social and civic organizations?
- What are two benefits and rationales to choosing to yield to stereotypes to fit in?
- What are two consequences and experiences of choosing to yield to stereotypes to fit in?

List three stereotypes that are often placed on Black women.

- Which of these stereotypes do you uphold?
- Which stereotypes do you deny?
- How did you choose these stereotypes to uphold? What reinforcers have you experienced to allow you to continue to uphold these stereotypes?
- How did you choose these stereotypes to deny? What reinforcers have you experienced to allow you to continue to deny these stereotypes?

PART II

Working With Black Women Clients

7

Working With Emotions

Think like a queen. A queen is not afraid to fail.
Failure is another stepping stone to greatness.

—Oprah Winfrey

Caring for myself is not self-indulgence, it is self-
preservation, and that is an act of political warfare.

—Audre Lorde

I was built this way for a reason, so I'm going to use it.

—Simone Biles

COMMON EMOTIONS THAT AFFECT BLACK WOMEN

The reality is that life has ups and downs. There are good days and tough days, there are lessons that are taught and lessons that are learned. There are moments when we question ourselves, our environments, and our experiences and we seek meaning for things that do not make sense. In these moments, we may experience incongruence with who we are, who we want to be, or how we want the world to be. These moments may also create a sense of dissonance when things do not seem to be what we thought they were. These are general life experiences that most humans encounter on their journeys. These moments, recurring or not, are not manifestations of a mental health disorder or a symptom of a mental health illness. Instead, they are elements of life.

Every troubled moment in our life does not mean that we have dysfunction or a disorder. It means we are human. And in the human experience, we are equipped with emotions, thoughts, behaviors, actions, reactions, and introspection.

In understanding that Black women's experiences are often layered with their marginalized experiences, it is also normal to understand that some of these general human moments are layered, labored, and intense for them, especially while trying to dissect and deconstruct what it means to be a human in a Black woman's body. While there are some experiences that are common for many people despite race and gender, such as a relationship breakup or a job loss, these may feel heavier and more complicated for a Black woman. Again, there may not be an associated diagnosis, but the experience can be or feel heavier because of the lived experiences and intersectionalities of Black women. There may even be some emotions that Black women experience more frequently (or not) only because they are Black women.

In this chapter, we will explore common emotions that affect Black women due to the intersections of being human, Black, and a woman and some common emotions that Black women experience but have been socialized to avoid or not experience.

Shame

Shame is defined as a painful feeling of humiliation or distress caused by the consciousness of wrong or foolish behavior (Dictionary.com, 2020).

In movies, one who experiences shame oftentimes walks around with a lowered face, lowered chin drawn close to midneck, shoulders hunched, and a visible expression that something negative, bad, or horrible has occurred. When faced the continued socialized messages of being a strong Black woman, a superhero, or any depiction that promotes more stoicism than range of emotion, and any superhuman narrative than abates raw feeling and vulnerability rather the depths of connectivity through a collective consciousness, a Black woman is left without the breathable space to experience shame. Yet, because she is human instead of a superhero, the emotion will still arise. Because she is a Black woman, she may push it away. Comparable to a tide that will continuously bring in a current, the emotion of shame for any given experience will return until accepted, addressed, and acknowledged.

Shame carries a notion of judgment (Choi, 2022). It is centered in the sentiment that one should have known better and consequently done better. However, what is common knowledge is based on what one has been exposed to experience (Halpern & Moses, 1990). A person may not know the dangers of a car unless they have been around a car. A person may not have known how to do better or be better in a specific situation unless the exposure occurred, first as an opportunity to learn and then as an opportunity to be tested. It could be argued that shame is only reserved for those who have been taught and failed versus those who have never been taught and failed.

As we contextualize to the lived experiences of Black women, whose most recent elders were segregated and whose foreign ancestors may have been enslaved, while pairing with the desires and purpose to break generational cycles or being the first to engage in collegiate learning experiences, it's quite possible that many Black women carry shame for experiences that are unfamiliar but they believe they should know.

Let us start with one factor: Should.

Should is a cognitive distortion defined as "the implicit or explicit rules we have about how we and others should behave" (Beck et al., 1979). In other words, there are times when one has a cognitive distortion that is implicitly or explicitly misaligned with one's preconceived expectations of another person's behaviors. When others break our rules, we are upset. When we break our own rules, we feel shame or guilt. For example, we may have agreed to our standard work hours occurring between 9 a.m. and 5 p.m.; however, we may continue sending emails until 7 p.m. We have broken our own rule by working later than our agreed time. And, we may be okay with breaking this rule. However, when our supervisor sends us an email at 6 p.m. and asks for a response by 7 p.m., we become upset. We note they have crossed our boundary. However, they have learned to cross that boundary because we crossed our boundary first. In acknowledging our error, we may feel ashamed that we created an expectation that does not honor our self-care and boundaries. Another example may be when a Black woman was raised in a very specific way that did not include intentional cultural connections to her Black identity. She may have been raised to fully assimilate in white culture or been coerced to deny her Black identity as a matter of social survival. Later, when interacting with other Black women, she may feel ashamed when she does not know or understand the cultural references that are made or she may feel ashamed if she says something that is culturally inappropriate or misaligned with the cultural consciousness of the group.

The distortion of shame occurs because the thinker believes there was information that must have been or was accessible to her and it needed to be applied at a particular moment.

The distortion of should places ownership solely on self or solely on someone else. "I should have known x, y, or z," "I needed to apply x, y, or z," or "They should have known x, y, or z."

Using this rationale, there is no shared responsibility for information given and taught or observed and learned. The distortion occurs because responsibility is considered one-sided and blame is placed on one entity, either self or another person, rather than multiple facets of learning, the nuances of dynamics, or the mere reality of ignorance being considered. Blame, as association with another distortion of personalization, is interwoven into the concept of should.

There is a responsible party, but who is it? Most people who consider themselves enlightened will lean into self-blame. Those whose egos remain fragile may blame others. In each scenario, the root of should is blame. The root of should and blame as distortions is the limited consideration of other factors that may be present such as access, learning style, understanding, opportunities to apply and practice, safe and nonconsequential reinforcements, and general consideration and care.

While previous chapters have highlighted the increased formal educational pursuits and completion of degrees of Black women, they have also noted the impacts and implications for legal or preferred segregation of Black women. The intersection of formal learning with the socialized reality of segregation has left many Black women thinking they should know something to which they have never been exposed.

Consider money. For generations in this country, most women including Black women were deemed second-class citizens, were unable to vote, open bank accounts or retain them in their names if married, have bills in their names, or manage finances for themselves or their families. The push for women's suffrage did not include racial equality. The concept of money was foreign in legal terms but real in terms of bills, expenses, and expenditures. As they thought about money, there was no formal experiential basis enabling application and correction. Centering on money and the complexities of financial literacy, many Black women think there are things they should know such as how to invest, the difference between stocks, and what an adjustable-rate mortgage is versus a fixed-rate mortgage. The shoulds extend to knowledge of high finance as much as they do to breaking generational cycles in order to have a healthy sense of self.

There are various thoughts and opinions on how one should interact with their family when they are breaking a generational cycle. Some people may tell a Black woman that she can have boundaries, but they do not apply to parents or elders. Some may reinforce societal values around family members being prime support figures and thus a Black woman should visit her family for holidays. Others may say that a Black woman can maintain distance from her family; however, she should create a replacement family. In these brief examples, a Black woman is being told what she should do. With a foundational understanding and lived experience on how to break a generational cycle or how to maintain healthy boundaries, these points are merely opinions, but they could be confusing to the Black woman's sense of her personal wants and desires and to her fear of consequences.

THERAPIST'S TIP: Utilizing a Feeling Wheel

Each emotion has a purpose. First, as a catalyst for a positive or challenging thought. Second, as a catalyst for a positive, challenging, or maladaptive behavior. When working with your client, ask her to have a printed *feeling wheel* or chart. The feeling wheel can be printed from an online site or can be purchased at various counseling stores.

For virtual sessions, ask the client to have the feeling wheel near her. For in-person sessions, have a copy printed in the office so she can refer to it.

The feeling wheel will allow the client to increase her emotional vocabulary, notice where the emotion may set in her body in a psychosomatic manner, and allow you the therapist to ensure you have a clear understanding of your client's emotion.

Catalyst Questions: Addressing Shame

When discussing shame with your client, consider these three questions:

- What is the root of your shame?
- With shame, we tend to believe that something is or was missing. What do you think is missing in your learning and understanding that has created this emotion of shame for this experience?
- Now that you know what you believe is missing, what would you like to learn? Please provide two or three things you would like to learn so we can begin to work on them.

Guilt

Guilt is one of those emotions that are complicated to describe and understand from a healthy perspective. Trying to make someone else feel guilty can be associated with manipulation, gaslighting, deflecting, and several Freudian defense mechanisms. Embracing one's own guilt does not allow for self-compassion or actionable change. Much like punitive discipline and consequences, the effects of guilt are short term because they are associated with avoidance of a stimulus versus motivation and positive reinforcement of a stimulus (Stewart et al., 2023). In other words, one may see a quick change in behavior but as the emotion subsides so does the consistency with that change agent.

In relationships and cycles in which guilt is used to shift behaviors, a person becomes accustomed to hearing statements that may make them feel guilty. However, as time progresses, the guilt that is imposed may turn into resentment toward the giver. Additionally, it is likely that your client, who is the receiver, is likely to feel self-doubt, frustration, or even hate, which, when turned inward or internalized, manifests as major depressive disorder. Again, this chapter is about challenges that do not reach a diagnostical level. However, the regularity of certain experiences or thoughts can evolve into a diagnosable disorder.

Considering guilt as a primary emotion, when your Black woman client comes to the therapy sessions, she may make statements that are rooted in a secondary emotion such as frustration, doubt, resentment, or anger but not the primary emotion of guilt. It becomes your professional responsibility to uncover the primary emotion and address its root causes. As with plant care, it is better to address the root than the leaf.

THERAPIST'S TIP: Pressure Technique

When aiming to uncover root issues, use the *pressure* technique.

> Ideal Step 1: Which emotion are/were you experiencing? Be sure to use your feeling wheel as a reference.

Ideal Step 2: Ah, _____ (emotion; e.g., resentment), okay. Thank you for using your feeling wheel and for sharing your emotion with me.

Ideal Step 3: Let us take it one step further, if _____ (emotion, e.g., resentment) was the tip of an iceberg, what is the emotion that is right underneath it? In other words, what other emotions do you have when you think about this experience?

Ideal Step 3: Ah, okay _____ (emotion) was right underneath _____ (emotion, e.g., resentment). I understand. Which emotion may be underneath that one?

Ideal Step 4: Ah, _____ (emotion). Got it. Thank you for continuing to share.

Ideal Step 5: And what is underneath _____ (emotion)?

Ideal Step 6: Ah, _____ (emotion). Yes. We are getting to the root of emotion. As we dive deeper into the root, we will be better able to address the first emotion you described and each one after it.

In these six steps, your client will identify three emotions and the depth associated with each one. This technique will allow for an increase in emotional vocabulary, emotional expression, self-awareness, and the onset of a solution or use of a protective skill or coping skill.

You can expand on this technique by continuing to prompt your client to identify deeper emotions.

Ideal Step 1: Previously, you mentioned that when _____ (provide the context in which an emotion or set of emotions were identified) you feel _____, _____, and _____ (the three emotions that were previously identified). I wonder if there is a deeper emotion there too. What do you think? What other emotions may be present?

Ideal Step 2: While we, as mental health clinicians, do not like to ask "why" questions because they can seem judgmental, I am going to ask you a series of why questions so we can explore the root.

Ideal Step 3: Tell me why you feel _____ (additional emotion that was identified).

Ideal Step 4: (After the client has answered the first "why" question) Why you do feel _____ (wait for another answer)?

Ideal Step 5: (After the client has answered the second "why" question) Why do you feel _____ (repeat the client's language)?

Ideal Step 6: (After the client has answered the third "why" question) Then why do you feel _____ (repeat the client's language)?

This process will go on until either you or the client have an "aha" moment.

At the point of an "aha" moment, you can describe your thought or analysis to your client, or you can allow her to describe her aha moment and how it may be connected to one or more experiences or thoughts in her life.

Doubt

Depending on the circumstances, doubt can be experienced as a feeling or a mental state. The difference between a feeling and mental state is that a feeling lasts for a brief time while a mental state can last longer due to the large-scale distribution across the brain networks (Oosterwijk et al., 2012). A feeling tends to be momentarily experienced and can be fleeting. However, a mental state lasts longer. It can become a more solidified emotion that has a frequent recurrence that is permanent, although it may just be stuck (Barrett, 2009). In other words, certain emotions, like doubt, can be temporarily experienced or more long-lasting if unaddressed and untreated. While this is not true for all emotions, it can be true for doubt.

Doubt, as a feeling or emotional state, is rooted in beliefs, knowledge, and confidence (Hermann et al., 2002). It orbits around past behaviors, observations, and patterns. Like the other emotions, it is sensorially experienced through the limbic system but forms into an emotional state related to the consistency of an observation or pattern that yields knowledge and information. This emotion is more logical than the other emotions because of its relationship to patterns.

In considering human development, an infant and toddler experience the world through observation and nonverbal communication due to the lack of formation of language acquisition and expression. From ages 0 to 3, humans have observed patterns as a way of learning before they can verbalize their thoughts and feelings related to an experience (Rosselli et al., 2014). As our verbal language increases, we continue to use observation as a form of information gathering, not only to have experience but also to make decisions.

Herein lies the challenge with the emotion of doubt. It is natural, developmental, and can be solidified through our development of observations solely without the understanding or expression of the feeling. In other words, doubt can form or be triggered without a clear or current observation. One feeling can trigger the other feeling of doubt.

Let us consider a common challenge for Black women, *imposter syndrome*. Imposter Syndrome was coined by Pauline Clance and Suzanne Imes (1978), two clinical psychologists who noticed that people were experiencing self-doubt despite external evidence of markers of progress or success. These people experienced a pervasive insecurity that yielded thoughts of undeserved or unearned success. Despite the acknowledgment of efforts exerted, lessons learned, or shifts made, people experienced imposter syndrome because of their self-doubt.

The challenges arose because the client's core beliefs, rooted in childhood experiences and messages, were triggered when they were presented with positive rewards or opportunities.

For Black women, the core beliefs that create self-doubt are usually connected to socialized messages that a young Black girl receives related to her worth, abilities, and strengths. When a young Black girl does not see images of people like her in positive situations, such as in television shows, movies, books, classrooms, workspaces, or even self-care spaces, she is left to use her imagination to determine her capabilities and sense of worth.

While using their imagination is a positive and beautiful experience all children should have, the launch of an imaginative thought is connected to a previously experienced observation. A child does not know how to color a leaf green if she has not seen a green leaf. If a child decides to color a leaf blue, the child may receive a message that leaves are supposed to be green or may be encouraged to continue to think creatively about blue leaves. In both situations, a reinforcer is usually present. Continuing this analogy, a Black woman may not believe she can do something if she has never seen it before or if, when she imagined it, someone told her she was incapable, unqualified, or simply wrong.

These statements create self-doubt. It impacts confidence, which is the emotion related to competence, which is the lived experienced related to patterns. Without a pattern of opportunity, competence cannot form, and confidence cannot be experienced. Doubt is based on patterns. And Black women, as double marginalized people, consistently observe patterns of isolation that challenge messages of worth, abilities, and opportunity. Our current society is set up to make Black women doubt themselves. This pattern of doubt is often correlated to the patterned messages that cause comparison to be destructive and unhealthy versus inspiring or ambitious.

THERAPIST'S TIP: Doubt

As a novice counselor, and even in recent years, I have had doubt that mirrors imposter syndrome. I am confident in my abilities as a therapist. I know my theoretical orientation. I create and utilize interventions connected to my preferred therapeutic modalities. I understand people, human development, psychosocial stages, and defense mechanisms. And I know Black people very well. However, there are times when a new client enters my space, either in person or virtually, and I begin to wonder "Am I the right therapist for them? Do I have what it takes to understand, analyze, or treat their personality or mood disorder? Is my language expression strong enough to help them understand, in their own words and terms, what is happening with them and their lives? Will they understand me? Will I understand them? Can transformative healing occur in this therapeutic relationship?" This is vulnerable to write, but I know it is more common than the singularly lived experience of my individual work. Therefore, I am sharing it with you as a tip.

Remember that even the most competent, confident, and skilled people can have doubts. So, when your client enters your therapeutic space, indicating doubt in areas that seem uncomplicated and rote for the client, explore the doubt by calling it by its name. Then pay close attention to your client's nonverbal communication. Does she shift in her seat? Raise her eyeglass frame? Correct you by using a defense mechanism? Look down? Shake her head? Or do anything that reflects shame or defense?

As you notice these nonverbal communication efforts, highlight each one to her and the depth from which it derives. An example is: "Rosemary, when I mentioned the word self-doubt, you shifted in your seat. As a therapist, I am trained in understanding nonverbal communication because it is 80% of our common expressive techniques. What do you want me to know when you shift in your seat? What is your raw thought? What is your refined thought? What is the desired thought? And what does this doubt mean to you?"

EMOTIONS AS CORE BELIEFS

In psychological history, hysteria is the only emotion that was only related to gender, specifically, women (Tasca et al., 2012). The original diagnosis of hysteria outlined symptoms related to being dramatic, suggestible, moody, impressionable, overly concerned with external appearance, seductive, and needing to be the center of attention (Sulz, 2010). While many of these symptoms can be associated with and represented in men, the ancient Egyptians, Greeks, Romans, and eventually Western Europeans through the work of Sigmund Freud, believed that these behaviors were related to a displaced womb and could only be assigned to women (Novais et al., 2015). Women who displayed several of these symptoms within a short period of time were formally or informally diagnosed with hysteria. During the active peak in diagnoses for this specific population, women were considered insane when they experienced any feelings or behaviors that did not align with how any given man wanted to see or perceive them. This created a ripple effect in which women began to suppress their emotions, only expressing them in women-centered spaces, and leaving the fun and drama to places of acceptable expression like theaters, art studios, and music rooms. The fear of misperception and misdiagnosis created the core belief that still is carried by many women: Only express emotions when the time is right and do not be dramatic when you do it because it can lead to consequences.

A similar process of self-repression and self-suppression, as a matter prevention of misunderstanding, misclassification, or mischaracterization occurred for

Black people too. It started during slavery, continued through the Reconstruction era and through the Jim Crow era with faint breaks in the structure at the end of the Civil Rights era. It continues through to the present day but can be fixed, starting in the therapeutic sessions between you and your client.

Ignorance is the root of misperception. However, the often-recurring consequence for Black people is a lack of physical, mental, or emotional safety when Black people express an emotion that is outside the realm of imagination or acceptance for the majority racial group. The consequences can lead to employment termination, housing loss, family separation, psychological disarray, and even death. In many Black homes, the origination of a core belief was created, as a matter of safety versus suppression. The phrase used was, "Do not air out your dirty laundry." The sentiment was that emotions can be dirty and expression allowing people to see them is unacceptable. The common core belief that formed is: It is unsafe to express your emotions around people who will misunderstand you, so do not do it.

At the intersected identity of being Black and being a woman, Black women often have a compounded core belief related to emotions: Do not share them with anyone because it is not safe, ever.

When many Black women enter therapy, their reluctance to share their emotions may not be related to you alone, but rather to the core beliefs that they have carried due to their intersected identity of race and gender.

COMMON EMOTIONS THAT BLACK WOMEN AVOID/ARE NOT ALLOWED TO EXPERIENCE

Grace

Biblically, grace is referred to as God's unmeasured and unearned favor to those who are unworthy (Staff, n.d.). Grace is the acknowledgment of mistakes and the space for correction. In other words, there is no need for grace without the presence of a mistake.

However, mistakes, especially those connected to morality, humanity, humility, decency, and simply right or wrong are not often afforded to minority and marginalized communities by other humans. There are social rules of engagement that dictate how one is expected to behave with oneself and around others. These social rules of engagement are usually made by the racial and gender majority groups to reflect what is culturally appropriate for them or what allows them to maintain their majority status and social power. These rules are often shared among the majority group members in a cultural manner that is passed down from one generation to the next.

As marginalized minorities, many Black women are not afforded the opportunity to access the social rules that were created by the majority groups. They are at a disadvantage because they will seemingly fail the social games, misunderstand certain social structures, or simply be disqualified from certain social opportunities that would allow them to make advances.

Consider it this way: A person is less likely to win a game when they have never been given the rules. They cannot determine if they are making the right game decisions, following the rules, understanding loopholes, creating strategy, or simply enjoying the game if they do not have access to the rules. They cannot ask for grace or utilize grace if they make decisions that they did not know were unwise or mistakes.

This similar experience can be true for our clients who have not been given the rules of the game but keep playing it, make mistakes, and do not have a person to give guidance, mentorship, or grace.

INSIGHT FROM A CLIENT: KM

KM is a skilled architect who has hit all the key elements in her career before age 40 and is eligible to be a partner in her firm. She stays at work late, rises early in the morning for self-care, and produces valuable and sustainable projects monthly. She is well respected and requested by her colleagues and clients. In attending her predominantly white institution (PWI), versus a historically Black college or university (HBCU), she learned the rules of the game related to her career, through observation, eavesdropping, and very rare direct conversations with her white peers and professors. However, she did not have accessible models or mentors on her career journey that looked like her, a Black woman. Challenges arose related to microaggressions, macro attacks on her character, and scrutiny of her about her work. She didn't find the space or room to give herself grace and when she was faced with challenges in her marriage due to her lack of presence, she retreated further into her work, challenging herself to be better than before, because that became her safety net in case her husband decided to divorce her.

When she entered therapy, the pressure that was on her was evident. I sensed several bricks on her shoulders that were causing a perpetual buckling in her knees. When we began to talk about grace, she referred to it as a foreign concept, one that was not awarded or afforded to her. We discussed the root feelings connected to grace or the lack thereof, along with the core beliefs that were created in her childhood and reinforced in adolescence and young adulthood. Over seven sessions, we talked about the challenges involved in understanding grace, internalizing it as a possibility, applying it to her life, and expressing her need for grace from self and others.

By simply asking two open-ended questions, "What is grace? When do you apply it to your life?" we were able to dive deeper into her self-awareness, areas of growth, communication skills, decisions that needed to be revisited, and sense of satisfaction in her life.

Consistent Happiness

While all emotions are temporary, even mental states versus fleeting emotions, there tends to be one emotion that many Americans strive for, and it is happiness. There are books, movies, articles, and even theories on how to achieve and maintain a consistent state of happiness. Although it is an easily accessible emotion when one has self-awareness related to their emotions, it can be tough to maintain and sustain within a society that is constantly challenging us to grow, evolve, move faster, do more, and achieve higher. It can be tough to acknowledge and maintain happiness when there is always a statement related to the next steps.

Joy and enjoyment are different from happiness. Joy is a more constant emotional state than the fleeting feeling of happiness. Joy is internally created and personally felt versus happiness that is externally triggered and dependent on extrinsic experiences. Enjoyment is a state of process that involves joy. It is not an emotion, but rather an experience that embraces the emotion of joy. It is different from happiness because it is neither an emotion nor anything that is fleeting. It is an experience that can be maintained and extended over time.

Happiness is an emotion connected to one's outlook. It encompasses how one sees and appreciates life, purpose and meaning, and contentment (Ryan & Deci, 2001). Again, this is easily accessible as one increases self-awareness around the sensory, relational, and spiritual experiences that amplify purpose, meaning, and values. While the most aware Black woman may be able to access happiness, it may be difficult for her to sustain this state of emotion.

Happiness, like many emotions, is individually centered but often influenced by external circumstances. Writer and podcaster Arthur C. Brooks (2022), notes that the killer of happiness is envy. Using a connection to Dante's *Divine Comedy*, Brooks notes that envy starts with what is seen and consequently what one feels challenged in achieving. Envy is different from inspiration—both states of wanting—because envy denotes a lack of ability or opportunity to achieve yet inspiration denotes the possibility of achievement through various steps and mindsets.

For Black women, envy may not be a primary emotion, but Black women constantly see the differences in their lives with those of the same gender but different racial groups. This is noted through the wealth gap, achievement gap, marriage gap, leadership and C-suite gap, capital funding for small businesses, and even how they are treated as consumers and customers in many stores and establishments.

A Black woman may have set herself up for happiness by listening to her music, watering her plants, talking on the phone with her cousins and yet lose the emotion by simply walking into a store and not being greeted by a representative or by looking at her pay stub and remembering the pay gap between herself and one of her coworkers who is less qualified but making more money.

The constant reminders, albeit avoided or not, can lead to a state of dissatisfaction that becomes the root of envy. In these examples, inspiration is not offered as a solution because the problem is centered on the systemic structures of the United States by which Black women were treated differently because of their race and gender. While Black women have benefited from the Women's Liberation movement and the Civil Rights movement, the disparities continue to exist and are visible to the naked eye. This becomes the killer of happiness. This is the reason that Black women cannot or have not been able to experience consistent happiness.

Yet, despite this reality, we note that many Black women prefer a cautious approach to happiness, consistently waiting for the proverbial shoe to drop. This is why and how many Black women experience more challenging emotions than positive ones and are often overdiagnosed with depression instead of addressing the systemic barriers that would allow them to decrease envy while increasing the opportunities or sustainability for happiness.

THERAPIST'S TIP: Advocacy

While teaching at Johns Hopkins University, I often reminded my students of the American Counseling Association Code of Ethics (2014) A.7.a. Advocacy. This code states, "When appropriate, counselors advocate at individual, group, institutional, and societal levels to address potential barriers and obstacles that inhibit access and/or the growth and development of clients."

Many times, therapists enter the mental health field focused on helping clients on an individual or micro level. We aim to see micro-progress that grows as self-awareness increases, skills are learned and utilized, distortions and defenses are decreased, and attachments are restored. However, rarely do we spend time actively advocating for our clients through societal addressing of barriers that are consistently affecting our clients and their mental health.

While a therapist may not go to their local town hall meeting to highlight the unhappiness epidemic of Black women, a therapist can go to events or visit their elected representatives to highlight the disparities that directly affect their clients such as the pay gap, the access to quality health care, the lack of safety in socialized segregated communities, or the outdated textbooks in schools that have a high population of Black students. These issues are observable, resolvable, and worth a therapist's time in advocacy.

Ask yourself: When is the last time you centered your politics and advocacy efforts on supporting the universal needs of your marginalized clients? Remember, you can start today.

NOW WHAT?

Each of my clients is encouraged to have a feeling wheel near them during the sessions and in random places in their homes and office. This tool allows them to properly identify their emotions while labeling and communicating them to others. It becomes a process of shared emotional awareness and expression. Five sessions into the therapeutic journey, clients ask: Now what? The question originates because they have become comfortable identifying, labeling, and expressing their emotions but they run into a series of situations in which they do not know what to do with the emotion because they have not been given the power or space to change the circumstances that catalyzed the emotion. In other words, a person can identify individual envy but does not have the power to change the systemic circumstances that created envy. In these situations, a client can be emotionally aware and yet feel powerless. The state of powerless can be triggering to a Black woman who carries the generational trauma of being unseen and unheard but present enough to be marginalized. She may only be seen when it is time to place her in the margin versus giving her power to make societal and structural change.

Consider that 2020 was the first year a Black woman was voted into the vice president office and 2022 was the first year a Black woman was sworn into the Supreme Court. Consider that Black women have been in this country, as enslaved people, since 1619, and it took over 400 years for them to achieve a powerful position in which they might be able to change elements of systemic structures that keep them marginalized. Four hundred years is a long time to feel powerless to change one's own circumstances. And even with the very few elected officials that may have the power to change systems, many Black women continue to present the question of: Now what?

It is likely that your Black women clients will gain the emotional awareness and expression skill set to identify, label, and communicate their feelings but still question if they should engage in this process regularly because they know or believe that their emotions may not or will not be a catalyst to change or a springboard to fairness. In these situations, it becomes a slippery slope for Black women to slide back into an emotional pit of pointlessness.

This is where the deeper level of the therapeutic work begins.

Since you will be engaging in advocacy, it is important to create the first of many safe spaces for Black women that will allow them to create change based on their individual and group needs. This starts with you allowing them to express how they feel about their therapeutic environment, postsession check-ins, your therapeutic approaches and modalities, and their general experiences with you. While there are times when you may feel misunderstood as a therapist, it is best that you create safety by being open, allowing for the feedback, making changes in the environment or approach, and demonstrating that their emotional expression and needs have value and can be met.

THERAPIST'S TIP: Utilizing the Sandwich Approach

In many graduate programs, therapists are taught how to start a session or how to engage throughout the duration of the session. Rarely are they consistently taught how to end a session. When engaging in a session, consider the sandwich approach:

The bread: *First 10 minutes.* Check in with the session. Ask about feelings, recurring thoughts, a few updates, and two or three things they may want to talk about during the session.

The meat: *Minutes 10–50.* Address any previous homework assignments, highlight which therapeutic goal or objective you all will be addressing today, dive deep into your therapeutic approach and aspects of the client's treatment plan, use your interventions, allow for processing and revelations.

The bread: *Last 10 minutes.* Begin to close out the session. Summarize the session, provide the homework for the next week, ask for their feedback for the session and what they may need to remain eager and engaged in the sessions and in the therapeutic process. Thank the client for their feedback and be sure to incorporate one or two elements of change for the next session if necessary.

Remember, there are several ways to do an end-of-session check-in with a client.

You can use these:

- A Likert scale approach: Tell me about your satisfaction in this session on a scale of 1–10.
- A miracle question approach: If you had the power to create a miracle, how would you change this session or what you felt in this session?
- Modeling: At the end of each session, I think about things that went well, things that were challenging, and ways I can improve. As you think about the end of each session, what thoughts come to mind for you?
- Simple: How was this session for you?

Additionally, there are several online resources targeted at helping therapists create end-of-session tools. Simply search for "end of session feedback counseling."

CONCLUSION

Many therapists entered the mental health field to help clients navigate their mental health experiences to include feelings, thoughts, and behaviors. The formal education of a therapist is centered on diagnostic symptoms and disorders; informal learning creates space for therapists to understand the nuances of emotions and behaviors that are beyond the scope of the *Diagnostical and*

Statistical Manual. In this chapter, we explored the emotions and factors that Black women experience but are encouraged to suppress or have difficulty navigating. As you work with your clients, consider these emotions and more, to allow them to have the space to learn, grow, express, and feel liberated within the wholeness of their being.

Therapist's Introspection

Personal	Professional
Before reading this chapter, what did you think about Black women and their expression of emotions?	Which clients came to mind while you read this chapter?
What were you taught or did you assume about Black women and how they express and demonstrate their emotions?	If you had an opportunity to redo a previous session with a Black woman client, what would you do differently, based on the information you learned in this session?
All of us have biases. What are two biases that arose for you while reading this chapter?	Whom do you need to talk to about this chapter's content? What do you want to say to them? How will you say it?
After reading this chapter, what did you learn and how will you put that information into application, both personally and professionally?	In thinking about your client's treatment plans, what new goals, objectives, and interventions need to be added?
What else did this chapter bring up for you?	

Therapeutic Guide

Therapy	Clinical Focus	Sample Therapeutic SMART Goal	Technique or Intervention
Cognitive Therapy	Mental illness arises from faulty cognitions Cognitions are schematic and formed from experiences that create a perception about self, others, and the world Cognitions can change, thus emotions and behaviors can change	Each session, for 10 minutes, the client will engage in psychoeducation to learn about the connection between thoughts and emotions, core beliefs, and cognitive restructuring to determine the role that she wants emotions to play in her life.	Cognitive restructuring Imagery-based exposure therapy Thought recording Catch, check, change (3 C's) Guided discovery Socratic questioning

Rational Emotive Behavioral Therapy (REBT)	Action-oriented, evidence-based approach to challenging emotions through thoughts Clients innately have rational and irrational thoughts Challenging thoughts create emotional change and subsequent behavioral change	For 10 minutes in each session, client will address challenging and patterned emotions through the use of one ABCDE worksheet. Client will explore the root of three of her emotional patterns through the use of pressure[1] techniques, to be achieved within 12 months.	Feeling wheels and charts Emotional labeling Emotional tracking Tracking emotions to circumstances and experiences Positive visualization Correlating emotions to thoughts Cognitive restructuring Challenging emotions ABCDE model
Narrative Therapy	Clients define themselves through stories All stories have meaning, thus one must determine the meaning for the stories they tell and the stories they do not tell Clients construct their identities and perception of others through the stories they tell themselves and tell others In unhealthy stories, narrative therapy helps to separate the person from the story	Client will examine the stories that she creates and recalls, to determine the role of emotions in her perceptions, beliefs, and actions, to be done for 10 minutes in each session. Client will create one story per month to construct the emotional self-identity that she wants to demonstrate to others, to be achieved within 12 months.	Externalizing the problem Deconstructing stories into manageable parts that allow for choice identification Emphasis on healthy collaborative relationships Reconstructing new stories Increasing identification and choices Unique outcomes technique

[1] Pressure technique is also referred to as the 5 Whys technique. With this technique, a clinician repeatedly asks why questions, to invoke deeper and strategic thinking to increase the awareness of cause and effect for a particular issue.

Journal Prompts

Which common life experiences have happened to you that affected you more harshly because you are Black and a woman? Springboard examples include: A job loss? A divorce from your children's father? A health issue?

How do you think your race and gender affected the harshness of this life experience?

What is something you think you should be able to do and in not doing it you experience shame?

What is the root of your shame?

With shame, we tend to believe that something is or was missing. What do you think is missing in your learning and understanding that has created this emotion of shame for this experience?

Now that you know what you believe is missing, what would you like to learn now? Please provide two or three things you would like to learn so we can begin to work on the learning.

What is doubt? How did you learn about doubt? What were the early messages that you received?

What is your earliest memory of doubt? What was the outcome of that circumstance?

What has doubt shown you or taught you about yourself?

What were the early messages you received and learned about grace?

What is the difference between grace and forgiveness?

In your life, do you give more grace or provide more forgiveness?

What does self-grace look like for you? Write three statements of grace-based self-talk. Write three statements of observable actions connected to self-grace.

8

Addressing Trauma

History, despite its wrenching pain, cannot be unlived,
but if faced with courage, need not be lived again.

—Maya Angelou

Take responsibility for yourself because no one's going to take
responsibility for you. I'm not a victim. I grow from this and I learn.

—Tyra Banks

I'm convinced that we Black women possess a special
indestructible strength that allows us to not only get
down, but to get up, to get through, and to get over.

—Janet Jackson

TREATING TRAUMA

As defined by the American Psychological Association (APA *Dictionary of Psychology*, n.d.), trauma is any disturbing experience that results in significant fear, helplessness, dissociation, confusion, or other disruptive feelings intense enough to have a long-lasting negative effect on a person's attitudes, behavior, and other aspects of functioning. Traumatic events include those caused by human behavior (e.g., rape, war, industrial accidents) as well as by nature (e.g., earthquakes) and often challenge an individual's view of the world as a just, safe, and predictable place.

Additionally, trauma is a mental health experience rooted in an experience that was outside one's realm of control and prediction. It continues to be one of the toughest concepts to explore with clients. For some, a trauma may have been so severe that they are unable to recall it or they avoid reliving the memory at all costs. For others, it is merely a matter of the past that they do not want to dwell on or to affect the future. Some forms of trauma are chronic and ongoing, such that it has merely become part of a person's everyday lived experience. For some Black women, one or all these phenomena can be true. Research suggests that unaddressed trauma is the catalyst for future trauma, either for that individual person or the people who are around them (Cruz et al., 2022). Most people who have experienced trauma do not want to cause trauma in another's life, yet research indicates that it is unavoidable without the intervention of therapy (Vallières et al., 2021). This may occur because traumatic experiences can create changes in the brain that can produce mental illness, skill regression, or faulty thoughts. These brain changes can cause behavioral actions that are dysfunctional and harmful. When involving other people, a person who has been traumatized may knowingly or unknowingly cause harm to others as a negative learned response to conflict a reaction to fear of a perceived reaction to threat, or as a matter of retaliation, not just to the person who caused the traumas but anyone who reminds the person who has been traumatized of their aggressor. With retaliation, there tends to be a sense of justification or foreshadowed self-defense.

There are many therapeutic modalities that can aid in the treatment of a client with trauma but first the trauma in its specificity must be identified and acknowledged so the treatment plan can be robust yet specific enough to heal the client and subsequently those directly and indirectly around her (Yadav & Gunturu, 2024).

For therapists, assisting and treating clients through their traumas can be complicated. It can result in countertransference, unchecked biases, and multiple psychodynamic defense mechanisms from which the client may walk away feeling more defeated and triggered than before she entered the therapeutic relationship. Addressing trauma can be tough for a counselor to treat because the trauma may trigger the therapist's own trauma or remind them of a time in which they may have explicitly or implicitly caused trauma for someone else. Many of the other mental health disorders, like depressive disorders or anxiety disorders, may allow there to be enough distance to form objectivity in treatment. These disorders may not be relatable for a counselor because these disorders may be organic, specific, or individually rooted. However, trauma is usually relational. It tends to involve one or more people creating trauma for another person. Rarely does the onset of trauma occur in complete isolation, but it is tricky to address because the person who caused the trauma may not be available to aid in the healing process and the client's perspective and experiences may overshadow the clarity needed to heal (Dalenberg, 2000). Additionally, if the therapist also is triggered, the healing process can be delayed.

Trauma may be one of the most common and universal experiences for Black people in the United States. In fact, it may be so common that it morphs into cultural phenomena that families try to prepare their kids to experience or an individual aims to predict so they can protect themselves. In some situations, one may even overhear a group of Black people laughing about their shared traumatic experiences because of the commonality of the experiences. It is important to note that the laughs may be a coping mechanism or a physiological release that symbolizes the relief that one is not alone in their traumatic experience (Wilkins & Eisenbraun, 2009). The latter can be another factor that confuses a therapist who is untrained in the intersection between trauma and Black experiences.

Researchers Frijda et al. (1991) noted that emotions last 90 seconds from the onset to the dissolution; however, the reoccurrence of a similar event can cause a reemergence of the emotion that may feel as though the emotion is lasting longer than 90 seconds. Additionally, recurring and intrusive thoughts about the incident may cause a reemergence of the emotion that, again, will seem as if it is lasting longer than the standard 90 seconds. When addressing trauma as an emotional response, one must consider the added complexity to brain chemistry that is more severe and less common than any other emotion. Trauma can cause damage to the brain. It can create fixed neural networks that derail how one responds to future challenging incidents, either making the person overreact or underreact to external stimuli. Additionally, it causes damage to the hippocampus, amygdala, and prefrontal cortex, which changes memory and how one thinks, makes decisions, and experiences other emotions (Bremner, 2006). Lastly, trauma is connected to the five senses and sensory recall (Kearney & Lanius, 2022). While clients may not remember the chronological details of a traumatic event due to the place in their brain where trauma is stored, they may have intrusive thoughts that occur based on a sensory register. Clients may see, touch, smell, hear, or taste something and then be flooded with disjointed but intense memories of the traumatic event.

In some situations, clients' trauma recall may occur in the subconscious state, so they are not explicitly aware of the cause of the emotional or physiological response that is associated with the traumatic event or trigger. In these situations, they may say, "I do not know what occurred, but it was something." In fact, one of the most complicated elements of trauma is the impact it has on the reticular activating system (RAS) that affects alertness (or hyperalertness), attention and focus, arousal and emotional responses, and learning. Additionally, trauma affects decision-making that can impact how one engages in the achievement of goals, participates in relationships and friendships, and perceives oneself. In these situations, trauma actively and negatively changes one's behaviors. Trauma is an emotional response to a terrible event; without therapeutic intervention, it can have lasting and generational impacts, create unhealthy relational experiences, and damage parts of the brain and subsequent physical functioning. While trauma may not be preventable, it is treatable. This mere fact is crucial when working with Black women, who may experience trauma due to their involuntary identities such as race or gender. You the therapist may not be able to single-handedly correct the causes of trauma such as racism and misogyny, but you can be competent, trained, skilled, and ready to intervene when your client experiences a traumatic event or when a past trauma is triggered.

THERAPIST'S TIP: Countertransference

In 1992, John Rowan, a humanistic-oriented therapist with an interest in psychoanalytic tradition, countered Sigmund Freud's identification of countertransference, suggesting that there were eight types of countertransference, not just one. There are still many educators and professors within the mental health fields who continue to teach the concept of countertransference through one sole and limited perspective. Furthermore, many mental health practitioners are taught that countertransference is a universally negative experience for therapists, which fails to account for cases of identification countertransference in which a therapist overly enjoys spending time with their client and crosses boundaries of objectivity by heavily leaning in on aspects of relatability—which are not for the benefit of their client.

Gelso and Hayes (2007) note that countertransference forms in three ways: physical, intellectual, and emotional. Additionally, Gelso and Hayes (2007) note that while the historical identification originated with Freud, the evolution of understanding of countertransference has expanded to include the therapist's experiential subjectivity when working with a client. Gelso notes that while countertransference can be managed, it must be explicitly and accurately identified first. Management may include acknowledgment, acceptance, the role of countertransference influence in a client's treatment plan, guidance from the clinical supervisors, and explicit tools to create physical, emotional, or intellectual boundaries.

In this context, countertransference is identified in three categories: defensive, reactive, and induced. Defensive countertransference occurs when a therapist's own personal issues influence their statements and reactions to a client (Flescher, 1953). They are consciously or subconsciously defending their personal lives based on what a client has said or done, unbeknownst to the client. Therefore, the client may experience a defensive, persuasive, or coerced experience from the therapist. Reactive countertransference refers to the manner in which a therapists responds when a client has expressed or demonstrated a distorted countertransference (Flescher, 1953). While clients may have distorted thoughts about reality, there may be times when the therapist reacts to the distortion as if it were real. This may manifest in a therapist engaging in the distortion instead of identifying it, addressing it, or challenging it. Here, we note that distortions can appear positive or negative, so a client may be overly complimenting a therapist due to their own distortion or need for validation and acceptance. A therapist may enjoy the distorted compliments and continue to react in a matter that never addresses why a client needs validation or acceptance. In this case, the client does not get the support or healing that is needed because the therapist is reacting to the distortion versus addressing it with the client. Therefore, the manner in which the therapist engages and responds reflects reactive countertransference. Lastly, induced countertransference occurs when a therapist consciously or unconsciously falls into the role that the client has created through her countertransference (Flescher, 1953). If a client needs a mother figure, the counselor may become a maternal role model. If the client needs a stern person to challenge their thoughts, the therapist may unconsciously take on that role. In this situation, the client's countertransference influences the way the therapist shows up in the session. The therapist's knowledge, education, and training become null and void as she turns into who the client needs her to be rather than who she is trained to be. Therefore, the countertransference causes a lack of professionalism and professional identity and the therapist is puppeteered by the client's needs versus the therapist's professional training and position.

Microaggressions

In the 2007 article "Racial Microaggressions in Everyday Life: Implications for Clinical Practice," Derald Sue et al. redefined racial microaggressions as "brief and commonplace daily verbal, behavioral, or environmental indignities, whether intentional or unintentional, that communicate hostile, derogatory, or negative racial slights and insults toward people of color." In a similar solely written 2010 book, *Microaggressions in Everyday Life: Race, Gender, and Sexual Orientation*, Sue expanded the definition of microaggressions to include gender and sexual orientations, explicitly noting that microaggressions are not solely limited to these three identities, but rather include all identities of those who are marginalized. These hidden messages may invalidate the group identity or experiential reality of target persons; demean them on a personal or group level; communicate that they are lesser human beings; suggest they do not belong with the majority group; threaten, intimidate, or relegate them to inferior status and treatment.

The intersection of race and gender places Black women farther in the margins and more likely to encounter microaggressions as daily, unpredictable, and hurtful experiences that are easily internalized to the frequency and intensity of the experience. To further complicate the lived experiences of Black women, microaggressions may be expressed by people who are within the same racial and/or gender group as the Black women, thus amplifying the collective experience of being unsafe.

The recurrence of unsafe experiences combined with emotional responses such as fear, judgment, rejection, and loneliness, create the onset of trauma through micro-events. Due to the delivery, the brain and body may register the insult sensorially before the mind has an opportunity to process the trauma or accompanying trigger. Since the presentation of these traumatic microaggressions is not physically aggressive, the Black woman receiving them may be unsure why she is experiencing the same physiological and psychological responses comparable to a physical trauma such as a natural disaster, abuse, or neglect. The formation of trauma is still real and true even in the absence of a physically aggressive event.

Even in a society that has attempted to lean into using politically correct terms, microaggressions seep into conversations and experiences due to explicit and implicit systemic undertones that challenge the receiver as a whole person because of her marginalized identities. The constant fight, both external and internal, can create a burnout that may neither be articulated nor nonverbally expressed but can be felt and thus shifts the behavior of Black women. In these situations, we find that Black women create two responses that may be used interchangeably or simultaneously when confronted with a microaggression. They can counter the confrontation with a piercing verbalized response of disgust, anger, and defense or they can withdraw and avoid, which can be internalized as diminished self-worth or self-value (Motro et al., 2022). With repeated experiences, there is greater activation in the limbic system of the brain that may create stress, a reduction of gray matter, and a decline in creativity and productivity (Kokubun et al., 2018).

You may notice that because of repeated microaggressions, your Black woman client begins to complain about a particular environment. Her productivity, in work, school, or hobbies declines and she loses zest for life. It is hard to feel safe when aggression is presented daily. It is challenging to be creative or produce when one does not feel safe.

Direct Aggression

The statistics are odious.

> Black women 23.4% more likely to experience sexual assault versus white women. (Bryant-Davis et al., 2010)

> Four in 10 Black women experience intimate partner violence (IPV) in their lifetime. (Black & Burton, 2011)

> Women have more adverse childhood experiences (ACE) than men (39% versus 21%). (Haahr-Pedersen et al., 2020)

> Black people have more ACEs than white people. (53% versus 36%) (Bernard et al., 2021)

> Black people are 19 times more likely to receive a wrongful conviction. (Gross et al., 2022)

> Black people account for 53% of legal exonerations for a wrongful conviction. (Gross et al., 2022)

Black people are twice as likely to be murdered by police than white people. (Rahman, 2021)

Black women earn on average $5,500 less per year and experience higher unemployment and poverty rates than the U.S. average for women. (Chinn et al., 2021)

Black women are subjected to higher levels of racism, sexism, and discrimination than Black men or white women. (Chinn et al., 2021)

The consequences of direct aggression toward Black women are not limited to just Black women. In a 2024 report, the World Health Organization (WHO) noted that direct aggression toward women has social and economic costs with an impact on work attendance and productivity, project completion and company reputation, work environment and general morale, children's physical and mental health, missed appointments and consequences to physicians, poor attendance at children's school events and extracurricular activities, and housing. Additionally, WHO noted that direct aggression is preventable. It does not have to occur. The population that tends to receive the brunt of this preventable social issue is Black women.

Exposure to violence, either in one incident or a repeated recurrence can lead to several mental health disorders including but not limited to depressive disorders, anxiety disorders, personality disorders, family relational disorders, and trauma disorders.

THERAPIST'S TIP: Tracking Trauma via Intake

As a therapist who is well versed in the intersection of trauma and minority communities, I have expanded the trauma section of my intake form to include topics that may be connected to trauma but not consistently discussed or labeled as trauma.

Consider adding these areas to your intake form too.

Physical Abuse	Sexual Abuse	Neglect
Interpersonal violence	Bullying (school or work)	Emotional abuse
Natural disaster	Refugee/asylum seeker	Relationship/breakup
Housing trauma	Financial trauma	Medical trauma
Employment trauma	Police/legal violence	Unrepairable rifts
Community violence (observer, participant, and/or victim)		War/terrorism

When gathering information about your clients via the intake process, remember that it is best to have a conversation around these topics versus simple and direct questions. The latter will seem like an interrogation and your therapeutic relationship is too new for a client to experience the pressure of thera-peutic intervention. The former method will demonstrate a higher level of care and concern for the client, even while you are gathering information for your formal case conceptualization.

Since a conversation around trauma is the best practice, be sure to set aside more time for your intake process. Instead of one hour, consider a full commitment of one to two sessions or a 90-minute session. Additionally, it is important that you provide context to each traumatic topic above. For instance, some clients may not have labeled a relationship breakup as trau-matic, yet it may have yielded a negative emotional response to an event that felt uncontrollable to them while also creating cognitive distortions, triggering negative core beliefs, or displaying as maladaptive or dysfunctional behaviors. Take a few minutes and think about how each of the abovementioned areas can be traumatic and demonstrated in one's life. Then create speaking notes for yourself so you can give context and examples for each topic so your client can fully understand and comprehend how some nontraditional or common experiences can be linked to traumatic experiences too.

Survival Aggression

There are times when members of a minority community engage in immoral or challenging activities as a way of survival. Their purest intent may be to live or provide for themselves, but the path, decisions, and actions may be difficult to process and consolidate. Their decision may have led to a personal trauma event; the recurring guilt around their decision may have led to a traumatic processing period; or their actions may have caused trauma for another person. In these situations, you may see a client who became a prostitute to earn money to survive or to escape a different traumatic environment. You may encounter a woman who placed her child in the foster care or adoption system because she did not think she could care for, love, or provide for the child. You may meet a client who once was or currently is in a gang and committed crimes to demonstrate loyalty to her gang family or to earn money for all to eat or have housing. In rare circumstances, you may encounter a client who engaged in child abuse because of misleading generational discipline practices or the uninformed continuation of generational traumas. This list is not exhaustive of the ethical dilemmas that marginalized people experience simply as a way of surviving in a culture in which they are not seen, heard, or appreciated and do not have the same paths and access to stability in finances, housing, relation-ships, or self-healing.

In these situations, consider the client's role but also the circumstances that led to her decisions. They may be the cause of aggression, and she may have experienced aggression that led to her becoming a cause of aggression. In either or both situations there is a connection between aggression and trauma that needs to be explored with the client (Rasche et al., 2016).

INSIGHT FROM A CLIENT: PP

PP entered therapy with her husband, RP. They have been married for 9 years and have three children together. Their oldest child was born to PP from a previous relationship; however, RP has been in that child's life since she was 3 months old and legally, financially, and emotionally claims that child as his own. While that child knows that RP is not her biological father, it is not a recurring topic in their home because she does not sense or see a difference in how she is treated by RP.

PP and RP entered therapy because they were having a challenge in how to parent their youngest child, a 5-year-old boy, who was the only boy child and the youngest in the family. PP noticed that RP was allowing him to have special privileges that their oldest daughters did not experience at his age. She was beginning to feel that he was becoming entitled and spoiled, thus shifting the relationship dynamics between him and his sisters and him and his parents. RP did not have a concern but agreed to counseling because he wanted to restore peace in his home while also catering to the needs of his only son, who was also named after him.

During the intake process, which was done individually, I asked each of them about trauma, in the form of relationship trauma and rifts. PP noted there was past infidelity in the relationship, initiated by RP and continued throughout her pregnancy with the youngest child. Separately, RP admitted to continuous infidelity with several women. He said that during their marriage, he had slept with over 80 women and was able to keep track based on his attendance at a local bar that he liked to visit. While at this bar, he challenged himself to meet, flirt, and sleep with at least one woman per month. Since the intake process is done separately, I did not share this information with PP but told RP that I would like us to build up the process to be able to share some of this information with his wife, so they could address any challenges in the marriage that caused him to seek companionship outside of the marriage. He agreed.

During treatment, PP and RP worked on their parenting and communication styles. RP noted the difficulties in his life as a Black man and his inherent desire to protect his son or delay the exposure of community and social violence that his son was likely to experience. The root of the differences in treatment was based on gender and past traumas, not an intentional lack of care or concern for their daughters.

Through this process, RP mentioned his infidelity in the context of finding pleasure with other women as an escape and a coping method with the daily challenges that he experienced as a Black man and the lack of comfort that he experienced at home with his wife and children. PP's response was full of anger, betrayal, confusion, and aggression. We extended the session time so that they could continue to process the complex layers of this experience. Within a week of the session, PP informed me that they would not be continuing couples therapy because she had initiated an interpersonal violence incident with RP and caused significant physical harm. He was in the hospital, and she was out on bond due to legal charges. She asked if once the process concluded, she could continue therapy and process her feelings of betrayal, her thoughts around their divorce, and her actions of aggression. The physical aggressions were uncharacteristic visceral reactions, and she was embarrassed that she lost control of herself and thus became a complex role model for her children, who had witnessed the incident but were not informed of the backstory. In their minds, their mother was the aggressor who was responsible for the father being in the hospital and the family splitting up. This caused an added layer of guilt for PP and trauma for her and her family.

Within a year, PP returned to therapy, divorced and alone. We created a new treatment plan that was focused on identifying themes of aggression, violence, and trauma along with her suppression, repression, and varied emotional and physical defense mechanisms. I provided a safe space for her to shed her embarrassment and guilt while replacing it with positive thoughts and mantras that could increase the positive emotions in her life. Additionally, she created plans for ways to interact with her ex-husband, restore the relationship and role modeling for her children, and determine her own self-work and self-love.

TRAUMA DISORDERS

Trauma is messy. It is hard, tough, cemented in a client's life, uncomfortable to confront and diagnose, and challenging to treat. For marginalized clients like Black women clients, trauma may be or seem like a daily part of their lives. From microaggressions to direct aggression to survival aggression, traumatic experiences may be unavoidable, unexplainable, and untreatable. However, it is our job to help and heal our clients.

Due to the challenges associated with trauma, many therapists do not explore the possibility of these disorders with clients. Since there is an overlap on the criteria specifiers in the *Diagnostic and Statistical Manual* that therapists consult to make diagnoses between some of the depressive and anxiety disorders and trauma, many therapists overdiagnose clients with a different mood disorder rather than taking the effort to explore the client's trauma and properly diagnosing her with PTSD or acute stress disorder.

While PTSD was initially introduced to the mental health community as a response to addressing and treating the needs of military personnel who fought and were returning from the Vietnam War, it became officially recognized in the *Diagnostic and Statistical Manual III* in 1970 (Andreasen, 2010). The most recent version, *DSM-5-TR* indicates that the primary and "most prominent clinical characteristics are anhedonic and dysphoric symptoms, externalizing angry and aggressive symptoms, or dissociative symptoms" (American Psychiatric Association, 2022). There are times when trauma and stress-related disorders can mirror other mood disorders; however, the abovementioned characteristics must be present for an accurate diagnosis to be given. Oftentimes, symptoms such as anger and aggression are overlooked in Black women as typical or stereotypical characteristics of this unique cultural group. With stereotypes such as angry Black woman or retaliatory statements such as "She was so aggressive," some therapists, amid their unaddressed biases, may see these as typical Black woman characteristics versus the demonstration of a posttraumatic stress disorder (Motro et al., 2022).

A therapist's biases along with common socialization stereotypes can cause a therapist to miss accurate symptoms and subsequently misdiagnose and mistreat a client.

THERAPIST'S TIP: The Suffering of Angry and Aggressive Black Women

Consider this: What if that angry Black woman or aggressive Black woman were simply suffering from repeated trauma, both direct events and indirect microaggressions? What if she was simply afraid and her only tool for self-protection was the facade of impenetrable toughness? What if she is coming to you for help but your biases prevent you from seeing her as a victim of trauma? How would that help her heal?

Posttraumatic Stress Disorder and Acute Stress Disorder

When working with Black women, some of the features of the diagnostic criteria may look different from those described in the *DSM*. Therapists should listen to what a client is saying and pay attention to what is not said, what is avoided, and what leaves a gap in understanding. Additionally, note how a client behaves in their sessions and which statements or topics cause a visible triggered response. Utilize a few humanistic theoretical concepts to encourage the client to continue to process and grow.

For Black women clients, PTSD, acute stress disorder, and the other trauma and stressor-related disorders may look like:

- Being acutely sensitive to 70% or more of things that are said or done to them: Since trauma is stored in the limbic system versus the frontal cortex, the client may not know or understand why she is sensitive around certain statements and actions but is still acutely aware that something is making her feel uncomfortable in the moment.

- Defensive body language: Crossing arms, rolling eyes, disconnecting via a spaced look that may not be reflective of the comments in the moment but rather the discomfort and trauma of the past.
- Self-numbing: Overeating or overdrinking before engaging with certain people or situations. This may occur because the client wants to reduce her sensitivities and not be on high alert. Self-numbing may relax her nervous system before she must engage with a person or situation that has been historically triggering.
- Tense muscles: Shoulders perked up and near ears. This may occur as a natural but subconscious reaction that is connected to a fight-or-flight response.
- Avoidance: Avoiding people and places that once brought pleasure although the client is not always conscious of the avoidance. This may occur because the client believes the experience may not be full of joy but also is tainted with memories of the past or unhinged confrontation from self or others. It is a conscious protection but also prevents the experiences of joy. It becomes a distorted thought that the experience is black or white, full of joy or no joy at all.
- Self-sabotage: In most given situations, especially those that have been traumatic, knowing what to do and when to do it, but not actually doing it. In this situation, the client may not trust herself. She may be blaming herself, even slightly, for the trauma or not trusting that she can protect herself if another situation arises.
- Feeling unsafe, insecure, or hyperalert: She may demonstrate actions that look as if she is walking on eggshells and is afraid to upset anyone at any given moment.
- Being inconsistent in her actions: She may have developed an insecure attachment style as a reflection of her trauma. She may want and act in closeness with someone and then without clear warning or understanding begin to pull away. Additionally, she may state a desire to be close with people but be emotionally unavailable or inaccessible.
- Being controlling or overplanning: She may want to know all the details before she decides and is very upset if anything alters the plan. This occurs because she may find a sense of safety in predictability and the lack of predictability makes her feel afraid, vulnerable, or exposed to the possibility of another traumatic experience.

For Black women clients, PTSD, acute stress disorder, and the other trauma and stressor-related disorders may sound like:

- Saying inauthentic things as a matter of protection: "It is what it is." "I do not care." These statements represent a sense of disconnection to avoid hurt. She may believe that if she disconnects early, she will experience less hurt or pain. This may be especially true if she blames herself for her trauma. These statements may make her feel that she has greater control to protect herself.
- Saying things that are fantasy-driven: Denial may have a negative connotation but, in this situation, a client may say things that align more of her wishes and fantasies versus reality. She does not want to experience trauma or must process through trauma; so she may choose to focus solely on what is positive, what could be or could have been, and what she wants versus what is real in the moment. This may be a coping technique to maintain hope for a future that is void of additional traumatic experiences.
- Saying things that create distance: In these situations, you may hear a client say, "I need a little time." This indicates that the client is overwhelmed with the messages and messaging. She may note that she is triggered but be unsure why it is occurring, or she may feel that the information will unravel her sense of safety. There are times when she receives a message that is counter to any self-talk she has used to make sense of her trauma. The presentation of an alternative thought or perspective may scare her because she thinks she will be vulnerable, or exposed, or will have to rebuild. She may not need time from you or therapy, but rather time to decide if the consideration of an alternative thought will cause her to unravel and rebuild herself. For her, that may be scarier than addressing the trauma directly.

THERAPIST'S TIP: Utilizing a Humanistic Therapeutic Approach

When working with Black women who have experienced trauma, it is best to use the humanistic theoretical approach to confrontation. The humanistic theoretical approach focuses on the present moment, the here and now, the idea that while humans are flawed, they have an internal capability to resolve their mental health and moral issues, primarily by going inward but also by being present in the moment. Additionally, this approach is self-centered, with a primary focus on self-concept as a matter of consistent perception about oneself.

When working with a Black woman who has experienced trauma, remember to be gentle and kind but call out the inconsistencies between what she said and did versus what she may have previously said she wants to do or how she wants to live. Using confrontation as a therapeutic intervention can encourage the client to learn more about herself, bring forth her inconsistencies from the unconscious or subconscious to a place of consciousness, and allow her to self-correct in moments where she may be tempted to default to a trauma response versus a healing response. Additionally, using confrontation as a therapeutic intervention could allow your client to experience therapy as a safe haven in which the confrontation and correction is gentle and warm versus harsh and unkind.

Consider using interventions that allow the client to regain a sense of trust within herself. Due to the messaging that many Black women receive such as "Black is bad," "Black people are dangerous," "Women are to blame for the issues in the world," "Women are temptresses," and more, your client may be blaming herself for having experienced trauma. She may have lost trust in herself, her sense of awareness of surroundings or people, her ability to predict when harm is approaching, and so on. She may benefit from writing daily affirmations, reading a daily devotional, or tracking her positive self-talk. These self-corrective moments should be action-based because the trauma was action-based. Additionally, they should involve a sensory element because trauma is stored sensorially. The client should consider burning a fragrant candle or incense, sitting on grass, drinking something flavor-forward but nutritious and doing things that activate one or more of the five senses of taste, touch, hearing, sight, or smell.

THERAPIST'S TIP: Diagnosing the Correct Trauma Disorder

There are six different types of trauma- and stressor-related disorders. Two of the six are specific to children or have an onset in childhood. If the onset occurred in childhood and was not diagnosed or was misdiagnosed or mistreated, it is likely that the specific disorder morphed into one of the adult-centered disorders, such as PTSD or acute stress disorder.

Set aside planning time to study the trauma- and stressor-related disorders so you can accurately distinguish them from the differential diagnostic options and understand the essential features and characteristics. For instance, acute stress disorder is like secondary trauma due to the criteria "learning that the event(s) occurred to a close family member or close friend" (American Psychiatric Association, 2022) but it is not limited to secondary trauma because the direct and primary traumatic event may have happened to your client. In other words, it can be a primary or secondary response. The onset of the symptoms may be delayed for up to 1 month after the traumatic event occurred.

Additionally, for one to be diagnosed with adjustment disorders, the emotional or behavioral symptoms must have developed within 3 months of the onset of the stressor. For Black women, the classification of one stressor may be difficult to identify, which is why it is important to have a conversation with the client during the intake and case conceptualization process rather than asking a series of interrogation-style questions.

Review and study the six trauma- and stressor-related disorders before diagnosing a client with a depressive or anxiety disorder.

- Reactive attachment disorder (children)
- Disinhibited social engagement disorder (children/adolescents)
- PTSD
- Acute stress disorder
- Adjustment disorders
- Other specified trauma- and stressor-related disorder

THERAPIST'S TIP: Utilizing Trauma Assessments and Tools

There are many times when the therapist completes the intake and case conceptualization process and foregoes a formal assessment period.

Oftentimes, assessments are the missing puzzle piece in accurately diagnosing the client and creating an effective treatment plan that will allow the client to achieve her treatment goals while also having lifelong sustainable tools for her to continue to be the person she wants to be.

Remember, when doing assessments with clients, therapists should start with a set of broadband assessments that will allow you to assess various disorders at once. Once a set of potential disorders is identified through the broadband assessment results, more diagnostic-specific assessments should be used. An example is using the Minnesota Multiphasic Personality Inventory-2-Restructured Form (MMPI-2-RF) as the broadband assessment, then the Beck Anxiety Inventory as a diagnostic-specific assessment.

Below is a list of diagnostic-specific assessments you can use when identifying a trauma- and stressor-related disorder:

- Clinician Administered PTSD Scale (CAPS)
- Davidson Trauma Scale (DTS)
- Distressing Event Questionnaire (DEQ)
- Evaluation of Lifetime Stressors (ELS)
- Global Psychotrauma Screen
- Impact of Event Scale Revised (IES-R)
- Mississippi Scale for Combat-Related PTSD (M-PTSD)
- Parenting Stress Index (PSI)
- Penn Inventory for Posttraumatic Stress Disorder
- Posttraumatic Diagnostic Scale (PDS)
- Posttrauma Risky Behaviors Questionnaire
- Primary Care PTSD Screen for *DSM-5*
- PTSD Checklist for *DSM-5* (PCL-5)
- PTSD Symptom Scale-Interview (PSS-I)
- PTSD Symptom Scale: Self-Report Version (MPSS-SR)
- Screen for Posttraumatic Stress Symptoms (SPTSS)
- Structured Interview for PTSD (SI-PTSD)
- Trauma Assessment for Adults (TAA)

- Trauma Assessment for Adults (TAA)–Self Report
- Trauma History Questionnaire (THQ)
- Trauma-Informed Mental Health Assessment
- Trauma Symptom Inventory (TSI)
- Traumatic Stress Schedule (TSS)

Most of these assessments can be found in the public domain or cost less than $30 and take less than 15 minutes for the client to complete and 15 minutes for the therapist to review, analyze, and draw diagnostic conclusions.

CONCLUSION

For many clients, experiencing, addressing, and healing from traumatic experiences, sole or recurring, may be the hardest thing that they will experience in life. It may feel like a lifetime of issues or a recurrence of triggers and emotions connected to the traumatic events. For many, the feeling of wanting to give up occurs when their trauma is unaddressed and unhealed; thus they live a life that is not reflective of their hopes, dreams, and goals, but rather limited to the engagement of traumatic responses and the fear of and avoidance of future hurt. This mentality will prevent a client from having the life she wants, instead living a life of fear and limits. In being marginalized and an involuntary minority, she may already sense uncontrollable limits in her life; addressing and healing beyond the trauma may be the powerful and self-induced liberation that she needs. You can be her guide to her personal freedom.

Therapist's Introspection

Personal	Professional
Before reading this chapter, what did you think about Black women and their experiences with trauma?	Which clients came to mind while you read this chapter?
What were you taught or did you assume about Black women and the types of trauma they experience?	If you had an opportunity to redo a previous session with a Black woman client, what would you do differently, based on the information you learned in this session?
All of us have biases. What are two biases that arose for you while reading this chapter?	Whom do you need to talk to about this chapter's content? What do you want to say to them? How will you say it?

After reading this chapter, what did you learn and how will you put that information into application, both personally and professionally?	In thinking about your client's treatment plans, what new goals, objectives, and interventions need to be added?
What else did this chapter bring up for you?	

Therapeutic Guide

Therapy	Clinical Focus	Sample Therapeutic SMART Goal	Technique or Intervention
Trauma-Focused Cognitive Behavioral Therapy (TF-CBT)	Psychoeducation about trauma, its impact and implication is important in the healing process Labeling the trauma and building hope and resilience are equally important All the components of cognitive behavioral therapy (CBT) apply with a specific clinical focus on trauma Narration and storytelling related to the traumatic event(s) allow clients to approach the traumatic memories and not avoid them Avoiding the cognitive processing of the traumatic events allows the impact of the trauma to be more long-lasting and sensitive to triggers	Client will learn and practice the TF-CBT skills of Psychoeducation, Relaxation, Affect Identification and Regulation, and Cognitive Coping (PRAC) 15 minutes each session to be achieved within 6 months. Client will decrease emotional sensitivity to triggers by narrating the traumatic event for no less than 30 minutes per month, in session, to be achieved within 18 months. Client will build hope by practicing five resilience-based skills, such as, self-care, developing a strong social network, labeling personal strengths, utilizing problem solving skills, and engaging with self-grace in the midst of personal change, to be achieved within 18 months.	Psychoeducation Relaxation Affect identification and regulation Cognitive coping Narration of traumatic event Building hope In vivo exposure Goal setting Self-care Enhancing safety Identifying distortions Labeling core beliefs Cognitive restructuring Behavioral experiments Behavioral reinforcements

Therapy	Clinical Focus	Sample Therapeutic SMART Goal	Technique or Intervention
Eye Movement Desensitization and Reprocessing (EMDR)	Reprocess trauma through brain bilateral stimulation by moving the eyes from one side of the brain to the other side of the brain Allows the brain to address unprocessed memories	Client will learn about EMDR by engaging in three psychoeducation sessions and reading two articles, to be achieved in 5 weeks. Client will identify two specific trauma targets to be addressed through EMDR, to be identified and achieved within 7 weeks. Client will engage in the 8 phases of EMDR to be achieved over 12 sessions.	Eight phases: 1. History-Taking and Treatment Planning 2. Preparation 3. Assessment 4. Desensitization 5. Installation 6. Body Scan 7. Closure 8. Reevaluation Worksheets Chronological Target Plan Congruent Breathing Belief Schema Focused History Wheel of Fortunate Resources EMDR Mechanics Sheet
Creative Arts Therapy (Art, Dance, Drama, Music, Writing)	Creative arts allow for the use of the right hemisphere of the brain. Talk therapy allows for the use of the left hemisphere of the brain. The combination of creative arts and talk therapy allows for more comprehensive processing and healing Encourages emotional processing when language or memories are not present	Client will facilitate traumatic event recall and healing through sensory stimulation and engagement (creative arts therapeutic approach) to be practiced for 1 hour per month. Client will increase life satisfaction through the childhood nostalgic actions of creative arts, to be done outside of the therapeutic space	Painting and coloring Finger painting Drawing Doodling and scribbling Collage Sculpting Ceramics Writing and singing songs Playing music

Allows for emotional processing when the memory is too difficult to express in words	environments, for 2 hours per month.	Improvising on unfinished lyrics and instrumental sounds
	Client will increase hope and optimism though the increased engagement of her imagination to be facilitated by the use of two of the four creative arts, to be practiced for 1 hour per week.	Listening to music with visualization
Supports creative approaches to goal setting and achievement		Listening to music without visualization
		Dance with music
		Dance without music
		Improvisation dance
		Writing prompts
		Story writing

Journal Prompts

When thinking about the traumatic events in your life, how have the events and the thoughts about the event affected your decision-making process? Honestly considering them, which areas of your life are underdeveloped because of your hesitation to make decisions or a history of self-sabotaging decisions?

What is your decision-making process? Consider it in five to seven steps. Write it down. Two days later, revisit your process and edit it. It may include additional steps.

Under what conditions have you experienced burnout? Was trauma, either explicit or implicit, a factor in the condition?

Have you ever decided, because of a need for survival, something that you later regretted? Did you make that decision because you did not think there was another choice? If you feel or felt guilty because of that decision, have you released the guilt? What needs to occur for you to comfortably reduce the guilt?

Have you ever been called an angry Black woman? Who said that to you? What were the conditions in which it was said? In accepting that you were angry, which other emotions may have been present? Was it easier to express anger rather than express the other emotions?

What if an angry Black woman or aggressive Black woman were simply suffering from repeated trauma, both direct events and indirect microaggressions? What if she or you were simply afraid and the only tool for self-protection was the facade of impenetrable toughness? How would therapy help you heal? What would you need from your therapist to feel protected and safe to heal?

9

Addressing Mental Health Disorders via a Cultural Lens

You can't focus on the bad thing, you have to focus on getting through it.

—Ciara

It's not the load that breaks you down, it's the way you carry it.

—Lena Horne

If you surrender to the wind, you can ride it.

—Toni Morrison

THE *DSM* AND CULTURAL REPRESENTATION

In the development of most mental health theories, Black people were not included in the research population (Davis, 2018). One could argue that they were not considered because they were not around, were not considered to be human, or were not a concern for the theorists or researchers. Others could argue that incorporating Black people into the research population was irrelevant because all people are the same in the face of science. Some could state that historical racial segregation created inaccessibility because people who believed they owned enslaved people did not allow others to see, spend time with, or care about their needs (Shim, 2021). Others could state that the lack of inclusion of Black people is simply an injustice to cultural representation and will impact the universal application of theoretical-based interventions.

Therapeutic approaches are different from theoretical orientations; therapeutic approaches are derived from theory. Most Black people were not utilizing therapy at the time when some approaches such as cognitive behavioral therapy and solution-focused therapy were being developed. One could simply acknowledge that the common theories and therapies do not include Black people, and consequently many of the acknowledged diagnoses do not include Black cultural engagements, either. More specifically, while the *DSM-5-TR* has sections that represent cultural sensitivity, the manual is rooted in theories, therapies, and approaches that consider culture as a component, not an integration (American Psychiatric Association, 2022).

When a person lives within a cultural identity such as race or gender, the socialization of who she should be occurs before the person is even aware of it (Martin et al., 2002). She receives messages that create structures of identity such as how she should behave, which religions she should practice, which clothes and colors she should wear, which sports she can play, how she can receive and express love, and, as it pertains to this chapter, how she should think and handle any mental health issues.

Many Black women are dealing with mental health issues that are manifested into symptoms that do not align with the *DSM* specifiers but are still true, relevant, and equally important (Garb, 2021). For instance, many Black women may be depressed but it is demonstrated in ways that are outside the bounds of the *DSM* criteria. A Black woman may enter the therapeutic space in search of a diagnosis and aligned treatment, but not fit the criteria. The result is a misdiagnosis, no diagnosis, an unaligned and unhelpful treatment plan, or no plan at all.

It is difficult to encourage people who have historical taboos about mental health to enter a therapeutic space only for that space to be unhelpful to that client. Entering an unhelpful therapeutic space would be counterproductive. Instead of helping the client address her own mental health, an unhelpful therapeutic space could extinguish the client's interest and motivation. Additionally the client may tell others about her ineffective and unhelpful therapeutic space, which would prevent others from seeking and engaging in therapy. This chapter is especially important because it directly addresses mental health disorders and symptoms that drive clients to therapy. These disorders are well known and oftentimes researched by the client. Careful consideration must be given in order to be helpful, effective, and transformative.

This chapter is divided into two common mental health disorders, depression and anxiety, and the cultural manifestations for Black women.

DEPRESSION

According to the World Health Organization (2017), depression is the leading cause of mental disability worldwide, with an estimated 4.4% of the population experiencing the disorder. As we consider the common terms related to diagnoses, *disorder* indicates a lack of order or function in one's life and *disability* relates to one's lack of ability to do a desired activity or have a desired experience. In considering depression, one is unable, due to mental disorder, to live a life of one's own desire due to a series of lacking abilities. While depression symptoms were identified as early as the 14th century, it was either considered a spiritual imbalance in which an individual had a depressed spirit or a biological issue with an impact on physical function and task completion (Tipton, 2014). Greek philosophers related depression to fear while Northern Europeans connected the disorder to moral disarray (Ahonen, 2018). These geographical areas were scarcely occupied by Black people during these centuries and the ways they experienced depression and the integration of their cultural identities were not included in the philosophical or experiential conception of depression. However, as theorists such as Freud, Beck, Bowlby, Frankl, Rogers, and others emerged, there were more Black people in proximity to include in the research populations and theoretical development. Yet there was an oversight.

In 1980, the *DSM III* introduced depression as a mental disorder; however, there remained much controversy circling the language and severity of a major depressive disorder and other mood disorders or mood changes within different disorders, like dementia (*DSM III-R*, p. xxii). As one of the key factors for revision, an advisory committee was formed to address theoretical orientations within the disorders, language specification, axial alignment, and other factors. This was important because the emergence of depression as a mental health disorder was being experienced by varying clients with other mental health disorders such as obsessive compulsive disorder, childhood developmental disorders, or organic disorders but was also a key specifier in other disorders such as bipolar disorder or a major depressive episode such as a seasonal pattern. Practitioners were having trouble creating a true and accurate diagnosis (*DSM III-R*, p. 16).

THERAPIST'S TIP: Research Depression History and Political Influence

Keep in mind that major depressive disorder is different from major depressive episodes. Major depressive disorders are related to the recurrent disorder one feels throughout a long duration of one's lifetime. Major depressive episodes are related to depressive symptoms that happen for a brief period and can often be correlated to a specific recent and acute experience. While some of the treatments may be the same, the distinction is important when explaining the diagnosis and treatment plan to the clients.

Additionally, it will be important to do a review of the history and changes of a particular disorder in the various editions of the *DSM*. In some editions major changes were made to create clarity and distinction between or within a diagnostic disorder. In most of our graduate programs, we had courses focused on diagnosis and pathologies, but those courses used the *DSM* that was current at the time. Since my own graduate education in 2003, there have been three versions of the *DSM*, the *DSM-4-TR*, *DSM-5*, and *DSM-5-TR*. It is important for us as professional mental health clinicians to know the history of the *DSM* and the explicit and subtle changes that occur in each edition before we diagnosis a client. We need to know what the criteria and specifiers were, what the current criteria and specifiers are, and what changes have occurred.

If you would like to take it one step further, conduct your own research on what was occurring socially and politically that amplified the focus on some disorders or the removal of others. For instance, the *DSM I* listed homosexuality as a sexual deviation with sociopathic personality disturbance; however, when the *DSM-III* was published there were significant changes in the language used for sexual orientation, and when the *DSM-5* was published, sexual orientation as a disorder had been completely removed. The political nature and climate related to same-gender relationships changed in the 1970s and 1980s, resulting in the change of language in the *DSM-III* and subsequent editions. When considering these social changes, we must consider what was occurring politically, even as we ponder and research the criteria for changes in depressive disorders too.

Doing your own research will amplify your experiences as a clinician, your ability and ease in explaining the disorders to your clients, and your accuracy in diagnosing. Your graduate school learning was a springboard to the continuation of your professional research, not the termination of learning, understanding, and applying new information.

CULTURAL FORMATIONS

In the fourth edition of the *DSM*, cultural formulations and a glossary of cultural-bound symptoms were introduced. According to Mezzich et al. (1999), "The cultural formulation supplemented the nomothetic or standardized diagnostic ratings with an ideographic statement, emphasizing the patient's personal experience and the corresponding cultural reference group" (p. 459). The introduction of the section was based on the growing immigrant population and the cultural factors aligned with their identity along with the variations of how the disorders may be demonstrated at the intersection of the client's cultural identity. While this was helpful, the section was an amendment to the disorder, not a clear integration of culture within the understanding and diagnostic process. Additionally, it was catalyzed by the acknowledgment of immigrants and not the citizens who were born within the United States and yet still had a varied cultural identity such as Black Americans.

Due to the movements within the mental health community, The Cross-Cutting Review Committee on Cultural Issues and Ethnoracial Equality and Inclusion Work Group created six distinct changes within the *DSM-5-TR* related to cultural inclusion (Norton, 2022). Pertaining specifically to Black women, four of the six changes are highlighted below:

1. The term "racialized" is used instead of "race/racial" to underscore that race is a social construct.
2. "Ethnoracial" is used to define and combine the U.S. Census categories that encompass both ethnicity and race, such as white, African American, and Hispanic.
3. "Minority" and "non-White" are no longer used, as they are thought to describe racial groups in relation to white people, creating a social hierarchy.
4. Data about the prevalence of certain disorders in specific ethnoracial groups were added when existing research included reliable data (American Psychiatric Association, 2022).

In relation to prevalent data for specific disorders in a specific ethnoracial group, the *DSM-5-TR* states

> [W]hile . . . findings suggest substantial cultural differences in the expression of major depressive disorder, they do not permit simple linkages between particular cultures and the likelihood of specific symptoms. Rather, clinicians should be aware that in most countries the majority of cases of depression go unrecognized in primary care settings . . . and that in many cultures, somatic symptoms are very likely to constitute the presenting complaint. (American Psychiatric Association, 2022, p. 166)

When considering the changes in the *DSM-5-TR*, it is also important to note that this is a movement toward advancing the recognition of the lived experiences of Black women, especially those who are seeking help. However, there continue to be limitations in the full understanding of when and how depression may show up for Black women who either do not have the experience and exposure to mental health criteria or who demonstrate their disorder in a nontraditional way.

For instance, one must consider that a common criteria symptom for major depressive disorder is a diminished ability to think or concentrate, or indecisiveness. However, McManus et al. (2022) note that when one is under a significant amount of recurring stress such as racism, misogyny, microaggressions, and/or stereotypical gaze, there is a significant loss of gray brain matter, which would result in a similar reflection of diminished ability to think or concentrate. Thus a client may meet a specific criterion for major depressive disorder but not be depressed, but instead will reflect the unfortunate reality of being a minority with two or more marginalized intersections.

Another example may be related to fatigue. The Center for American Progress (CAP) notes that Black women earn $0.64 to every $1.00 that a white man earns (Bleiweis et al., 2021). To create a comfortable or comparable lifestyle, it is likely that a woman will have to work more hours per day, week, or year than a white man. This is the reason many Black women have second jobs or multiple careers. A Black woman who reports fatigue may not be experiencing fatigue in a traditional manner but rather a reflection of the fact that she must overwork just to maintain a particular lifestyle. Her fatigue may not be related to depression but rather a reflection of the unfortunate reality of sitting at the intersection of two marginalized identities and having to work more than the others just to maintain an average American lifestyle.

Another incongruence for Black women and depression is the lack of opportunity to demonstrate depressive symptoms like a change in hobbies. This may occur for multiple reasons to include by not limited to:

- Work, family, the added pressure of being an involuntary double minority.
- Traumatic histories related to microaggressions that prevent the onset or continuation of hobbies.
- It may not be that the Black woman client wants to have a reduction in hobbies or has a lack of interest in her established hobbies, but rather a realization that because she is an involuntary double minority, she does not have the time or resources to engage in her hobbies due to significantly more pressure to excel.

While there are truly times when a Black woman is depressed and accurately meets the criteria for a depressive disorder diagnosis, one must consider if the demonstration of her symptoms is organic, authentic, or learned from family members who are depressed and have normalized their behaviors or the symptoms of a depressive disorder.

The intersection of race and gender may yield a Black woman's demonstration of depression differently from the general or common criteria in the *DSM-5-TR*. For some Black women, depression may look like perfectionism, martyrdom, or avoidance.

Perfectionism

When considering the link between perfectionism and the diagnostic criteria for major depressive disorder, some Black women may lean into fastidiousness as a coping strategy to combat the scrutiny they are likely to experience from others. In acknowledging that Black women are often doubted for their intellect, contributions, or mere presence, the active and intentional skill of perfectionism leaves less room for statements, behaviors, or work products to be deconstructed or mislabeled and more room for Black women to be seen.

However, the repetitiveness of engaging in perfectionistic behaviors can cause a Black woman to feel that her best is not good enough, leading to a state of hopelessness that she will never be seen for who she truly is and not just what she can do for others. The thoughts and efforts that are required for perfectionism can be emotionally and chronologically time-consuming. As previously mentioned, the learned relationship with perfectionism can contribute to a lack of engagement in pleasurable activities. Therefore, it is less likely that she lost interest in pleasure but more likely that she began to interchange pleasure and perfectionism with a subconscious goal of protection. When one is at the intersection of two marginalized identities, protection may be more valuable than pleasure.

Martyrdom

Defined by Carl Jung (1959) as "a display of feigned or exaggerated suffering to obtain sympathy or exaggeration," martyrdom is loosely connected to the intersected archetypes as both the sage and the caregiver. In historical records and cultural stories, the martyr is often a person who believes there is a greater purpose or cause in the world and their life is only of worth if given to support the cause (DeSoucey et al., 2008). While perceived as remarkable and giving, this selfless perception is indeed a persona assumed to give meaning to feelings of worthlessness and despair.

Situated between the wisdom of a sage and the act of caring for others, many Black women take on the mask of a martyr to find a sense of worth within a society that embeds messages of their invisibility, marginalization, and worthlessness. Many Black women lean into this persona because it is a learned behavior that has elements of positivity, care, and uplift that have often been supported and reinforced by society, religious institutions, and even family members.

Considering the enslavement of Black people, caretaking in the United States historically was not a positive act or position for Black women. Oftentimes, enslaved people who took care of their masters did so begrudgingly. Yet, these same people were often given additional privileges because they were caretakers, as opposed to their enslaved counterparts who worked in the fields or on the farms. These caretakers were granted additional food, access to books (even if they were not permitted to read), access to and overhearing conversations, and the shelter of the master's house. Because of these reinforcements, caretaking became a position of privilege and being a martyr was celebrated. However, the perverted nature of caretaking was less addressed and overtly hidden by the persona of a martyr. There are many Black women who don the mask of martyrdom simply to feel a sense of worth, privilege, or admiration. However, in these experiences of taking care of the slavemaster, it meant that the enslaved person did not and could not take care of herself. Her personal needs were not a priority at all. She learned to sacrifice herself, her time with her family, nursing her own children, sleeping, bathing, nutrition, and community. Oftentimes, her role as a caretaker also meant that she had to suppress her own thoughts and ideas to prioritize the thoughts and ideas of her master, submitting to direction and leadership that was beneficial to him but harmful to her.

The current day experience of caretaking for Black women who don the mask of martyrdom is quite similar. We see Black women who will sacrifice their self-care, personal needs, short-term and long-term goals, time with their children, and opportunities to date, marry, or travel simply to take care of someone else. Additionally, these same women may stay quiet on issues that harm them, hope that someone chooses to prioritize them, or begin to devalue themselves while prioritizing someone else.

The human desire to be seen is a challenging position for Black women who are often placed in the margins of invisibility unless they are doing something that would benefit someone else. This is a learned pattern of behavior that is reinforced socially, politically, and economically and within religion and families. It is difficult to address and harder to break and is to the detriment and destruction of the Black woman.

When considering depression and one of the *DSM* criteria specifiers, feelings of worthlessness or excessive or inappropriate guilt, it becomes clearer that many Black women who are depressed will demonstrate it through the experience of martyrdom that must be acknowledged and addressed by you the therapist.

Guilt is often a feeling experienced by Black women but when it is coupled with feelings of worthlessness and the awareness of marginalized identity, many Black women may believe their best option to being acknowledged is to a create a life that is dedicated to the greater cause of serving others. This perception is often overlooked by therapists because it is self-sacrificing and positively reinforced and often seen as positive. Yet, for a Black woman it could be her manifestation of depression even though presented as a loving and positive nature.

INSIGHT FROM A CLIENT: CM

CM is a wonderful Black woman with a long-lasting career as a real estate attorney in Washington, DC. Hailing from a well-established nuclear family, she attended the most prestigious secondary schools and colleges, played elite sports, and earned a reputation as a wonderful and caring friend. Her personal accolades and the accomplishments of her parents mattered less to her than the perception of others. She cared about what people thought of her and it was not particularly a negative trait. However, her presenting issue orbited around concerns of being misperceived or misunderstood.

During the intake process, I asked several questions to explore her identity and persona. When answering, the most joyful responses aligned with a self-sacrificing, yet very proud acknowledgment of being a martyr. For her it was vital and her destined experience to serve others. In return, she wanted admiration, a sense of being needed, and invitations to highly exclusive events, which temporarily heightened her sense of worth.

In the process of exploration, CM met a man who needed to be taken care of. His emotional state was inconsistent, his sense of identity was fractured, and his ego was easily bruised. These attributes were the very things that drew CM to him. She believed that if she took care of him as nobody else had, he would love her in a way she had imagined but never felt.

She married him, stopped counseling, and allowed distance to form between herself and her family.

A few years later, she returned to counseling with a fuller understanding and lived experiences of the consequences of being a present-day martyr. She articulated the notion that martyrs start with a well-intended and conscious mindset of helping and healing others but are not aware of the consequential implications of constantly self-sacrificing. In short, if one continues to self-sacrifice, eventually, they will sacrifice all of who they are and have nothing to be left with in the end, including self-identity.

When she returned to counseling, she wanted to address the path that allowed her to create the very persona that was nearly destroying her. During this process, we explored her early childhood experiences and her sense of being unseen, not from the world, but from her family. Since her parents had well-established careers, they were often at work or at networking and social events to continue to allow their careers to thrive. CM helped the family by making sure the house was clean, laundry was folded, younger siblings were taken care of, and older siblings were reminded of the family rules and boundaries. During this time, so much effort and energy was placed on the external care of others that she learned to thrive on the little bit that was left over to her. She learned to do her best with very little for herself but a lot that was given to others. Her parents thanked her and rewarded her for her visible and invisible sacrifices. Through this, she learned that she was valued by authority when she took care of them and she was respected by peers when she took care of them too. Her whole life was centered on taking care of others and sacrificing her own wants, dreams, and desires.

Several weeks into the new round of therapy, I diagnosed her with major depressive disorder. Initially, it was hard for her to acknowledge or accept. The online sources she read about did not fully list what she was experiencing, but she was clear that she felt worthless unless she was taking care of someone else, and when she was not taking care of others she felt guilty. While there were other specifiers present, she accepted the diagnosis, signed the treatment plan, and begin to work on goals that would restore her sense of worth, while creating boundaries, first with herself, on how she engaged with others, to protect herself from herself and her default learned behavior of martyrdom.

Avoidance

While avoidance is not explicitly stated in the *DSM-5-TR* under major depressive disorder, it may be a function of persistent depressive disorder, formerly known as dysthymia. The World Health Organization (2017) stated that "Worldwide it is estimated the prevalence of depression (including persistent depressive disorder/dysthymia) is 12%. In the United States, the prevalence is slightly higher, with the estimation of major depressive disorder being 17% and persistent depressive disorder being 3%." One of the factors to explain the lower prevalence of persistent depressive disorder is that it often masks one's personality. The *DSM-5-TR* specifier is that a client will be in a depressed mood for no less than 2 years, which allows the person and their family or friends to become accustomed to this state of being (American Psychiatric Association, 2022). A client may not notice that there is something abnormal occurring within herself because the depressed mood has become normalized and integrated into her life.

Persistent depressive disorder is not defined by an episode or experience, but rather a mood that has morphed into a way of being (Schramm et al., 2020). With all the pressures that a Black woman faces, this disorder may present as a functional personality trait versus a disorder or dysfunction in her life. The added complication is that many Black women live and thrive in community with other Black women. If several Black women are experiencing persistent depressive disorder unknowingly, they may perceive it as normal functioning.

Avoidance is an action versus a feeling and is defined by Webster's as "the action of preventing something from happening." Many things happen to and around Black women that may be out of their control, thus leaving them exposed, vulnerable, and feeling alone. Many Black women may avoid dreaming, hoping, or fantasizing about the future because they know and anticipate that there will be negative things that can derail or destroy their dreams. Black women may subconsciously choose to avoid dreaming, completing tasks that will lead to their success, or making strides in personal growth and evolution because they simply do not want to be disappointed.

While avoidance may seem to be a form of self-sabotage, for many Black women it is a protective mechanism that allows them to have a sense of control through an action and a sense of safety through prediction.

The added complexity of avoidance, particularly for Black women, is the stereotypical perception of Black people as lazy. Oftentimes, people overlook this stereotype when considering there may be a large group of people within the Black community that are persistently depressed versus simply lazy. This occurrence is common because, oftentimes, Black people were not properly included in the research and reporting of many of the disorders in the *DSM-5-TR*. The misconceptions lead to claims of laziness versus treatments for persistent depressive disorder.

INSIGHT FROM A CLIENT: OMF

OMF entered therapy as 44-year-old Black woman with four children spanned across 2 decades. With two children in their 20s and two children in primary school, OMF committed to therapy with the simple goal of learning more about herself. With her first child having been born before she was 21 years old, she identified as a woman who spent most of her life raising children instead of understanding herself. Each hour of therapy was a personal treat to herself, because the whole hour was dedicated to her, and she did not have to share with anyone. While this may seem silly, it was a positively oriented self-centered action that would allow her to focus and heal while being the primary focus of someone else's attention (mine).

Toward the end of a two-session intake process, I asked OMF a few questions that loosely aligned with the mental status exam. While this exam is assessed subjectively through the lens of the therapist, I engage my client's thoughts and feelings to ensure I have a comprehensive conceptualization of who they are and how they function in the world. When assessing and talking about OMF's most common moods, she did not mention a depressed state. Instead, she gave examples that mirrored martyrdom, self-sacrificial actions, and a complicated avoidance of her personal goals. Gently, I dived deeper (which is why our intake process takes several sessions) by asking a modified version of Bloom's taxonomy aligned questions, only to discover that the onset of her depressive symptoms occurred after the birth of her second child, when she was still in her early 20s. At the time of that birth, postpartum depression was rarely discussed in mass media and when it was, it was described in extreme and unrelatable examples. Additionally, she was experiencing complications in her relationship with her partner while also trying to raise her first child, who was a toddler at the time. She waited 10 years to have another child, explaining it was because she did not want to "go there" again. Her sense of "not wanting to go there" was what we now know to be depression.

At some point in her life, the symptoms of postpartum depression disorder morphed into symptoms that mirrored persistent depressive disorder. In a study conducted by Cheng et al. (2022), these researchers noted that there are common neuromarkers in the brain between postpartum depression and major depressive disorder. Postpartum depression affects a different set of brain functions versus major depressive disorder; however, the commonality between postpartum depression disorder, major depressive disorder, and persistent depressive disorder is the link in neuromarkers. In 2018, Jollans and Whelan defined neuromarkers as "biological indicators of the presence or progression of a disease or condition." For OMF, this progression took place over a 20-year span resulting in the 44-year-old client in my office, unaware of the reason that she had not been able to focus on her personal goal achievement, which we concluded was due to the transition from postpartum depressive disorder to persistent depressive disorder.

Due to this realization and diagnosis, I was better equipped to support OMF and developed a treatment plan that was less focused on skills development and a behavioral approach related to goal achievement, but instead on the resolution of her long-standing depressive state and neurological chemistry. We used therapeutic approaches to change neurological functioning, catalyzed by a prescribed psychotropic and a high-frequency set of therapeutic services. By the end of her therapeutic treatment, she earned two degrees, developed a hobby, and met with her friends more often. She felt she had found her passion and purpose.

THERAPIST'S TIP: Mental Status Exam

The mental status exam (MSE) is an assessment tool that is used to evaluate a client's mental functioning at different intersections of therapy (Donnelly et al., 1970). Comparable to physical exams given by physicians, the MSE is given by mental health providers to assess and document signs of mental illness and as conversation starters for changes in a client's life. Mental status exams are easy to find. A simple internet search can render variations that fit your theoretical style, therapeutic orientation, or approach with clients.

Oftentimes, clinicians conduct the MSE only during the intake process and do not utilize it in the remaining sessions. However, it is important that the MSE is used every session to track patterns, inconsistencies, or discrepancies and to be able to determine seasonal and lifestyle changes that may impact a client's mental well-being and personal functioning. If there are areas that require you to ask questions directly to the client, consider using the assessment at the beginning of each session as a standard check-in.

In my company, Onyx Therapy Group, our MSE includes:

Appearance/Behavior:

☐ person ☐ place ☐ time describe: _____

Psychomotor:

☐ unremarkable ☐ hyperactivity ☐ agitated ☐ hypoactive
☐ tics ☐ tremor ☐ abnormal movements ☐ repetitive behavior
☐ stereotyped behavior ☐ impaired coordination: ☐ fine motor
☐ gross motor ☐ other: _____

Speech/Language:

☐ unremarkable ☐ pressured ☐ incoherent ☐ loud ☐ soft
☐ hypotalkative ☐ hypertalkative ☐ mute ☐ limited comprehension
☐ limited expression ☐ nonverbal ☐ articulate
☐ other: _____

Mood/Predominant Emotion States:

☐ elation   ☐ fearful   ☐ sad   ☐ angry   ☐ anxious
☐ shame   ☐ curious

Affect:

☐ WNL   ☐ dysphoric   ☐ labile   ☐ intense   ☐ flat   ☐ restricted
☐ situationally inappropriate

Emotion Regulation:

☐ over controlled   ☐ under controlled

Thought Process:

☐ linear   ☐ circumstantial   ☐ tangential   ☐ loose   ☐ flight of ideas
☐ racing thoughts   ☐ blocking   ☐ slowed   ☐ unable to assess
☐ other: _____

Thought Content:

☐ developmentally appropriate   ☐ fears   ☐ dreams/nightmares
☐ guilty   ☐ worthless   ☐ inadequate   ☐ hopeless   ☐ delusions
☐ obsessions   ☐ unable to assess   ☐ other: _____

Attention:

☐ easily distracted   ☐ poor focus   ☐ poor sustained attention
☐ hypervigilance

Perception:

☐ unremarkable   ☐ hallucinations   ☐ flashbacks   ☐ disassociation

Judgment/Reason:

☐ unremarkable   ☐ fair   ☐ poor   ☐ developmentally appropriate
☐ other: _____

Relatedness to Clinician/Manner/Attitude:

☐ cooperative   ☐ guarded   ☐ hostile   ☐ withdrawn
☐ poor boundaries   ☐ proximity seeking   ☐ exploration
☐ disorganized   ☐ indifferent   ☐ ambivalent   ☐ participation limited
☐ participation via props (e.g., puppets)   ☐ other: _____

Insight/Self-Awareness:

☐ unremarkable   ☐ fair   ☐ poor   ☐ developmentally appropriate
☐ other: _____

Suicidal Ideation:

☐ plan   ☐ intent   ☐ means   ☐ describe: _____

Homicidal Ideation:

☐ plan   ☐ intent   ☐ means   ☐ describe: _____

THERAPIST'S TIP: Know the Difference—Eight Depressive Disorders

When assessing a client for depression, remember there are eight depressive disorders to include:

- Disruptive mood dysregulation disorder (children based)
- Major depressive disorder
- Persistent depressive disorder
- Premenstrual dysphoric disorder
- Substance/medication-induced depressive disorder
- Depressive disorder due to another medical condition
- Other specified depressive disorder
- Unspecified depressive disorder

During your intake process, formal and informal assessment process, and case conceptualization process, you should gather enough information to make a proper and accurate diagnosis for your client.

Be cautious against making a diagnosis too quickly, based on two to three specifiers. A wrong diagnosis will lead to an ineffective treatment plan, which may lead to a client feeling untreated because of a lack of progress and growth. As with a physical diagnosis, if the diagnosis is wrong, the treatment is wrong and the client will remain in pain and may even lose hope for the mental health field, simply because we did not take time to properly diagnose a client.

THERAPIST'S TIP: Careful Consideration of Comorbidity of Depression and Anxiety

Counselors often diagnose clients with one of the depressive disorders and one of the anxiety disorders. While there is a small chance that a client has both depression (one of the eight) and anxiety (one of the ten) it is more likely that a client has only one of the diagnoses, with added specifiers that resemble another disorder.

For instance, most of the depressive disorders have a specifier of "with anxious distress." In this case, the client should not be diagnosed with both a depressive disorder and an anxiety disorder but rather with one depressive disorder and a specifier that highlights anxious symptoms of distress.

Be cautious of overdiagnosing a client; the disorders carry individual and social labels that could complicate the client's life and functioning while leaving them feeling hopeless and in despair and still trying to address their needs. An accurate diagnosis creates an accurate treatment plan.

ANXIETY

M. A. Crocq (2015) outlined the nosology of anxiety and the several renditions of the disorder before it became officially recognized in the *DSM* in 1980. Initially categorized as a medical disorder, especially due to the physiological responses that accompany a perceived threat, anxiety was misunderstood for centuries and loosely interchanged with the emotion of fear. However, researchers and scholars have taken great effort to distinguish anxiousness from fear and fear from anxiety (Daniel-Watanabe & Fletcher, 2022). The *DSM* states the difference as: "Fear is the emotional response to real or perceived imminent threat, whereas anxiety is anticipation of future threat" (American Psychiatric Association, 2022).

While it is likely that one who has been diagnosed with one of the 12 anxiety disorders will be afraid, it is not always appropriate to assume that one who is afraid is also anxious or has anxiety.

THERAPIST'S TIP: Correcting the Improper Use of Mental Health Jargon

As laypeople are learning to reduce the taboos linked to mental health, we find more people comfortable talking about their own mental health and using psychological jargon. These laypeople lack formal education in mental health but have lived experiences that make them experts in their own lives.

While being careful not to invalidate their feelings and experiences, we, as trained, certified, and licensed mental health therapists must help correct the improper use of mental health jargon. For instance, if you overhear a person describing fear but calling it anxiety, take a moment to think of a response and lean into the boundaries of the profession and the call for psychoeducation; then inform the person about the difference between anxiousness as an emotion, fear as an emotion, and anxiety as a stated disorder. This one simple step can save a lot of people from continued dissemination of miseducation.

When assessing a client for anxiety, remember there are 12 anxiety disorders, all linked to a commonality of fear about the future. They are distinguished by developmental age of onset, specifically separation anxiety and likely selective mutism, and also by the types of fears and situations that strike the feelings of fear and anxiousness. In the latter one may see the onset of a specific phobia or social anxiety disorder (formerly known as social phobia). The disorders may be linked or distinguished between each other due to the engagement of avoidance of the catalyst for the fear.

THERAPIST'S TIP: Know the Difference—11 Anxiety Disorders

The 11 anxiety disorders are:

- Separation anxiety disorder
- Selective mutism, specific phobia
- Social anxiety disorder
- Panic disorder
- Panic attack specifier
- Agoraphobia
- Generalized anxiety disorder
- Substance/medication-induced anxiety disorder
- Anxiety disorder due to another medical condition
- Other specified anxiety disorder
- Unspecified anxiety disorder

During your intake process, formal and informal assessment process, and case conceptualization process, you should gather enough information to make a proper and accurate diagnosis for your client.

Be cautious against making a diagnosis too quickly, based on two to three specifiers.

A wrong diagnosis will yield to an ineffective treatment plan, which may lead to a client feeling untreated because of a lack of progress and growth. As with a physical diagnosis, if the diagnosis is wrong, the treatment is wrong and the client will remain in pain and may even lose hope for the mental health field, simply because we did not take time to properly diagnose a client.

Researchers Pavolva et al. (2022) stated that

> Anxiety in parents appears to be more closely associated with anxiety in offspring. The risk of anxiety disorder in an individual offspring may depend on which parent is affected. We found that the transmission of anxiety disorders is accounted for by same-sex transmission.

This research and other studies conclude that anxiety can be passed down from generation to generation maternally and that girls are predisposed to anxiety disorders if their mother has an anxiety disorder, diagnosed or undiagnosed.

It is worth noting that one in five women will develop an anxiety disorder during their pregnancy. Stephanie Collier (2021b) noted that this reported number is still relatively low because many women suffer in silence and do not report their symptoms related to anxiety disorder. Estriplet et al. (2022) reported that "Black mothers experience a higher prevalence of maternal mental health issues, including postpartum depression and anxiety, in comparison to the United States national estimates." Given Black women's higher percentages of negative experiences with the medical world, it is likely that they may have a higher, yet unreported rates of an anxiety disorder during pregnancy. This may be due to the higher than average risk of death (three times more likely than white mothers) and preterm birth deliveries (1 in 6 Black women deliver prematurely) (Sethi, 2020). These maternal mental health challenges, such as anxiety, may be passed to her children while in utero.

The transmission of anxiety from a mother to a daughter may not be the only factor that determines if a Black woman will have an anxiety disorder. Many political and environmental factors can lead to belief in or anticipation of a future threat. Issues such as the disproportionate number of Black students enrolled in a special education program that is aligned to the preschool to prison pipeline, lower SAT scores due to a lack of rigorous academic programming in local schools that have a disproportionate number of Black students and thus less probability of admission to high-ranking universities, the disproportionate rates of unhoused Black people in comparison to white people, the disproportionate rate of Black people who die due to an engagement with a law enforcement official, the disproportionate rate of Black people who are incarcerated for petty crimes versus the larger population of incarcerated individuals, and more. The list and research are quite extensive relating to the differences in how Black people are treated, live, and die in this country versus members of other racial groups. For many Black women, the anticipated fear of threat for the future is based on the reality and series of facts that she and her community are not safe. For many Black women, it is simply a waiting game to see when the fear will manifest into reality.

While the *DSM-5-TR* has sections detailing a culture-related diagnostic lens, listings of several disorders do not address the cultural differences for Black people and anxiety disorders; other racial and cultural groups are considered more often. However, for a few of the disorders, such as panic disorder, it is stated that ". . . among individuals of African descent, the criteria for panic disorder may be met only when there is substantial severity and impairment" (American Psychiatric Association, 2022). This statement occurred after explaining that there are generally "lower rates of panic disorder overall in both African American and Afro-Caribbean groups." The lived manifestations of these experiences are that many Black people may have an anxiety disorder, such as a panic disorder, but since they believe they must or are required to keep functioning, they do not meet all the criteria until their severity or impairment is high.

The push for Black women to continue to function, which is a result of learned generational experiences, is backhandedly used to underdiagnose or undertreat Black people for anxiety disorders. While this is a grave injustice, the lack of functioning for Black women may equate to additional harm or threat such as losing their job, having their children removed from the home, or being hospitalized and experiencing racial biases from medical professionals, thus exacerbating the ruminations of anticipated fear. In other words, the systems and institutions within the United States may be the justification of why and how Black women demonstrate one of the anxiety disorders, so they do not experience social, occupational, or economic consequences.

From an early age, many Black girls that live life with an anxiety disorder, diagnosed or undiagnosed, may be misunderstood and treated based on how they demonstrate their symptoms. Within the Black community, words like "funny acting," "siddity," or "snobbish" are often used to describe girls and women who may have fears of anticipated threats related to how one perceives them, engages with them, or even misunderstands them. Concerning social anxiety disorder a Black woman may avoid social settings or avoid being emotionally vulnerable for fear of being judged and the correlating consequences of being misperceived. So, while she may walk into a space with a head held high and a confident look on her face, all of which may be a persona that aligns with the Jungian archetype of a powerful magician, she may choose to sit in the corner alone or engage in a deep conversation too quickly or in a shallow manner (Granrose, 2021). This demonstration is less about being socially awkward than about being mutable so that she can avoid the fear of being misjudged and the social consequences that accompany these experiences.

INSIGHT FROM A CLIENT: KIM

KIM is a 35-year-old educator. She is a single woman who desires lifelong partnership, children, and a life of international living and travel. She is well-versed in multiple languages, mostly self-taught, and is an avid reader. Her favorite pastime includes linking with her very small group of book club members and discussing complex topics through the safety of fictional characters versus the exposure of personal experiences. KIM entered therapy because she stated she wanted to grow socially so she can meet her future partner and raise well-balanced children who were not as fearful as she was. She wanted skills to address her self-diagnosed social anxiety so she could conquer the world.

During the treatment process with KIM, I used motivational interviewing to explore the roots of her fear, to determine if they were based in the past, present, or future. Most of her fears were rooted in the past and patterns of experiences, judgments, and rejections that she had experienced from others. She started to experience distress during dating, changing jobs and meeting new colleagues, or engaging with the parents of her students. She was acutely aware of the consequences of being misunderstood and the implications it could have on her job, her comfort at work, and the small mental space that was not overrun by her anxious ruminations.

In the beginning of treatment, we met often—once a week for 6 months. She was assigned homework that required her to submit information to me between sessions so that she could replace some of her ruminations with purpose-driven activities. Additionally, she enjoyed activities that allowed her to dream about her future self free of anxiety and worries. It was a reversal of the self-fulfilling prophecy concept. Additionally, we created mantras and preplanned response statements when she was called "funny acting," "weird," "awkward," or "snobbish." Over time, layers of vulnerability were added to the response statements, to allow her to experiment with the true power of authentic communication and to recreate her perception of safety. Additionally, we assessed her definition of friendship and what she needed in friends as she increased her social engagement. This checklist and these criteria allowed her to maintain a couple of friendships, release a couple of friendships, and seek new friendships and networks based on the healthy version of herself.

Through this process, KIM became a version of herself that was authentically secure and confident. While there were other factors at play, KIM did meet a person who is currently her life partner. While they are not married, they are considering living together and talking about the future.

Of the 12 anxiety disorders, panic disorder may be the only one that is consistently demonstrated by Black women and all other racial and ethnic groups. This is particularly true because this disorder is defined by physiological responses that are universal among all humans. It is difficult to weave in cultural concepts when describing chest pains and discomfort. The reasons for the onset of a panic episode may vary based on the thoughts and cultural alignment of the client. In other words, panic disorder may be present, but the onset and the outcomes may be different. Previously, it was mentioned that panic disorder may be hard for clinicians to diagnose because Black people may not demonstrate dysfunction in their daily living because the risk of impairment is too consequential so they may choose to persistently live their life instead of acknowledging or treating their panic attacks.

The first criteria specifiers for panic disorder are "palpitations, pounding heart, or accelerated heart rate." A meta-analysis by researchers Chalmers et al. (2014) stated, "Anxiety disorders increase risk of future cardiovascular disease (CVD) and mortality, even after controlling for confounds including smoking, lifestyle, and socioeconomic status, and irrespective of a history of medical disorders." This research indicates that panic disorder may be related to heart disease. The Centers for Disease Control stated that 44% of all U.S. American women are living with some form of heart disease (CDC, 2024). The percentage is higher for Black women. In an evidence-based research study, Jacobsen (2024) noted that Black women are 2.4% more likely to develop heart disease versus white women, leading to a 40–percentage point difference in death rates for Black women versus white women. Additionally, a Black woman within this category has an aged heart that is 13 years older than her chronological age, thus causing her heart to age faster and death to approach more quickly (Ebong & Breathett, 2020).

The correlation between heart disease and anxiety disorders is clear, and panic attacks are anxiety disorders (*Anxiety and Heart Disease*, 2023). And yet, panic disorders are underdiagnosed in Black women simply because they do not allow themselves to be impaired by their attacks.

Catalyst Questions: Panic Disorder

Many Black women underreport panic attacks simply because the right questions are not being asked. Since a Black woman is unlikely to lean into impairment, it is important for therapists to meet her where she is by using language, examples, and scenarios instead of mental health jargon or *DSM* wording.

When talking with or assessing Black women for panic disorder, consider asking questions such as:

> Are there moments when you are sitting still and your heart begins to race?

> Are there moments when you can feel the pulse in your throat without touching your neck?

> How often do you feel numbness in your toes or hands?

> When you think about certain things, does your head start to hurt and you feel you cannot breathe? If so, what are those things and thoughts that cause that discomfort?

Consider stating that there is a correlation between panic attacks and heart disease, and while you are treating the client for their presenting and root issues, you want to help prevent the growing rates of heart disease in Black women and specifically want to make sure your client is paying attention to the warning signs that may start as repeated panicked moments. This will allow her to see the correlation between physical and mental health but to also feel seen and appreciated by you.

CONCLUSION

The depressive disorders and anxiety disorders are the most diagnosed mental health disorders in the United States. Therefore, it is likely that one of your Black women clients will need to be diagnosed with one of the 20 options listed in the *DSM-5-TR*. This chapter highlights the importance of seeing your client for who she is and making the right correlations, to the *DSM* disorders versus expecting her symptoms to fit into the cookie cutter and generalized language of the manual. In this context, the correct correlations to the *DSM* may include but are not limited to cultural factors, transdiagnostic descriptors, disorder specifiers, language descriptors, and perception of self.

As a marginalized person, generalized language may not apply to her. Increasing the application of your cultural competency may allow you to properly diagnose and treat your client, thus allowing her to become free from any debilitating symptoms that may prevent her from fulfilling her life dreams and satisfaction. While it is a heavy statement, you may have the power, by properly seeing and treating her, to help her become the woman she wants to be. What a wonderful position for you to be in.

Therapist's Introspection

Personal	Professional
Before reading this chapter, what did you think about Black women and their experiences with diagnostic mental disorders?	Which clients came to mind while you read this chapter?
What were you taught or did you assume about Black women and the ways they demonstrate their diagnostic mental health disorders?	If you had an opportunity to redo a previous session with a Black woman client, what would you do differently, based on the information you learned in this session?
All of us have biases. What are two biases that arose for you while reading this chapter?	Whom do you need to talk to about this chapter's content? What do you want to say to them? How will you say it?
After reading this chapter, what did you learn and how will you put that information into application, both personally and professionally?	In thinking about your client's treatment plans, what new goals, objectives, and interventions need to be added?
What else did this chapter bring up for you?	

Therapeutic Guide

Therapy	Clinical Focus	Sample Therapeutic SMART Goal	Technique or Intervention
Psychoanalytic Psychotherapy	The mind has three parts: unconscious, subconscious, conscious Subconscious motivations influence conscious behaviors Understanding the subconscious provides insight into the conscious Trauma and trauma responses may be lodged in the subconscious and not easily identified in consciousness or behaviors Uncovering our root thoughts can lead to overcoming and healing from trauma	Client will identify two of her default defense mechanisms through the role of reflection, introspection, memory recall, and current tracking, to be achieved within 6 months. Client will understand her internalizations of her mental health, from onset to present, through the exploration of her subconscious and conscious, to be achieved within 18 months.	Explore the 15 defense mechanisms (acting out, altruistic surrender, avoidance, compartmentalization, compensation, conversion, denial, displacement, dissociation, introjection, projection, reactive training, rationalization, repression, and sublimation) Free association Dream analysis Freudian slip Rorschach inkblots Clarifications Interpretations
Cognitive Behavioral Therapy (CBT)	Triadic connection between thoughts, feelings, and behaviors Most cognitions connect to core beliefs that are developed in childhood Many negative emotions are associated with distorted cognitions that are a result of core beliefs, personality concerns, improper learning, or unaligned application Most behaviors are conditioned and reinforced over time, generally, unknowingly Mental health disorders are a combination of thoughts, feelings, and behaviors	Client will learn two skills to that will allow her to recognize and challenge irrational thoughts that are a result of her specific mental health, to be accomplished within 12 months. Through the use of guided discovery and the SOLVE technique, the client will learn to create personal solutions that will assist in the management of her specific mental health disorder. Client will track her thoughts, emotions, and behaviors 2 days per week, to explore the triadic dynamic and influence in her life, to be achieved weekly for 12 months.	Cognitive restructuring Behavioral experiments Exposure therapy Flooding Guided discovery Homework Thought recording Relaxation Role-play SOLVE technique (problem solving)[1] Successive approximation Systemic desensitization Worksheets

Therapy	Clinical Focus	Sample Therapeutic SMART Goal	Technique or Intervention
Psychophar-macological Therapy	Biological and chemical influences can cause or contribute to mental health disorders

Prescription medications are made of chemicals that can offset natural chemical influences that may be contributing to mental health disorders

Prescription medication can address some mental health disorders such as the depressive disorders, anxiety disorders, and other mood disorders

Medication can be used to facilitate in other experiences that may exacerbate mental health disorders such as insomnia and substance use engagement | As an addition to talk therapy, client will explore the use of one or two psychopharmacological treatments, to be decided with her primary care physician or psychiatrist, to be determined within 3 months.

Client will maintain the consistent and exact use of psychopharmacological medication as prescribed by her primary care physician or psychiatrist, to be assessed one time per week for 12 months.

Client will assess the impact of psychopharmacological treatment on four areas of her life (self-concept, engagement with others, mood and memory, and symptoms), to be evaluated one time per week for 12 months. | Antidepressants: used to treat depressive disorders, anxiety disorders, insomnia, and pain

Anxiolytics: used to treat anxiety symptoms

Stimulants: used to treat depressive disorders and attention deficit hyperactivity disorder (ADHD)

Antipsychotics: Used to treat schizophrenia and bipolar disorder

Mood stabilizers: Used to treat bipolar disorder

Weekly medication evaluation on mood, behavior, judgment, memory, focus, and self-concept

Weekly medication evaluation on side effects[1] |

[1] The SOLVE technique is a framework that allows for constructive thinking when approaching challenges in one's life. The systematic approach uses identification, analysis, and structured implementation to create sustainable solutions.

Journal Prompts

What is the role of perfectionism in your life? How do you want others to perceive you when you aim toward or deliver perfection?

How do you see yourself when you fail at being perfect?

Do you aim for perfectionism at work, in relationships, in your body image, or with your self-talk?

Have you ever chosen to be a martyr? Under which circumstances did you make that choice?

When most of us were younger, we dreamt of what our lives could be. It included what types of jobs we would have, the work we would do, how we would look, who we would marry, and how we would be perceived in this world. Do you still dream? If not, why?

Have you given up on the action of dream, particularly for your life? Is the action of not dreaming a form of avoidance of disappointment?

For the next 2 days, reignite a few dreams for your life. Start with a hobby. Imagine the hobby. What would you be doing? How would it look? How would you feel? Who would be with you?

Are there other areas of your life that you avoid? Are those areas of avoidance associated with a fear of disappointment? Where is your control in those areas? How can therapy empower you to lean into those areas versus avoiding them?

Have you been anxious? How is anxiousness different from anxiety for you?

If there is a correlation between anxiousness and fear, what were you most afraid of during the moment that you were anxious?

In thinking over the next 6 months, 1 year, and 5 years, what are you most afraid to experience? What is your greatest fear?

In thinking about being anxious in social settings, which settings make you feel the most anxious? How do you end up showing up in those spaces? How do you want to show up in those spaces?

How do you cope when you are anxious? What are three redirective thoughts that you say to yourself? What are three redirective behaviors that you do?

Conclusion

Whether you are a clinician working with a Black woman client, a student who is learning to be a culturally aware clinician, or a Black woman who is seeking to learn more about yourself and those around you, you did it. You made it to the end of this guidebook.

In traditional guidebook format, I want to leave you with a few takeaways.

1. Handle with Care

Black women are strong, wise, fragile, and sensitive. They should be handled with care—the same care that you use when handling an expensive gem, your favorite treasure, or your mother's feelings. Avoid stereotypes that limit the Black woman to being single-faceted. She is complex and should be embraced with curiosity and care. Return to this guidebook to remind yourself of the uniqueness of Black women and to remember that they are more than the stories you have been told or the stereotypes you have absorbed through media. They are complex, heavy, deep, and sensitive.

2. History is in the Present

Different from some other racial or gender groups, Black women's lives are shaped by the past. History has created the path for many Black women. However, many are aiming to create their own paths, and break free of the limits historically placed on them. Therefore, their minds are constantly working to determine which road to walk, which path to forge, and when to sit still. They are breaking cycles and sitting in intersections. This is challenging work. This is a form of mental and emotional gymnastics. This is when they need you. Return to this book to review the ways that history influences the lives of Black women. Some of your clients' decisions will not be easy, and some will be made with their eyes on the rearview mirror, as well as on their vision of the future. Remember this fact and remind your clients too.

3. Double Minority

Black women are a double minority—as a racial group and as a gender group. Therefore, they are often expected to live their lives from the margins, to watch others achieve what they dream for themselves, and to be happy with the limitations of assisting others without experiencing fulfillment on their own. As a double minority, they are socialized to be appreciative for less and to see themselves as an exception if they achieve more. They are socialized based on their race, they are socialized based on their gender, and they are told that their dreams should not exceed the expectations placed on them. However, your role is to empower them: to hold a mirror up to them so they can see their value, their worth, their dreams, and their goals. Your job is to guide them to the realization of their dreams by clearing away some of the muck and murk that is placed on them through limiting socialized thoughts. Return to this book as you guide your clients to their own empowerment and a life in the center of their dreams.

4. Guide, but Do Not Advise

Our job is to guide through questions, analysis, and insight. It is tempting to give advice or to coach. It is tempting to want someone to do what you want them to do. However, this Black woman is your client, and she may have a few things figured out already and need you to be a thought partner, a mirror to her decisions, or a listening ear while she decides her next steps and decisions. In times when you want to provide more than a listening ear, a guided question, or a therapeutic intervention, remember that she can figure out her life and create a future that she wants for herself.

5. It Takes Time to Unlearn and Learn Again

Through socialization, there are some things that Black women may not be comfortable doing. By the time she comes to you, she may be in her 20s, 30s, 40s, or older. Therefore, she has had 2, 3, or 4-plus decades of socialized messages. One hour per week with you may not be enough to unravel 4 decades of living. However, return to this book and review all the cited research, catalyst questions, journal prompts, and theoretical and therapeutic resources to aid her in her transformative process.

6. Pros and Cons

For many experiences in life, there are pros and cons. As Black women gain, earn, or experience something new, they may lose something too. For some women, the pursuit of a transformed life may mean that they lose friends, end relationships, lose familiarity in a location, or even grieve an old version of themselves. Therefore, it is important to allow our clients space to grieve amid creating or experiencing something new. Return to this book as you assist your client in grief, even if it is during the most beautiful times of her life. Be explicit.

Ask questions. Allow for space to process, and provide journal prompts so she can live a life of fullness and awareness.

7. Emotions For All
Some Black women have not been taught to identify or access their emotions. They have been socialized to express emotions that align with stereotypes or to suppress emotions that do not benefit others. While they enter therapy to process emotions and feelings, this may be a learning curve. Return to this book to review resources that can help guide you and the client in emotional identification, emotional vocabulary, and emotional processing.

8. Community Matters
Black women, especially Black American women, sit in another intersection. While you are familiar with their intersection of being a double involuntary minority because they are Black and women, you must also consider, and include in your work, their intersection of having ancestral predisposition to communities and villages while being individualized Americans. Therefore, your Black woman client may have internal struggles and cognitive dissonance in choosing between self and others. Return to this book to refamiliarize yourself with the "Insight from a Client" sections while creating questions that increase awareness. And, if you find that you tend to guide your clients toward individualization only, consult with your supervisor to ensure you are remaining culturally competent, addressing any countertransference and biases, and are ready to hold space for your client as she navigates her additional cultural identity as a community-oriented individual.

9. Further Research Is Needed
While the *DSM* is the most used diagnostic manual in the United States, it does not fully capture the lived experiences of Black women. The culture-related diagnostic issues section is a brief paragraph that reminds the reader to consider the culture of the client. However, it does not cite references, provide guidance, or demonstrate how a particular diagnosis is demonstrated in culturally diverse clients. Therefore, when you are in the conceptualization and planning phase of your treatment, use this guide and the cited resources to deepen your research so you can provide the most accurate diagnosis and develop the most effective and culturally rich treatment plan for your client.

10. Make SMART Treatment Goals
Make treatment goals that are Specific, Measurable, Achievable, Relevant, and Time-Bound. While many Black women are entering therapy and are open to counseling, there is still a taboo connected to needing and accessing mental health services. Therefore, there needs to be clear, objective, and observable evidence that therapy works. This is the primary way to combat subjective

taboos. Thus, data that is derived from SMART goals allows the client to quantify their progress and match it with their internal and qualitative changes too. Use this guide as a reference for developing SMART goals and refer to the table at the end of each chapter, which has sample SMART goals you can use with and for your client.

11. Your Professional Development and Self-Care

Be sure to seek supervision and therapy. This book contains a lot of information. Some of it may be enlightening while some of it may be shocking. Some of it may have triggered your own trauma, highlighted your own biases, or made you feel insecure or guilty based on your own misinformation or lack of information. It is okay. Books are supposed to teach us. They are meant to expand our worldview. They are meant to make us see the world a little clearer, even if we do not agree with every single point. So, whatever thoughts and feelings you had while reading this book, process them with someone. Return to this book as you process your thoughts and feelings with a culturally aware and competent supervisor or your personal therapist. While you work with a coach, process through peer supervision, talk to a colleague, or journal, share this book with them so both of you are using the same guide, language, research, and resources.

12. Advocate

There will be rooms you walk in that your Black woman client may never have had a chance to see or experience. There may be conversations that you engage in or overhear that include topics your client may not know about. There may be misinformation disseminated that causes direct or indirect harm to your client. You may be in a position that your Black woman client may never be in. Use your access, privilege, and resources to advocate for your Black woman client and her experiences. Return to this book to refresh yourself on certain statistics, history, vocabulary, insights from clients, and language so you can articulate, express, and advocate for the lived experiences of your Black woman client.

References

2002 Survey of Business Owners (SBO). (n.d.). https://web.archive.org/web/2005103009 5723/http:/www.census.gov/csd/sbo/

About the religious landscape study. (2024, April 14). *Pew Research Center.* https://www .pewresearch.org/about-the-religious-landscape-study/

ACES. (1990). *Standards for counseling supervisors.* ACES-Standards-for-Counseling-Supervisors-1990.pdf (acesonline.net)

ACES. (2011). *Best practices in clinical supervision.* ACES-Best-Practices-in-Clinical-Supervision-2011.pdf (acesonline.net)

Adani, S., & Cepanec, M. (2019). Sex differences in early communication development: Behavioral and neurobiological indicators of more vulnerable communication system development in boys. *Croatian Medical Journal, 60*(2), 141–149. doi:10.3325/ cmj.2019.60.141

Adeshay. (2024, February 8). *Data Chart: Black children, two-parent households, and Black fatherhood.*

Ahlers-Schmidt, C. R., Schunn, C., Engel, M., Dowling, J., Neufeld, K., & Kuhlmann, S. (2019). Implementation of a statewide program to promote safe sleep, breastfeeding and tobacco cessation to high risk pregnant women. *Journal of Community Health, 44*(1), 185–191. doi:10.1007/s10900-018-0571-4

Ahonen, M. (2018). Ancient philosophers on mental illness. *History of Psychiatry, 30*(1), 3–18. doi:10.1177/0957154x18803508

Allen, B. J. (1998). Black womanhood and feminist standpoints. *Management Communication Quarterly, 11*(4), 575–586.

Almeida, R., Wood, M., Messineo, T., & Font, R. (1998). The cultural context model: An overview. In M. McGoldrick (Ed.), Revisioning family therapy: Race, culture, and gender in clinical practice (pp. 414–432). Guilford.

American Counseling Association Code of Ethics. (2014). https://www.counseling.org/ resources/ethics

American Psychiatric Association. (2022). *Diagnostic and Statistical Manual of Mental Disorders. Fifth Edition, Text Revision (DSM-5-TR).* doi:10.1176/appi. books.9780890425787

American Psychiatric Association. (2022). *Diagnostic and statistical manual of mental disorders* (5th ed., text rev.). https://doi.org/10.1176/appi.books.9780890425787

Ananthaswamy, A., & Douglas, K. (2018). The origins of the patriarchy. *The New Scientist, 238*(3174), 34–35. doi:10.1016/s0262-4079(18)30707-3

Andreasen, N. C. (2010). Posttraumatic stress disorder: A history and a critique. *Annals of the New York Academy of Sciences, 1208*(1), 67–71. doi:10.1111/j.1749-6632.2010.05699.x

Anthony, M., Jr, Nichols, A. H., & Del Pilar, W. (2021, December 21). *Raising undergraduate degree attainment among Black women and men takes on new urgency amid the pandemic*. The Education Trust. https://edtrust.org/resource/national-and-state-degree-attainment-for-black-women-and-men/

Anxiety and heart disease. (2023, October 30). Johns Hopkins Medicine. https://www.hopkinsmedicine.org/health/conditions-and-diseases/anxiety-and-heart-disease

APA Dictionary of Psychology. (n.d.). American Psychological Association. https://dictionary.apa.org/

Arczynski, A. V., & Morrow, S. L. (2016). The complexities of power in feminist multicultural psychotherapy supervision. *Journal of Counseling Psychology, 64*(2), 192–205.

Arrendondo, P., Toporek, M. S., Brown, S., Jones, J., Locke, D. C., Sanchez, J., & Stadler, H. (1996). *Operationalization of the multicultural counseling competencies*. AMCD. http://www.counseling.org/Resources/Competencies/Multcultural_Competencies.pdf

Ashley, W. (2013). The angry Black woman: The impact of pejorative stereotypes on psychotherapy with Black women. *Social Work in Public Health, 29*(1), 27–34. doi:10.1080/19371918.2011.619449

Atske, S. (2024, April 17). *'What's the difference between income and wealth?' and other common questions about economic concepts*. Pew Research Center. https://www.pewresearch.org/decoded/2021/07/23/whats-the-difference-between-income-and-wealth-and-other-common-questions-about-economic-concepts/

Bargard, A., & Hyde, J. S. (1991). Women's studies: A study of feminist identity development in women. *Psychology of Women Quarterly, 15*, 181–201.

Barrett, L. F. (2009). The future of psychology: Connecting mind to brain. *Perspectives on Psychological Science, 4*(4), 326–339. doi:10.1111/j.1745-6924.2009.01134.x

Batmaz, S., & Altinöz, A. E. (2023). Thought content and thinking processes in psychotherapy: Cognitive versus metacognitive approaches. *Integrated Science Brain, Decision Making and Mental Health* (pp. 365–393). doi:10.1007/978-3-031-15959-6_18

Battle, J., & Wright, E. (2002). W.E.B. Du Bois's talented tenth. *Journal of Black Studies, 32*(6), 654–672. doi:10.1177/00234702032006002

Baylor, A. A. (2014). *Sankofa: Traditions of mentoring among Black women educators* (Doctoral dissertation, The University of Wisconsin). Retrieved from ProQuest Dissertations Publishing. (UMI 3633327)

Beck, A. T., Rush, A., Shaw, B., & Emery, G. (1979). *Cognitive therapy of depression*. Guilford.

Beck, J. S. (1964). *Cognitive therapy: Basics and beyond*. Guilford.

Beck, J. S. (2020). *Cognitive behavior therapy: Basics and beyond* (3rd ed.). Guilford.

Bell, E. L. (1990). The bicultural life experience of career-oriented black women. *Journal of Organizational Behavior, 11*(6), 459–477. doi:10.1002/job.4030110607

Berg, A., Hudson, S., Klitsch Weaver, K., Lesko Pacchia, M., Ahmed, I. (2023, May 22).

The beauty market in 2023: *A special state of fashion report.* McKinsey & Company. https://www.mckinsey.com/industries/retail/our-insights/the-beauty-market-in-2023 -a-special-state-of-fashion-report

Berg, I. K., & de Shazer, S. (1993). Making numbers talk: Language in therapy. In S. Friedman (Ed.), *The new language of change: Constructive collaboration in psychotherapy.* Guilford.

Berk, L. E. (2007). *Exploring lifespan development* (4th ed.). Pearson. BB18695220

Bernard, D. L., Smith, Q., & Lanier, P. (2021). Racial discrimination and other adverse childhood experiences as risk factors for internalizing mental health concerns among Black youth. *Journal of Traumatic Stress,* 35(2), 473–483. https://doi.org/10 .1002/jts.22760

Bernard, J. M., & Goodyear, R. K. (2014). *Fundamentals of clinical supervision.* Pearson.

Berrey, S. A. (2009). Resistance begins at home: The Black family and lessons in survival and subversion in Jim Crow Mississippi. *Black Women, Gender & Families,* 3(1), 65–90. doi:10.1353/bwg.0.0000

Besharov, D. J., & West, A. (2002). *African American marriage patterns* (p. 95). Hoover Press: Thernstrom.

Bhutta, N., Bricker, J., Chang, A., Dettling, L., Goodman. S., Hsu, J., Moore, K., Reber, S., Henriques Volz, A., & Windle, R. (2020). Changes in U.S. family finances from 2016 to 2019: Evidence from the Survey of Consumer Finances. *Federal Reserve Bulletin* 106(5). https://www.federalreserve.gov/publications/files/scf20.pdf

Black, M. C., & Burton, T. (2011, April 18). *NISVS research briefing* [PowerPoint slides]. https//: vawnet.org

Black-Americans | The United States Army. (2024). https://www.army.mil/blackamericans/

Blanchfield, T. (2022, July 27). *What to know about the DSM-5-TR.* Verywell Mind. https://www.verywellmind.com/what-to-know-dsm-5-tr-changes-5521765

Blazina, C. (2024, April 14). *Global population skews male, but UN projects parity between sexes by 2050.* Pew Research Center. https://www.pewresearch.org/short -reads/2022/08/31/global-population-skews-male-but-un-projects-parity-between- sexes-by-2050/

Bleiweis, R., Frye, J., & Khattar, R (2021, November 17). *Women of color and the wage gap.* Center for American Progress. https://www.americanprogress.org/article/ women-of-color-and-the-wage-gap/

Bonavia, T., & Brox-Ponce, J. (2018). Shame in decision making under risk conditions: Understanding the effect of transparency. *PLoS ONE,* 13(2), e0191990. doi:10.1371/ journal.pone.0191990

Borders, L. D. (2014). Best practices in clinical supervision: Another step in delineating effective supervision practice. *American Journal of Psychotherapy,* 68(2), 151–162. doi:10.1176/appi.psychotherapy.2014.68.2.151

Bradley, L. J., & Whiting, P. P. (2001). Supervision training: A model. In L. J. Bradley & N. Ladany , *Counselor supervision: Principles, process & practice* (3rd ed., pp. 207–229). Routledge.

Bradley, W. J., & Becker, K. D. (2021). Clinical supervision of mental health services: A systematic review of supervision characteristics and practices associated with formative and restorative outcomes. *The Clinical Supervisor,* 40(1), 88–111. doi:10.1080/07 325223.2021.1904312

Bremner, J. D. (2006). Traumatic stress: Effects on the brain. *Dialogues in Clinical Neuroscience*, 8(4), 445–461. doi:10.31887/dcns.2006.8.4/jbremner

Brooks, A. C. (2022, October 20). How to stop being so envious. *The Atlantic.* https://www.theatlantic.com/family/archive/2022/10/envy-happiness-social-media/671786/

Brown, K. W., & Ryan, R. M. (2003). The benefits of being present: Mindfulness and its role in psychological well-being. *Journal of Personality and Social Psychology*, 84(4), 822–848. doi:10.1037/0022-3514.84.4.822

Bryant-Davis, T., Ullman, S. E., Tsong, Y., Tillman, S., & Smith, K. (2010). Struggling to survive: Sexual assault, poverty, and mental health outcomes of African American women. *American Journal of Orthopsychiatry*, 80(1), 61–70. doi:10.1111/j.1939-0025.2010.01007.x

Burkard, A. W., Knox, S., Clarke, R. D., Phelps, D. L., & Inman, A. G. (2014). Supervisors' experiences of providing difficult feedback in cross-ethic/racial supervision. *The Counseling Psychologist*, 42(3), 314–344.

Burnes, T. R., Wood, J. A., Inman, J. L., & Welikson, G. A. (2012). An investigation of process variables in feminist group clinical supervision. *The Counseling Psychologist*, 41(1), 1–24.

Burnett-Zeigler, I. (2022). *Nobody knows the trouble I've seen: The emotional lives of Black women.* Amistad.

Byrd, A., & Tharps, L. (2001). *Hair story: Untangling the roots of Black hair in America.* St. Martin's Press.

Cambridge University Press. (n.d.). Woman. In Cambridge Dictionary. https://dictionary.cambridge.org/dictionary/english/woman

Cameron, S., & turtle-song, i. (2002). Learning to write case notes using the SOAP format. *Journal of Counseling & Development*, 80, 286–292.

Campbell, A. F., & Campbell, A. F. (2022, January 28). *Black women are still dropping out of the workforce. Here's why.* Center for Public Integrity. https://publicintegrity.org/inside-publici/newsletters/watchdog-newsletter/black-women-jobs-dropping-out-of-workforce/

Cardin, B. (2023, July 15). Women's Small Business Ownership and Entrepreneurship Report. *U.S. Senate Committee on Small Business and Entrepreneurship*, 1–13. https://www.sbc.senate.gov/public/_cache/files/b/9/b99ffab8b62a-48e1-95ba-b14c5451880b/D779F6653743546214AD6E09EAED29F7.women-entrepreneurship-report.pdf

Carlton, P. G., & Klassen, D. A. (2008). *Black Women Executives Research Initiative Finding.* pp. 1–28. The Executive Leadership Council.

CDC (Centers for Disease Control and Prevention). (2024, May 15). *About women and heart disease.* https://www.cdc.gov/heart-disease/about/women-and-heart-disease.html

CDC (Centers for Disease Control and Prevention). (n.d.). Maternal mortality rates in the United States, 2021. https://www.cdc.gov/nchs/data/hestat/maternal-mortality/2021/maternal mortality-rates-2021.htm

Chalmers, J. A., Quintana, D. S., Abbott, M. J., & Kemp, A. H. (2014). Anxiety disorders are associated with reduced heart rate variability: A meta-analysis. *Frontiers in Psychiatry*, 5. doi:10.3389/fpsyt.2014.00080

Chapman, G. (2015). *The 5 love languages: The secret to love that lasts.* Northfield.

Cheeks, M. (2018, January 10). *How Black women describe navigating race and gender in the workplace.* Harvard Business Review. https://hbr.org/2018/03/how-black-women-describe-navigating-race-and-gender-in-the-workplace

Cheng, B., Guo, Y., Chen, X., Lv, B., Liao, Y., Qu, H., Hu, X., Yang, H., Meng, Y., Deng, W., & Wang, J. (2022). Postpartum depression and major depressive disorder: the same or not? Evidence from resting-state functional MRI. *Psychoradiology, 2*(3), 121–128. doi:10.1093/psyrad/kkac015

Cherepanov, E. (2020). *Understanding the transgenerational legacy of totalitarian regimes: Paradoxes of cultural learning.* Routledge.

Child and Adolescent Health Measurement Initiative. (2022). *2021 National Survey of Children's Health, Sampling and Survey Administration.* https://www.cahmi.org.

Chinn, J. J., Martin, I. K., & Redmond, N. (2021). Health equity among Black women in the United States. *Journal of Women's Health, 30*(2), 212–219. doi:10.1089/jwh.2020.8868

Chisholm, S. (1970). *Unbought and unbossed.* Houghton Mifflin.

Choi, H. (2022). Feeling one thing and doing another: How expressions of guilt and shame influence hypocrisy judgment. *Behavioral Sciences, 12*(12), 504. doi:10.3390/bs12120504

Churchwell, S. (2021, Winter). A brief history of the American dream. *The Catalyst,* George W. Bush Institute. https://www.bushcenter.org/catalyst/state-of-the-american-dream/churchwell-history-of-the-american-dream.

Civil Rights Act of 1964, Pub. L88-352, 78 Stat. 241 (1964). http://civil.laws.com/civil-rights-act-of-1964

Clance, P. R., & Imes, S. A. (1978). The imposter phenomenon in high achieving women: Dynamics and therapeutic intervention. *Psychotherapy, 15*(3), 241–247. doi:10.1037/h0086006

Clark, T. T., Yang, C., McClernon, F. J., & Fuemmeler, B. F. (2014). Racial differences in parenting style typologies and heavy episodic drinking trajectories. *Health Psychology, 34*(7), 697–708. doi:10.1037/hea0000150

Cohen, A. (2017). *Imbeciles: The Supreme Court, American eugenics, and the sterilization of Carrie Buck.* Penguin.

Collier, S. (2021a, June 25). How can you manage anxiety during pregnancy? *Harvard Health.* https://www.health.harvard.edu/blog/how-can-you-manage-anxiety-during-pregnancy-202106252512

Collier, S. (2021b, July 30). Postpartum anxiety is invisible, but common and treatable. *Harvard Health.* https://www.health.harvard.edu/blog/postpartum-anxiety-an-invisible-disorder-that-can-affect-new-mothers-202107302558

Collins, E. M. (2013, March 4). *Black soldiers in the Revolutionary War.* U.S. Army. https://www.army.mil/article/97705/Black_Soldiers_in_the_Revolutionary_War/

Collins, P. H. (2000). *Black feminist thought: Knowledge, consciousness, and the politics of empowerment.* Psychology Press.

Collins, W. J. (2020). The Great Migration of Black Americans from the US South: A guide and interpretation. *Explorations in Economic History, 80,* 101382. doi:10.1016/j.eeh.2020.101382

Conley, D. (1999). Getting into the Black: Race, wealth, and public policy. *Political Science Quarterly, 114*(4), 595–612. doi:10.2307/2657785

Cook, S. G. (2011). Strategies for success in the academy for Black women. *Women in Higher Education, 20*(10), 22–23.

Crenshaw, Kimberlé (1989). "Demarginalizing the intersection of race and sex: A Black feminist critique of antidiscrimination doctrine, feminist theory and antiracist policies." University of Chicago Legal Forum, *1,*139–167.

Crocq, M. (2015). A history of anxiety: From Hippocrates to DSM. *Dialogues in Clinical Neuroscience, 17*(3), 319–325. doi:10.31887/dcns.2015.17.3/macrocq

CROWN Act of 2020 (2020 - H.R. 5309). (n.d.). GovTrack.us. https://www.govtrack.us/congress/bills/116/hr5309

Cruz, D., Lichten, M., Berg, K., & George, P. (2022). Developmental trauma: Conceptual framework, associated risks and comorbidities, and evaluation and treatment. *Frontiers in Psychiatry, 13.* doi:10.3389/fpsyt.2022.800687

Dalenberg, C. J. (2000). *Countertransference and the treatment of trauma.* American Psychological Association. doi:10.1037/10380-000

Daniel-Watanabe, L., & Fletcher, P. C. (2022). Are fear and anxiety truly distinct? *Biological Psychiatry Global Open Science, 2*(4), 341–349. doi:10.1016/j.bpsgos.2021.09.006

Davidson, J., & Hannaford, D. (2022). Opting out: Women messing with marriage around the world. Rutgers University Press.

Davies, K. (1992). Zora Neale Hurston's poetics of embalmment: Articulating the rage of Black women and narrative self-defense. *African American Review, 26*(1), 147. doi:10.2307/3042084

Davis, D. J., Chaney, C., Edwards, L., Thompson-Rodgers, G. K., & Gines, K. T. (2012). Academe as extreme sport: Black women, faculty development, and networking. *Negro Educational Review, 62 & 63*(1–4), 167–187.

Davis, J. T. M., & Hines, M. (2020). How large are gender differences in toy preferences? A systematic review and meta-analysis of toy preference research. *Archives of Sexual Behavior, 49*(2), 373. doi:10.1007/s10508-019-01624-7

Davis, K. (2018). 'Blacks are immune from mental illness.' *Psychiatric News, 53*(9). doi.org/10.1176/appi.pn.2018.5a18

DeSoucey, M., Pozner, J., Fields, C., Dobransky, K., & Fine, G. A. (2008). Memory and sacrifice: An embodied theory of martyrdom. *Cultural Sociology, 2*(1), 99–121. doi:10.1177/1749975507086276

Dictionary.com | Meanings & Definitions of English Words. (2020). In *Dictionary.com.* https://www.dictionary.com/browse/shame

Dixon, E. (2021, July 3). Breaking the chains of generational trauma. *Psychology Today,* The Flourishing Family (blog).

Donnelly, J., Rosenberg, M., & Fleeson, W. P. (1970). The evolution of the mental status—Past and future. *American Journal of Psychiatry, 126*(7), 997–1002. doi:10.1176/ajp.126.7.997

Dreifus, C. (1989, August). Alice Walker "Writing to save my life." Interview. *The Progressive, 53,* 29–32.

Du Bois, W. E. B. (1898). The study of the Negro Problems. The Annals of the American Academy of Political and Social Science, 11(1), 1–23. https://doi.org/10.1177/000271629801100101

Du Bois, W. E. B. (1903). *The souls of Black folk: Essays and sketches.* https://muse.jhu.edu/chapter/2141188/pdf

Ebong, I., & Breathett, K. (2020). The cardiovascular disease epidemic in African American women: Recognizing and tackling a persistent problem. *Journal of Women's Health, 29*(7), 891–893. doi:10.1089/jwh.2019.8125

EEOC releases Annual Performance Report for Fiscal Year 2022. (2024). US EEOC. https://www.eeoc.gov/newsroom/eeoc-releases-annual-performance-report-fiscal-year-2022

Eriksen, K., & Kress, V. (2006). The DSM and the professional counseling identity: Bridging the gap. *Journal of Mental Health Counseling, 28*(3), 202–217.

Estriplet, T., Morgan, I., Davis, K., Perry, J. C., & Matthews, K. (2022). Black perinatal mental health: Prioritizing maternal mental health to optimize infant health and wellness. *Frontiers in Psychiatry, 13.* https://doi.org/10.3389/fpsyt.2022.807235

Ethnic groups. (n.d.). *The World Factbook.* https://www.cia.gov/the-world-factbook/field/ethnic-groups/

Eurich, T. (2018). *Insight: The surprising truth about how others see us, how we see ourselves, and why the answers matter more than we think.* Crown Currency.

Falendar, C. A., Burnes, T. R., & Ellis, M. V. (2013). Multicultural clinical supervision and benchmarks: Empirical support for informing practice and supervision training. *The Counseling Psychologist, 41,* 6–25.

Fanon, F. (1952/2008). *Black skin, white masks.* Grove Press.

Federal laws prohibiting job discrimination: Questions and answers. (n.d.). U.S. EEOC. https://www.eeoc.gov/fact-sheet/federal-laws-prohibiting-job-discrimination-questions-and-answers

Feinberg, M. E. (2003). The internal structure and ecological context of coparenting: A framework for research and intervention. *Parenting, 3*(2), 95–131. https://doi.org/10.1207/s15327922par0302_01

Feinstein, R. A. (2018). *When rape was legal: The untold history of sexual violence during slavery.* https://openlibrary.org/books/OL28850536M/When_Rape_Was_Legal

Fenn, K., & Byrne, M. (2013). The key principles of cognitive behavioural therapy. *InnovAiT Education and Inspiration for General Practice, 6*(9), 579–585. doi:10.1177/1755738012471029

Fenton-O'Creevy, M., & Furnham, A. (2022). Money attitudes, financial capabilities, and impulsiveness as predictors of wealth accumulation. *PloS One, 17*(11), e0278047. doi:10.1371/journal.pone.0278047

Field, K. (2014). The violence of family formation: Enslaved families and reproductive labor in the marketplace. *Reviews in American History, 42*(2), 255–264. doi:10.1353/rah.2014.0039

Flescher, J. (1953). On different types of countertransference. *International Journal of Group Psychotherapy, 3,* 357–372.

Freud, S. (1894). "The neuro-psychoses of defense," in J. Strachey (Ed.), *The Standard Edition of the Complete Psychological Works of Sigmund Freud (1893–1899) Early Psycho-Analytic Publications* (Vol. 3). Hogarth.

Frey, W. H. (2018). *Diversity explosion: How new racial demographics are remaking America.* Brookings Institution Press.

Frijda, N. H., Mesquita, B., Sonnemans, J., & Van Goozen, S. H. M. (1991). The duration of affective phenomena or emotions, sentiments and passions. In K. T. Strongman (Ed.), *International Review of Studies on Emotion* (Vol.1, pp.187–225). Wiley.

Fürsich, E. (2010). Media and the representation of others. *International Social Science Journal, 61*(199), 113–130. doi:10.1111/j.1468-2451.2010.01751.x

Gaines, J. (2024, July 25). Mental status exams: 10 best templates, questions & examples. *PositivePsychology.com.* https://positivepsychology.com/mental-status-examination/

Gallup-Lumina Foundation. (2022). *The State of Higher Education 2022 Report: Quantifying the perspectives of the currently, previously, and never enrolled after unprecedented disruptions to higher education.* https://www.luminafoundation

.org/wp-content/uploads/2022/04/gallup-lumina-state-of-higher-education-2022-report.pdf

Gallup-Lumina Foundation. (2024). State of Higher Education 2024 Report. https://www.gallup.com/

Garb, H. N. (2021). Race bias and gender bias in the diagnosis of psychological disorders. *Clinical Psychology Review, 90*, 102087. doi:10.1016/j.cpr.2021.102087

Gardner, H. (2011). *Frames of mind: The theory of multiple intelligences.* Basic Books.

Gelso, C. J., & Hayes, J. (2007). *Countertransference and the Therapist's Inner Experience: Perils and Possibilities* (1st ed.). Routledge. https://doi.org/10.4324/9780203936979

Giano, Z., Wheeler, D. L., & Hubach, R. D. (2020). The frequencies and disparities of adverse childhood experiences in the U.S. *BMC Public Health, 20*(1). doi:10.1186/s12889-020-09411-z

Girma, L. L. (2023, February 15). Bloomberg. https://www.bloomberg.com/news/articles/2023-02-15/why-black-women-are-banding-together-to-leave-america-behind

Gold, M. S. (1981). Diagnosis of depression in the 1980s. *JAMA, 245*(15), 1562. doi:10.1001/jama.1981.03310400044029

Granrose, J. (2021). The Archetype of the Magician (Philosophy). Eyecorner Press.

Grant, A. M., Franklin, J., & Langford, P. (2002). The Self-Reflection and Insight Scale: A new measure of private self-consciousness. *Social Behavior and Personality, 30*(8), 821–835. doi:10.2224/sbp.2002.30.8.821

Green, C. E., & Greene King, V. (2001). Sisters mentoring sisters: Afrocentric leadership development for Black women in the academy. *Journal of Negro Education, 70*(3), 156–165.

Griffin, K.A., & Reddick, R.J. (2011). Surveillance and sacrifice: Gender differences in the mentoring patterns of Black professors at predominantly white research universities. *American Educational Research Journal, 48*(5), 1032–1057.

Griffin, R. A. (2012). I am an angry black woman: Black feminist autoethnography, voice and resistance. *Women's Studies in Communication, 35*(2), 138–157.

Gross, S. R., Possley, M., Otterbourg, K., Stephens, K., Paredes, J., & O'Brien, B. (2022). Race and wrongful convictions in the United States 2022. *Social Science Research Network.* doi:10.2139/ssrn.4245863

Gutowski, E. R., Freitag, S., Zhang, S., Thompson, M. P., & Kaslow, N. J. (2022). Intimate partner violence, legal systems and barriers for African American women. *Journal of Interpersonal Violence, 38*(1–2), 1279–1298. doi:10.1177/08862605221090561

Haahr-Pedersen, I., Perera, C., Hyland, P., Vallières, F., Murphy, D., Hansen, M., Spitz, P., Hansen, P., & Cloitre, M. (2020). Females have more complex patterns of childhood adversity: implications for mental, social, and emotional outcomes in adulthood. *European Journal of Psychotraumatology, 11*(1). https://doi.org/10.1080/20008198.2019.1708618

Hadley, C. N. (2021, August 27). "Employees are lonelier than ever. Here's how employers can help." *Harvard Business Review.* https://hbr.org/2021/06/employees-are-lonelier-than-ever-heres-how-employers-can-help

Halpern, J. Y., & Moses, Y. (1990). Knowledge and common knowledge in a distributed environment. *Journal of the ACM, 37*(3), 549–587. doi:10.1145/79147.79161

Harper's Weekly. (1862, June 21). Illegal to teach slaves to read and write. Retrieved from http://www.sonofthesouth.net/leefoundation/civil-war/1862/june/slaves-read-write.htm

Harris-Perry, M. V. (2011). *Sister citizen: Shame, stereotypes, and Black women in America*. Yale University Press.

Harrison, P. (1990). *"Religion" and the religions in the English enlightenment*. Cambridge University Press.

Hatchett, G. T. (2017). Monitoring the counseling relationship and client progress as alternatives to prescriptive empirically supported therapies. *Journal of Mental Health Counseling*. 39(2), 104–115.

Henley, N. M., Meng, K., O'Brien, D., McCarthy, W. J., & Sockloskie, R. J. (1998). Developing a scale to measure the diversity of feminist attitudes. *Psychology of Women Quarterly*, 22, 317–348.

Hermann, A. D., Leonardelli, G. J., & Arkin, R. M. (2002). Self-doubt and self-esteem: A threat from within. *Personality and Social Psychology Bulletin*, 28(3), 395–408. doi:10.1177/0146167202286010

Hernandez, P. (2008). The cultural context model in clinical supervision. *Training and Education in Professional Psychology*, 2(1), 10–17.

Hernandez, P., & McDowell, T. (2010). Intersectionality, power, and relational safety in context: Key concepts in clinical supervision. *Training and Education in Professional Psychology*, 4(1), 29–35.

History.com editors. (2022, November 22). *Black Civil War soldiers: Facts, death toll & enlistment* https://www.history.com/topics/american-civil-war/black-civil-war-soldiers.

Hoffschwelle, M. S. (2015). A Black woman "in orthority": Claiming professional status in Jim Crow Alabama. *The Journal of Southern History*, 81(4), 843–886.

Homeownership rates by race and ethnicity: Black alone in the United States. (2024, April 30). *Federal Reserve Bank of St. Louis*. https://fred.stlouisfed.org/series/BOAAAHORUSQ156N

hooks, b. (1989). *Talking back: Thinking feminist, thinking black*. SouthEnd Press.

Howell, E. A. (2018). Reducing disparities in severe maternal morbidity and mortality. *Clinical Obstetrics & Gynecology*, 61(2), 387–399. doi:10.1097/grf.0000000000000349

Isobel, S., McCloughen, A., Goodyear, M., & Foster, K. (2020). Intergenerational trauma and its relationship to mental health care: A Qualitative inquiry. *Community Mental Health Journal*, 57(4), 631–643. https://doi.org/10.1007/s10597-020-00698-1

Jacobsen, J. (2024, January 25). *Heart disease in Black women statistics: Facts for 2024.* EHProject. https://www.ehproject.org/health/longevity/heart-disease-in-black-women-statistics

Jollans, L., & Whelan, R. (2018). Neuromarkers for mental disorders: Harnessing population neuroscience. *Frontiers in Psychiatry*, 9. doi:10.3389/fpsyt.2018.00242

Jung, C. (1959). *The collected works: The archetypes and the collective unconscious* (Vol. 9, pt. 1). Princeton University Press.

Junge, C., Valkenburg, P. M., Deković, M., & Branje, S. (2020). The building blocks of social competence: Contributions of the Consortium of Individual Development. *Developmental Cognitive Neuroscience*, 45, 100861. doi:10.1016/j.dcn.2020.100861

Kaduvettoor, A., O'Shaughnessy, T., Mori, Y., Beverly III, C., Weatherford, R. D., & Ladany, N. (2009). Helping and hindering multicultural events in group supervision: Climate and multicultural competence. *The Counseling Psychologist*, 37(6), 786–820.

Kearney, B. E., & Lanius, R. A. (2022). The brain-body disconnect: A somatic sensory basis for trauma-related disorders. *Frontiers in Neuroscience, 16.* doi:10.3389/fnins.2022.1015749

Keith, V. M., Lincoln, K. D., Taylor, R. J., & Jackson, J. S. (2010). Discriminatory experiences and depression symptoms among African American women: Do skin tone and mastery matter? *Sex Roles, 62,* 48–59.

Kelch-Oliver, K., Smith, C. O., Johnson, K., Welcom, J. S., Gardner, N. D., & Collins, M. H. (2013). Exploring the mentoring relationship among African American women in psychology. *Advancing Women in Leadership, 33*(1), 29–37.

Kilpatrick, D. G., Resnick, H. S., Ruggiero, K. J., Conoscenti, L. M., & McCauley, J. (2007). Drug-facilitated, incapacitated, and forcible rape: A national study [Dataset]. In *PsycEXTRA Dataset.* doi:10.1037/e667182007-001

King, L. (2013). The relevance and redefining of Du Bois's talented tenth: Two centuries later. *Papers & Publications: Interdisciplinary Journal of Undergraduate Research, 2*(1), 9.

King, T. (2015, July 14). Parenting in the Black community: Why raising children is different for us. *Atlanta Black Star.* https://atlantablackstar.com/2015/07/14/psychology-parenting-exploring-new-ideas-black-motherhood-fatherhood

Kitchener, K. S., & King, P. M. (1981). Reflective judgment: Concepts of justification and their relationship to age and education. *Journal of Applied Developmental Psychology, 2,* 89–116.

Kokubun, K., Nemoto, K., Oka, H., Fukuda, H., Yamakawa, Y., & Watanabe, Y. (2018). Association of fatigue and stress with gray matter volume. *Frontiers in Behavioral Neuroscience, 12.* doi:10.3389/fnbeh.2018.00154

Kretz, D. (2022). *Administering freedom: The state of emancipation after the Freedmen's Bureau.* University of North Carolina Press.

Kroeber, A. L., & Kluckhohn, C. (1952). Culture: a critical review of concepts and definitions. *Papers. Peabody Museum of Archaeology & Ethnology, Harvard University, 47*(1), viii–223.

Kühne, F., Maas, J., Wiesenthal, S., & Weck, F. (2019). Empirical research in clinical supervision: A systematic review and suggestions for future studies. *BMC Psychology 7,* 54. doi:10.1186/s40359-019-0327-7

LaFromboise, T. D., Coleman, H. L. K., & Hernandez, A. (1991). Development and factor structure of the Cross-Cultural Counseling Inventory–Revised. *Professional Psychology: Research and Practice, 22,* 380–388.

Leahey, T. H. (2017). *A history of psychology: From antiquity to modernity.* Routledge.

Lee, A. T., Chin, P., Nambiar, A., & Haskins, N. H. (2023). Addressing intergenerational trauma in Black families: Trauma-informed socioculturally attuned family therapy. *Journal of Marital and Family Therapy, 49*(2), 447–462. doi:10.1111/jmft.12632

Liao, K. Y., Wei, M., & Yin, M. (2019). The misunderstood schema of the strong black woman: Exploring its mental health consequences and coping responses among African American women. *Psychology of Women Quarterly, 44*(1), 84–104. doi:10.1177/0361684319883198

Library of Congress. (n.d.). *Abraham Lincoln and emancipation.* https://www.loc.gov/collections/abraham-lincoln-papers/articles-and-essays/abraham-lincoln-and-emancipation/#:~:text=Draft%20Preliminary%20Emancipation

Lim, M., Qualter, P., Ding, D., Holt-Lunstad, J., Mikton, C., & Smith, B. (2023). Advancing loneliness and social isolation as global health challenges: Taking three priority actions. *Public Health Research & Practice, 33*(3). doi:10.17061/phrp3332320

Lindquist, K. A., MacCormack, J. K., & Shablack, H. (2015). The role of language in emotion: predictions from psychological constructionism. *Frontiers in Psychology, 6.* doi:10.3389/fpsyg.2015.00444

Lister, R. L. (2019). Black maternal mortality: The elephant in the room. *World Journal of Gynecology & Women's Health, 3*(1). doi:10.33552/wjgwh.2019.03.000555

Lloyd, B. C. (2023, July 21). Black women in the workplace. *Gallup.com.* https://www.gallup.com/workplace/333194/black-women-workplace.aspx

London, M., Sessa, V. I., & Shelley, L. A. (2022). Developing self-awareness: Learning processes for self- and interpersonal growth. *Annual Review of Organizational Psychology and Organizational Behavior, 10*(1), 261–288. doi:10.1146/annurev-orgpsych-120920-044531

Lusardi, A., & Mitchell, O. S. (2014). The economic importance of financial literacy: Theory and evidence. *Journal of Economic Literature, 52*(1), 5–44. doi:10.1257/jel.52.1.5

MacKenzie, K. R. (1983). The clinical application of a group climate measure. In R. R. Dies & K. R. MacKenzie (Eds.), *Advances in group psychotherapy: Integrating research and practice* (pp. 159–170). International Universities Press.

Malone, A. (2023). Black students: Involuntary minorities, teacher disposition, and the impact of professional development [Dissertation, Morgan State University].

Marazziti, D., Baroni, S., Mucci, F., Piccinni, A., Moroni, I., Giannaccini, G., Carmassi, C., Massimetti, E., & Dell'Osso, L. (2019). Sex-Related differences in plasma oxytocin levels in humans. *Clinical Practice and Epidemiology in Mental Health, 15*(1), 58–63. doi:10.2174/1745017901915010058

Martin, C. L., Ruble, D. N., & Szkrybalo, J. (2002). Cognitive theories of early gender development. *Psychological Bulletin, 128*(6), 903–933. doi:10.1037/0033-2909.128.6.903

McDaniel, A., DiPrete, T. A., Buchmann, C., & Shwed, U. (2011). The Black gender gap in educational attainment: Historical trends and racial comparisons. *Demography, 48*(3), 889–914. doi:10.1007/s13524-011-0037-0

McGiffert, M., & Axtell, J. (1976). The school upon a hill: Education and society in Colonial New England. *American Historical Review, 81*(2), 440. doi:10.2307/1851311

McLean, M. A., Humphreys, K. L., & Zeanah, C. H. (2023). Infant development: The first 3 years of life. In A. Tasman (Ed.) *Tasman's Psychiatry* (pp. 1–33). Springer. doi:10.1007/978-3-030-42825-9_97-1

McManus, E., Haroon, H., Duncan, N. W., Elliott, R., & Muhlert, N. (2022). The effects of stress across the lifespan on the brain, cognition and mental health: A UK biobank study. *Neurobiology of Stress, 18,* 100447. doi:10.1016/j.ynstr.2022.100447

Mental Health, Brain Health and Substance Use (MSD). (2017, January 3). *Depression and other common mental disorders.* https://www.who.int/publications/i/item/depression-global-health-estimates

Meyers, D. T. (1986). The politics of self-respect: A feminist perspective. *Hypatia, 1*(1), 83–100. doi:10.1111/j.1527-2001.1986.tb00523.x

Mezzich, J. E., Kirmayer, L. J., Kleinman, A., Fabrega, H., Parron, D. L., Good, B. J., Lin, K., & Manson, S. M. (1999). The place of culture in *DSM-IV. The Journal of Nervous and Mental Disease, 187*(8), 457–464. doi:10.1097/00005053-199908000-00001

Miceli, M., & Castelfranchi, C. (2018). Reconsidering the differences between shame and guilt. *Europe's Journal of Psychology, 14*(3), 710–733. doi:10.5964/ejop.v14i3.1564

Miller, C. D. (2015). A phenomenological analysis of the crabs in the barrel syndrome. *Academy of Management Proceedings, 2015*(1), 13710. doi:10.5465/ambpp.2015.13710 abstract

Miller, G., & De Shazer, S. (1998). Have you heard the latest rumor about . . . ? Solution-Focused therapy as a rumor. *Family Process, 37*(3), 363–377. doi:10 .1111/j.1545-5300.1998.00363.x

Mitchell, T., & Mitchell, T. (2024a, April 14). 1. *Trends and patterns in intermarriage.* Pew Research Center. https://www.pewresearch.org/social-trends/2017/05/18/1 -trends-and-patternsinintermarriage

Mitchell, T., & Mitchell, T. (2024b, July 15). 3. *Religious beliefs among Black Americans.* Pew Research Center. https://www.pewresearch.org/religion/2021/02/16/religious -beliefs-among-black-americans/

Money, J. (1955). Hermaphroditism, gender and precocity in hyperadrenocorticism: Psychologic findings. *Bulletin of the Johns Hopkins Hospital, 96*, 253–264.

Money, J., & Ehrhardt, A. A. (1974). *Man and woman, boy and girl: Differentiation and dimorphism of gender identity from conception to maturity.* New American University.

Mosley, E. A., Prince, J. R., McKee, G. B., Carter, S. E., Leone, R. M., Gill-Hopple, K., & Gilmore, A. K. (2021). Racial disparities in sexual assault characteristics and mental health care after sexual assault medical forensic exams. *Journal of Women's Health, 30*(10), 1448–1456. doi:10.1089/jwh.2020.8935

Motro, D., Evans, J. B., Ellis, A. P. J., & Benson, L. (2022). Race and reactions to women's expressions of anger at work: Examining the effects of the "angry Black woman" stereotype. *Journal of Applied Psychology, 107*(1), 142–152. doi:10.1037/apl0000884

Mtshali, L. (2020, December 6). Everything you ever wanted to know about those sousou savings clubs African and Caribbean women love. *Essence.*

Muse-Burke, J. L., Ladany, N., & Deck, M. D. (2001). The supervisory relationship. In L. J. Bradley & N. Ladany, N. (Eds.). *Counselor supervision: Principles, process & practice* (3rd ed., pp. 29–62). Routledge.

National Center for Education Statistics. (2024). *Master's degrees conferred by postsecondary institutions, by race/ethnicity and sex of student: Selected academic years, 1976–77 through 2021–22.* https://nces.ed.gov/programs/digest/d23/tables/dt23_323 .20.asp

National Center for Health Statistics. (2022). National Health Interview Survey 2021 survey description. https://ftp.cdc.gov/pub/Health_Statistics/NCHS/Dataset_Doc umentation/NHIS/2021/srvydesc-508.pdf

National Women's Law Center. (2018, August 2). *Black women disproportionately experience workplace sexual harassment, New NWLC report reveals.* https://nwlc.org/press -release/black-women-disproportionately-experience-workplace-sexual-harassment -new-nwlc-report-reveals/

"Negroes and Mullattoes" (1847). *Missouri Secretary of State.* https://www.sos.mo.gov/ CMSImages/MDH/AnActRespectingSlaves,1847.pdf

Noroozi, M., Gholami, M., & Mohebbi-Dehnavi, Z. (2020). The relationship between hope and resilience with promoting maternal attachment to the fetus during pregnancy. *Journal of Education and Health Promotion, 9*(1), 54. doi:10.4103/jehp. jehp_386_19

Norton, A. (2022). *What's new with the DSM-5-TR?.* American Counseling Association.

www.counseling.org. https://www.counseling.org/publications/counseling-today
-magazine/article-archive/article/legacy/what-s-new-with-the-dsm-5-tr

Novais, F., Araújo, A., & Godinho, P. (2015). Historical roots of histrionic personality disorder. *Frontiers in Psychology, 6.* doi:10.3389/fpsyg.2015.01463

NPR. (2013, August 28). Women were "second class citizens at '63 March." https://www.npr.org/transcripts/216550412?storyId=216550412?storyId=216550412

Ogbu, J. (1978). *Minority education and caste: The American system in cross-cultural perspective.* Academic Press.

Ogbu, J. U., & Simons, H. D. (1998). Voluntary and involuntary minorities: A cultural-ecological theory of school performance with some implications for education. *Anthropology & Education Quarterly, 29*(2), 155–188. doi:10.1525/aeq.1998.29.2.155

Oosterwijk, S., Lindquist, K. A., Anderson, E., Dautoff, R., Moriguchi, Y., & Barrett, L. F. (2012). States of mind: Emotions, body feelings, and thoughts share distributed neural networks. *NeuroImage, 62*(3), 2110–2128. doi:10.1016/j.neuroimage.2012.05.079

Organization for Economic Cooperation and Development OECD/ILO. (2017). Better use of skills in the workplace: Why it matters for productivity and local jobs. OECD Publishing. doi:10.1787/9789264281394-e

Otani, K., Suzuki, A., Matsumoto, Y., & Shirata, T. (2017). Relationship of negative and positive core beliefs about the self with dysfunctional attitudes in three aspects of life. *Neuropsychiatric Disease and Treatment, 13,* 2585–2588. doi:10.2147/ndt.s150537

Papalia, D. E., & Martorell, G. (2021). *Experience human development* (14th ed.). McGraw Hill.

Park, C. L., Holt, C. L., Le, D., Christie, J., & Williams, B. R. (2018). Positive and negative religious coping styles as prospective predictors of well-being in African Americans. *Psychology of Religion and Spirituality, 10*(4), 318–326. doi:10.1037/rel0000124

Patsides, N. (1998). *William M. Banks, Black intellectuals: Race and responsibility in American life.* (p. 335). W. W. Norton. doi:10.1017/s0021875898406030

Pavlova, B., Bagnell, A., Cumby, J., Vallis, E. H., Abidi, S., Lovas, D., Propper, L., Alda, M., & Uher, R. (2022). Sex-Specific transmission of anxiety disorders from parents to offspring. *JAMA Network Open, 5*(7), e2220919. doi:10.1001/jamanetworkopen.2022.20919

Pederson, A. B. (2023). Management of depression in Black people: Effects of cultural issues. *Psychiatric Annals, 53*(3), 122–125. doi:10.3928/00485713-20230215-01

Pew Research Center. (2025). *Religious landscape study.* https://www.pewresearch.org/religious-landscape-study/

Piaget, J., & Cook, M. T. (1952). *The origins of intelligence in children.* International University Press.

Pierik, B. (2022). Patriarchal power as a conceptual tool for gender history. *Rethinking History, 26*(1), 71–92. doi:10.1080/13642529.2022.2037864

Rabelo, L. Z., Bortoloti, R., & Souza, D. H. (2014). Dolls are for girls and not for boys: Evaluating the appropriateness of the Implicit Relational Assessment Procedure for School-Age Children. *The Psychological Record, 64*(1), 71–77. doi:10.1007/s40732-014-0006-2

Racy, F., & Morin, A. (2024). Relationships between self-talk, inner speech, mind wandering, mindfulness, self-concept clarity, and self-regulation in university students. *Behavioral Sciences, 14*(1), 55. doi:10.3390/bs14010055

Rahman, K. (2021, December 28). Full list of Black people killed by police in 2021. *Newsweek.* https://www.newsweek.com/black-people-killed-police-2021-1661633

Rasche, K., Dudeck, M., Otte, S., Klingner, S., Vasic, N., & Streb, J. (2016). Factors influencing the pathway from trauma to aggression: A current review of behavioral studies. *Neurology, Psychiatry & Brain Research/Neurology, Psychiatry and Brain Research, 22*(2), 75–80. doi:10.1016/j.npbr.2016.01.009

Ratts, M. J., Singh, A. A., Nassar-McMillan, S., Butler, S. K., & McCullough, J. R. (2016). Multicultural and social justice counseling competencies: Guidelines for the counseling profession. *Journal of Multicultural Counseling and Development, 44*(1), 28–48. doi:10.1002/jmcd.12035

Reilly, A. J. (1998). *Three approaches to organizational learning.* The Pfeiffer Library (Vol. 16, 2nd ed.), Jossey-Bass/Pfeiffer.

Reupert, A., Straussner, S. L., Weimand, B., & Maybery, D. (2022). It takes a village to raise a child: Understanding and expanding the concept of the "Village." *Frontiers in Public Health, 10.* doi:10.3389/fpubh.2022.756066

Reynolds-Dobbs, W., Thomas, K. M., & Harrison, M. S. (2008). From mammy to super-woman: Images that hinder black women's career development. *Journal of Career Development, 35*(2), 129–150. doi:10.1177/0894845308325645

Rico, B., Kreider, R. M., & Anderson, L. (2018, July 9). *Growth in interracial and inter-ethnic married-couple households.* U.S. Census Bureau. https://www.census.gov/library/stories/2018/07/interracial-marriages.html

Riina, E. M., & Feinberg, M. E. (2018). The trajectory of coparenting relationship quality across early adolescence: Family, community, and parent gender influences. *Journal of Family Psychology, 32*(5), 599–609. doi:10.1037/fam0000426

Robenstine, C. (1992). French colonial policy and the education of women and minorities: Louisiana in the early eighteenth century. *History of Education Quarterly, 32*(2), 193. doi:10.2307/368985

Rothwell, C., Kehoe, A., Farook, S. F., & Illing, J. C. (2021). Enablers and barriers to effective clinical supervision in the workplace: A rapid evidence review. *BMJ Open, 11*(9), e052929. doi:10.1136/bmjopen-2021-052929

Rosselli, M., Ardila, A., Matute, E., & Vélez-Uribe, I. (2014). Language development across the life span: A neuropsychological/neuroimaging perspective. *Neuroscience Journal, 2014,* 1–21. doi:10.1155/2014/585237

Rowan, J. (1992). *The reality game: A guide to humanistic counselling and therapy.* Psychology Press.

Rudman, L. A., & Saud, L. H. (2020). Justifying social inequalities: The role of social Darwinism. *Personality and Social Psychology Bulletin, 46*(7), 1139–1155.

Ruffin, J. E. (1985). *An exploratory study of adult development in black professional women.* (Doctoral dissertation, City University of New York). Retrieved from ProQuest Dissertations Publishing. (UMI8515656)

Rush, B. (1773). *An address to the inhabitants of the British settlements in America, upon slave-keeping.* Internet Archive. https://archive.org/details/addresstoinhabit00rush_0

Ryan, R. M., & Deci, E. L. (2001). On happiness and human potentials: A review of research on hedonic and eudaimonic well-being. *Annual Review of Psychology, 52*(1), 141–166. doi:10.1146/annurev.psych.52.1.141

Safran, J. D., & Muran, J. C. (2000). Resolving therapeutic alliance ruptures: Diversity and integration. *Journal of Clinical Psychology: In Session: Psychotherapy in Practice,* 56, 233–243.

Saini, A. (2023). *How did patriarchy actually begin?* https://www.bbc.com/future/article/ 20230525-how-did-patriarchy-actually-begin

Saleem, F. T., English, D., Busby, D. R., Lambert, S. F., Harrison, A., Stock, M. L., & Gibbons, F. X. (2016). The impact of African American parents' racial discrimination experiences and perceived neighborhood cohesion on their racial socialization practices. *Journal of Youth and Adolescence,* 45(7), 1338–1349. doi:10.1007/ s10964-016-0499-x

Schlossberg, N. K., Lynch, A. Q., & Chickering, A. W. (1989). *Improving higher education environments for adults: Responsive programs and services from entry to departure.* Jossey-Bass.

Schramm, E., Klein, D. N., Elsaesser, M., Furukawa, T. A., & Domschke, K. (2020). Review of dysthymia and persistent depressive disorder: History, correlates, and clinical implications. *The Lancet. Psychiatry,* 7(9), 801–812. doi:10.1016/ s2215-0366(20)30099-7

Schwyck, M. E., Du, M., Li, Y., Chang, L. J., & Parkinson, C. (2023). Similarity among friends serves as a social prior: The assumption that "birds of a feather flock together" shapes social decisions and relationship beliefs. *Personality and Social Psychology Bulletin,* 50(6), 823–840. doi:10.1177/01461672221140269

Seales, D. J. (1987). *Factors which influence the professional success of Black women: Implications for career development* (Doctoral dissertation, Fairleigh Dickinson University). Retrieved from ProQuest Dissertations Publishing. (UMI 8811710)

Sethi, S. (2020, April 21). Advancing racial equity in maternal mental health policy. Center for Law and Social Policy (CLASP). https://www.clasp.org/publications/ report/brief/advancing-racial-equity-maternal-mental-health-policy/.

Sexual harassment in our nation's workplaces. (2022, April). Office of Enterprise Data and Analytics (OEDA) Data Highlight No. 2. U.S. Equal Employment Opportunity Commission (EEOC).

Sheu, L., Kogan, J. R., & Hauer, K. E. (2017). How supervisor experience influences trust, supervision, and trainee learning. *Academic Medicine,* 92(9), 1320–1327. doi:10.1097/acm.0000000000001560

Shim, R. S. (2021). Dismantling structural racism in psychiatry: A path to mental health equity. *American Journal of Psychiatry,* 178(7), 592–598. doi:10.1176/appi. ajp.2021.21060558

Slavery before the trans-Atlantic trade: African passages.(n.d.). Lowcountry Digital History Initiative. https://ldhi.library.cofc.edu/exhibits/show/africanpassageslowcountry adapt/introductionatlanticworld/slaverybeforetrade

Speer, D. (2024). How many Americans live abroad? Association of Americans Resident Overseas (AARO). https://aaro.org/living-abroad/how-many-americans-live-abroad

Staff, Y. (n.d.-c). *Romans* 3:23–24. https://www.bible.com/bible/111/ROM.3.23-24.niv

Stanley, J. T., & Chukwuorji, J. C. (2024). Sankofa: Learning from the past to build the future—Introduction to the special issue on aging in Sub-Saharan Africa. *Innovation in Aging,* 8(4). doi:10.1093/geroni/igae031

Statista. (2024, September 5). *Number of births in the United States 1990-2022.* https:

//www.statista.com/statistics/195908/number-of-births-in-the-united-states-since-1990/

Steinmetz, K. (2020, February 20). She coined the term 'Intersectionality' over 30 years ago. Here's what it means to her today. *TIME*. https://time.com/5786710/kimberle-crenshaw-intersectionality/

Stewart, C. A., Mitchell, D. G., MacDonald, P. A., Pasternak, S. H., Tremblay, P. F., & Finger, E. (2023). The psychophysiology of guilt in healthy adults. *Cognitive Affective & Behavioral Neuroscience*, 23(4), 1192–1209. doi:10.3758/s13415-023-01079-3

Sue, D. W., Capodilupo, C. M., Torino, G. C., Bucceri, J. M., Holder, A. M. B., Nadal, K. L., & Esquilin, M. (2007). Racial microaggressions in everyday life: Implications for clinical practice. *American Psychologist*, 62(4), 271–286. doi:10.1037/0003-066X.62.4.271

Sue, D. W. (2010). *Microaggressions in everyday life: Race, gender, and sexual orientation*. John Wiley & Sons.

Sue, D. W. (n.d.). Microaggressions. Unitarian Universalist Association. https://www.uua.org/files/pdf/m/microaggressions_by_derald_wing_sue_ph.d._.pdf

Sue, D. W., Arredondo, P., & McDavis, R. J. (1992). Multicultural counseling competencies and standards: A call to the profession. *Journal of Counseling & Development*, 70(4), 477–486. doi:10.1002/j.1556-6676.1992.tb01642.x

Sulz, S. (2010). [Hysteria I. Histrionic personality disorder. A psychotherapeutic challenge]. *PubMed*, 81(7), 879–887; quiz 888. https://doi.org/10.1007/s00115-010-3016-6

Surowiec, A., Snyder, K. T., & Creanza, N. (2019, July 15). A worldwide view of matriliny: using cross-cultural analyses to shed light on human kinship systems. *Philosophical Transactions of the Royal Society B. Biological Sciences*, 374(1780), 20180077. doi:10.1098/rstb.2018.0077.

Sutton, A., Williams, H. M., & Allinson, C. W. (2015). A longitudinal, mixed method evaluation of self-awareness training in the workplace. *European Journal of Training and Development*, 39(7), 610–627. doi:10.1108/EJTD-04-2015-0031

Szymanski, D. M. (2003). The Feminist Supervision Scale (FSS): A rational/theoretical approach. *Psychology of Women Quarterly*, 27, 221–232.

Szymanski, D. M. (2005). Feminist identity and theories as correlates of feminist supervision practices. *The Counseling Psychologist*, 33(5), 729–747.

Tasca, C., Rapetti, M., Carta, M. G., & Fadda, B. (2012). Women and hysteria in the history of mental health. *Clinical Practice and Epidemiology in Mental Health*, 8(1), 110–119. doi:10.2174/1745017901208010110

Taylor, B. K., & Westlund, K. N. (2016). The noradrenergic locus coeruleus as a chronic pain generator. *Journal of Neuroscience Research*, 95(6), 1336–1346. doi:10.1002/jnr.23956

Taylor, R. J., Taylor, H. O., Nguyen, A. W., & Chatters, L. M. (2020). Social isolation from family and friends and mental health among African Americans and Black Caribbeans. *American Journal of Orthopsychiatry*, 90(4), 468–478. doi:10.1037/ort0000448

Tipton, C. M. (2014). The history of "exercise is medicine" in ancient civilizations. *Advances in Physiology Education*, 38(2), 109–117. doi:10.1152/advan.00136.2013

Trapnell, P. D., & Campbell, J. D. (1999). Private self-consciousness and the Five Factor

Model of Personality: Distinguishing rumination from reflection. *Journal of Personality and Social Psychology, 76*(2), 284–304. doi:10.1037/0022-3514.76.2.284

Trautwein, A. (2022, April 22). The rise in popularity of the baby shower. *The Mom Kind – Autism, Parenting, & Mental Health.* https://themomkind.com/the-rise-in-popularity-of-the-baby-shower/

Tribble, B. L. D., Allen, S. H., Hart, J. R., Francois, T. S., & Smith-Bynum, M. A. (2019). "No [right] way to be a Black woman": Exploring gendered racial socialization among Black women. *Psychology of Women Quarterly, 43*(3), 381–397. doi:10.1177/0361684318825439

The Great Migration (1910–1970). (2021, June 28). National Archives. https://www.archives.gov/research/african-americans/migrations/great-migration

UpToDate. (n.d.). DSM-5-TR diagnostic criteria for a major depressive episode, https://www.uptodate.com/contents/image?imageKey=PSYCH%2F89994

U.S. Census Bureau. (2022a, June 10). *2020 census illuminates racial and ethnic composition of the country.* Census.gov. https://www.census.gov/library/stories/2021/08/improved-race-ethnicity-measures-reveal-united-states-population-much-more-multiracial.html

U.S. Census Bureau. (2022b, July 19). *District of Columbia had lowest percentage of married Black adults in 2015–2019.* Census.gov. https://www.census.gov/library/stories/2022/07/marriage-prevalence-for-black-adults-varies-by-state.html

U.S. Census Bureau. (2022c, December 15). *Public use Microdata Sample (PUMS).* Census.gov. https://www.census.gov/programs-surveys/acs/microdata.html

U.S. Census Bureau. (2024, June 25). *National population by characteristics: 2020–2023.* Census.gov. https://www.census.gov/data/tables/time-series/demo/popest/2020s-national-detail.html

U.S. Surgeon General Advisory. (2023). Our epidemic of loneliness and isolation. U.S. Department of Health and Human Services. https://www.hhs.gov/sites/default/files/surgeon-general-social-connection-advisory.pdf

Vallières, F., Hyland, P., & Murphy, J. (2021). Navigating the who, where, what, when, how and why of trauma exposure and response. *European Journal of Psychotraumatology, 12*(1). doi:10.1080/20008198.2020.1855903

Van Deburg, W. L. (1977). Slave drivers and slave narratives: A new look at the "dehumanized elite." *The Historian, 39*(4), 717–732. http://www.jstor.org/stable/24444658

Walker, A. (1989). *In search of our mother's gardens: Womanist prose.* Mariner Books.

Walsh, K., Danielson, C. K., McCauley, J. L., Saunders, B. E., Kilpatrick, D. G., & Resnick, H. S. (2012). National prevalence of posttraumatic stress disorder among sexually revictimized adolescent, college, and adult household-residing women. *Archives of General Psychiatry, 69*(9), 935. doi:10.1001/archgenpsychiatry.2012.132

Watkins, M. B., Ren, R., Boswell, W. R., Umphress, E. E., Del Carmen Triana, M., & Zardkoohi, A. (2011). Your work is interfering with our life! The influence of a significant other on employee job search activity. *Journal of Occupational and Organizational Psychology, 85*(3), 531–538. doi:10.1111/j.2044-8325.2011.02050.x

Webb, S. H. (2015). *The disparity of racial diversity in counselor education and supervision.* (Doctoral Dissertation, Walden University). Retrieved from ProQuest Dissertations Publishing. (UMI 3723217)

White-Davis, T., Stein, E., Karasz, A. (2016). The elephant in the room: Dialogues about race within cross-cultural supervisory relationships. *The International Journal of Psychiatry in Medicine, 51*(4), 347–356.

Wilkins, J., & Eisenbraun, A. J. (2009). Humor theories and the physiological benefits of laughter. *Holistic Nursing Practice, 23*(6), 349–354. doi:10.1097/hnp.0b013e3181bf37ad

Williams, D. K. (2023, September 5). What happens when Americans stop going to church. *The Atlantic.* https://www.theatlantic.com/ideas/archive/2023/09/christianity-religion-america- church-polarization/675215/

Williams, H. A. (2009). *Self-Taught: African American education in slavery and freedom.* University of North Carolina Press.

Williams, H. A. (2012). *Help me to find my people: The African American search for family lost in slavery.* https://muse.jhu.edu/chapter/1724691/pdf

Wolfe, Brendan. (2020, December 07). Racial integrity laws (1924–1930). In *Encyclopedia Virginia.* https://encyclopediavirginia.org/entries/racial-integrity-laws-1924-1930.

Women in the labor force: A databook. (2022, March 21). Bureau of Labor Statistics. https://www.bls.gov/opub/reports/womens-databook/2021/

Women's Business Ownership Act of 1988 Text of H.R. 5050 (100th): Women's Business Ownership Act of 1988 (Passed Congress/Enrolled Bill version). GovTrack.us

Wong, L. C. J., Wong, P. T. P., & Ishiyama, F. I. (2013). What helps and what hinders in cross-cultural clinical supervision: A critical incident study. *The Counseling Psychologist, 41*(1), 66–85.

World Health Organization. (2017, January 3). *Depression and other common mental disorders: Global health estimates.* https://www.who.int/publications/i/item/depression-global-health-estimates

World Health Organization. (2023, November 15). WHO launches commission to foster social connection. https://www.who.int/news/item/15-11-23-who-launches-commission-to-foster-social-connection

World Health Organization. (2024, March 25). *Violence against women.* https://www.who.int/news-room/fact-sheets/detail/violence-against-women

Yabusaki, A. S. (2010). Clinical supervision: Dialogues on diversity. *Training and Education in Professional Psychology, 4*(1), 55–61.

Yadav, G., & Gunturu, S. (2024, June 8). *Trauma-Informed therapy.* StatPearls. National Library of Medicine. https://www.ncbi.nlm.nih.gov/books/NBK604200/

Yanguas, J., Pinazo-Henandis, S., & Tarazona-Santabalbina, F. J. (2018). The complexity of loneliness. *Acta Biomedica, 89*(2), 302–314. doi:10.23750/abm.v89i2.7404

Yarwood, M. (n.d.). *The duration of an emotion.* Pressbooks. https://psu.pb.unizin.org/psych425/chapter/the-duration-of-an-emotion/

Index

Header note: Tables are noted with a *t*.

ABCDE model, 139*t*
abuse, 50, 146
acceptance of one's own decisions, 97
accidents in childhood, Black children and
    disproportionate rate of, 60
ACEs. *see* adverse childhood experiences
    (ACEs)
achievement gap, 134
acute stress disorder, 154, 155
    PTSD and, what they look like for Black
        women clients, 151–52
    PTSD and, what they sound like for Black
        women clients, 152–53
"Addressing Intergenerational Trauma in
    Black Families: Trauma-Informed Socio-
    cultural Attuned Family Therapy" (Lee,
    et al.), 64
adjustment disorders, 154, 155
adverse childhood experiences (ACEs)
    parental, healing for, 62
    women *vs.* men and, 146
advocacy
    clinician's role in, 109, 188
    creating safe spaces and, 136
    therapist's tip on, 135
aggression
    direct, 146–47, 150
    survival, 148–50
agoraphobia, 175
"aha" moment, in uncovering root issues, 129
Ahlers-Schmidt, C. R., 11
Ainsworth, M., 76
Akan people, Ghana, xix
Allen, B. J., xxi

Alpha Kappa Alpha, 77
American Baptist Mission Home Society, 35
American Counseling Association Code of
    Ethics, 135
American dream
    Black women and increased alignment to,
        26
    having more money than previous genera-
        tions and, 33–35
American Psychological Association (APA),
    trauma as defined by, 141
American Sociological Association, authoritar-
    ian parental approach study, 60
amygdala, trauma and, 143
analysis, in Bloom's taxonomy, 31, 32
analytical psychology therapy, clinical focus,
    sample therapeutic SMART goal, tech-
    nique or intervention, 68*t*
Angelou, M., 72, 141
angry Black woman stereotype, 82, 106
Antecedent, Behavior, Consequences (ABC)
    Chart, 69*t*, 118*t*
antiliteracy state laws, 27
anxiety, 161, 174–77
    in Black children and youth, disproportion-
        ate rate of, 60
    depression comorbid with, careful consider-
        ation of, 173–74
    fear *vs.*, 174
    journal prompts on, 183
    mother to daughter transmission of, 175, 176
anxiety disorders, 142, 179
    Black people and underdiagnosis/under-
        treatment of, 176–77

anxiety disorders (*continued*)
    culture-related diagnostic lens for, 176
    distinguishing among types of, 174–75
    due to another medical condition, 175
    pregnancy and, 175, 176
APA. *see* American Psychological Association
    (APA)
application, in Bloom's taxonomy, 31, 32
appreciation, in five-dimensional framework of
    mattering, 95
Aptaclub, baby shower research findings, 10
Asexualization Act of California, 11
"ashy" skin, 116
Asian Americans, interracial marriages
    between white Americans and, 98
assets, wealth and value of, 34
associate's degrees, Black women and earning
    of, statistics on, 29
Association of American Residents Overseas,
    on immigration of Black women, 95–96
attachment formation, friendships and, 72–73
attachment styles, friendships and, understand-
    ing, 80
attachment theory, 73, 74, 76
attention, in five-dimensional framework of
    mattering, 95
authenticity, 107, 108
authoritarian parenting style, mental health of
    children and, studies on, 60, 61
avoidance
    Black women, depression, and complexity
        of, 165, 169
    journal prompts on, 183
    trauma, acute stress disorder, and, 152

babies, friend-based connections between, 84
baby dolls, early maternal socialization of girls
    and, 10, 22
"baby mama" label, 113, 114
baby showers, maternal socialization of girls
    and, 10–11
bachelor's degrees
    Black women and earning of, statistics on, 29
    percentage of Americans with, 79
Baker, J., 5
balanced parenting style, 60
Banks, T., 141
beauty standards, Black girls and negative mes-
    sages around, 51, 53
Beck, A., 51, 162
behavioral interviews, 118*t*

behavioral modeling, 118*t*
behavioral rehearsals, 12
behavioral therapy
    clinical focus, sample therapeutic SMART
        goal, technique or intervention, 69*t*, 118*t*
    moving beyond stereotypes and, 118*t*
behaviorism, 76
Berk, L. E., 76
bias(es)
    stereotypes and awareness of, 112
    unchecked, trauma treatment and, 142
    see also stereotypes
Biles, S., 123
bipolar disorder, 162
birth control, nonconsensual, 11
births in United States, drop in annual num-
    ber of, 1990–2020, 11
Black Americans
    American dream and obstacles faced by, 33
    identifying as Christian, percentage of
        church attenders and, 14
    as involuntary minorities, xviii
    loneliness and, 37
    median household income for, 33
    postslavery period and educational obstacles
        for, 27–28
Black boys, historically excluded from baby
    showers, 10
Black children
    coparenting relationships and, 66
    lack of fullness of love languages and, 73
Black community, talented tenth and responsi-
    bilities to, 35–36
Black enslaved drivers, lack of Black American
    community support and, 42–43
Black families
    intergenerational trauma in, addressing,
        64–65
    nurturance as afterthought to survival in,
        60–61, 73
Black family wealth, white family wealth *vs.*, 34
Black Girl Magic, counterproductive aspect
    of, 115
Black girls
    anxiety disorders and, 177
    changing media-based beauty standards
        and, 53–54
    early maternal socialization of, 10–11
    media messages and, 51–52
    self-doubt and, 130
Black identity, beauty of, 111

Black men
  educational and professional attainments
    of, compared with Black women, 18
  historically excluded from baby showers, 10
  percentage of, in interracial marriages, 98
  role of religion in lives of, xx
Black mothers
  learning new parenting skills, 62
  postpartum depression and, 176
Black-owned businesses, 92
Black parents
  nurturance as secondary to sternness and
    fear and, 60–61, 73
  racism and parenting style of, 60
  in relation to generational cycles, 61
Black people
  direct aggression and, statistics on, 146–47
  limitations: from Black people to, 92–94
  not included in research population, 160,
    169
  self-repression and self-suppression among,
    131–32
  trauma as common experience for, 142
Black Skin, White Masks (Fanon), 107
Black trans women, stereotypes of, 106
Black women
  angry and aggressive, suffering of, 151
  being seen and, xvi–xvii
  church attendance and new choices made
    by, 14
  closing of wealth gap and, 34
  common emotions affecting, 123–31
  consistent happiness and, 134–35
  crabs in the barrel toxic mentality and, 43, 44
  cultural shock and intersected cultural
    identities of, 25, 27, 28
  direct aggression and, statistics on, 146–47
  divorce and, 6
  doubt felt by, 129–31
  DSM-5-TR and cultural inclusion-related
    changes pertaining to, 164
  dual masks and, burden of, 107
  educational and professional attainments
    of, compared with Black men, 18
  educational attainment rate of, pros and
    cons of, 25–27, 28
  education in the United States and, 27–29
  entering therapy and existential needs of, 93
  friendships and contributions of, 82–83
  further research needed on lived experi-
    ences of, 187
  gender roles for, considerations related to,
    18
  grace and, 132–33
  Great Migration and, 93
  guiding, but not advising, 186
  guilt felt by, 127–29
  hairstyling, racial discrimination, and,
    110–12
  handling with care, 185
  historical significance of friendships among,
    74
  history in the present for, 185
  intersection of race and gender and double
    minority status of, xiv, xvi, xx–xxiii, 24,
    92, 145, 186, 187
  as largest demographic of women with chil-
    dren, in US, 11
  loneliness in the workplace and, 37
  marriage rate among, drop in, 6
  microaggressions and lived experiences of,
    145–46
  microaggressions and sexual harassment
    and, 41–42
  money and, 126
  need for friendships, safe havens, and, 77
  operational definition of, in text, xv
  panic disorder, heart disease, and, 178–79
  percentage of, in interracial marriages, 98
  polarities in lives of Malcolm X and Martin
    Luther King Jr. and impact on, 37
  question of now what? and, 136
  religion and incongruence experienced by,
    15
  religion in lives of, xx
  self-actualization and, xiv
  self-doubt and, 130
  shame experienced by, 124–27
  stereotyping of, unfair and unfounded,
    105–6
  talented tenth issues and, 36
  therapy and re-empowerment of, xxi
  trauma, strong Black woman persona, and,
    56
  well-intended but culturally incompetent
    therapists and, 14
  in the workforce, statistics on, 25
  workforce-related research on, 38
blame, should and root of, 125
bleaching skin, 107
Bloom's taxonomy, 35, 170
  catalyst questions, 31–33

Bloom's taxonomy (*continued*)
  therapist's tip, 30–31
bodily-kinesthetic intelligence, 55
bondage, feelings of, journal prompts on, 101,
  102
book clubs, as safe havens, 77
boundaries, 168
  breaking generational cycles and, 65
  deal-breakers and, 84, 85
  friendships and, 79
  setting, 36
  should and, 125
  skill deficits related to, 56
  see also self-awareness; self-care
BOW Collective, 77
Bowlby, J., 162
boys, gender stereotypes and, 76, 77
brain, trauma and, 142, 143, 151
Bribri people, of Costa Rica, xix
Bronfenbrenner, U., 76
Brooks, A. C., 134
Brooks, G., 5
Bryant, K., 72
Buck v. Bell, 11
Burke, T., 41
Burnes, T. R., clinicians' role, identity, and
  intentions study, xxii
Burnett-Zeigler, I., 55, 56
Burns, U., xiii
business collaborations, as safe havens, 77
business market in the United States, value
  of, 110
business ownership
  Black women and percentage increase in,
    26
  discrimination against Black Americans
    and, xviii

capital, American dream and, 33
CAPS. *see* Clinician Administered PTSD
  Scale (CAPS)
cardiovascular disease (CVD), anxiety disorders and, 178
career, improving experience with, journal
  prompts for, 48
career-driven woman, 82
career legacies, 5, 6
career opportunities, Black women, educational success, and, 26
caregiver archetype, martyrdom and intersection with sage archetype and, 166

caring ethic, conflictual encounters and dialectic tensions in, xxi
catalyst questions, 186
  Bloom's taxonomy, 31–33
  core beliefs addressed with, 53
  fictive relationships, 75–76
  imposter syndrome, 40
  panic disorder, 179
  reforming counterproductive statements, 115
  on shame, 127
  stereotypes explored with, 106, 108
  use of, xxiii–xxiv
catch, check, change (3 C's), 138*t*
CBT. *see* cognitive behavioral therapy (CBT)
CDC. *see* Centers for Disease Control (CDC)
Center for American Progress (CAP), on
  earnings for Black women *vs.* for white
  men, 164
Centers for Disease Control (CDC), on heart
  disease and American women, 178
Chalmers, J. A., 178
Chapman, G., 73
Cheeks, M., 39
Cherepanov, E., 64
childhood messages, that no longer apply,
  51–54
childhood sexual abuse, question of children
  and history of, 8
children
  hope and raising of, 54, 55
  trauma- and stressor-related disorders in,
    154
children, question of, 8–14
  choice-based factors and, 11
  circumstantial factors and, 11
  exploration of having children: catalyst
    questions, 13
  exploring the mother role: catalyst ques-
    tions, 9
  insight from client: FY, 12
  insight from client: SH, 8–9
  socialization of women and, 10
China, Mosuo people of, xix
Chisholm, S., 25
choice for Black women, power of, 6
church attendance, question of, 14–17
  insight from a client: TR and ZR, 15–17
  Pew Research Center religious landscape
    study, 14
Civil Rights Act of 1964, xviii, 25
Civil Rights era, 132

Civil Rights movement, intersection with Women's Liberation movement and, 26, 28, 34, 93, 135

Civil War, Black people and history of fighting in, xviii, 91

Clance, P., 39, 129

Clark, T., 60

Clinician Administered PTSD Scale (CAPS), 155

clinicians
  advocacy and role of, 109, 188
  history x identity = culturally responsive approach for, xvii–xxiii
  see also therapists

code switching, 107

cognitions, faulty, mental illness and, 138*t*

cognitive behavioral therapy (CBT), 13, 160
  clinical focus, sample therapeutic SMART goal, technique or intervention, 181*t*
  core beliefs and, 51

cognitive development theory (Piaget), 76

cognitive restructuring, 97, 138*t*, 139*t*

cognitive therapy, clinical focus, sample therapeutic SMART goal, technique or intervention, 138*t*

Cohen, A., 11

collectivism *vs.* individualism, survival and, 105

college attendance, Black women and percentage increase in, 26

college education, talented tenth and acquisition of, 35

Collier, S., 175

Collins, M., 49

communication, 7, 17
  healthy, creating therapeutic goals for, 59
  with ourselves, 78
  skill deficits related to, 56

communication process
  breaking generational cycles and importance of, 65
  coparents and, 66
  steps in, 57

community
  Black women and orientation toward, 187
  survival and, 106

competence, confidence and, 130

confidence, self-doubt and impact on, 130

conflictual encounters, Black women and, xxi

congruence, in person-centered therapy, 20*t*, 117*t*

consumerism, American dream and, 33

contingency management contract, 118*t*

controlling and overplanning, trauma, acute stress disorder, and, 152

coon stereotype, 106

coparenting
  journal prompts on, 71
  success of, factors related to, 66

coping behaviors, replacement practices and, 17

coping strategies, core beliefs and, 51

core beliefs, 65, 96, 116
  authoritarian parenting style and, 61
  catalyst questions on, 53
  cognitive behavioral therapy model and, 51
  demonizing teacher of, avoiding, 52
  emotions as, 131–32
  formation and reinforcement of, 51, 52
  foundation of, understanding, 80
  historical stereotypes and, 112–15
  imposter syndrome and, 130
  repeated messages and, 53
  self-talk and, 78
  stereotypes and, insight from a client: SRJ, 113–15
  strong Black woman persona and, 56
  that no longer apply, 51–54
  utilizing workbooks and worksheets for, 54

Cosby Show, The, 111

Costa Rica, Bribri people of, xix

counterproductive statements, reforming, catalyst questions for, 115

countertransference, 36, 105
  formation and categories of, 144–45
  marriage choices and issue of, 7, 8
  stereotypes and, 112
  trauma treatment and, 142

COVID-19 pandemic, loneliness and impact of, 37

crabs in a barrel phenomenon
  enslaved Black drivers and, 43
  marginalized people and, journal prompts on, 102

creative arts therapy, clinical focus, sample therapeutic SMART goal, technique or intervention, 158*t*–59*t*

Crenshaw, K. W., 24, 91

Crocq, M. A., 174

Cross-Cutting Review Committee on Cultural Issues and Ethnoracial Equality and Inclusion Work Group, 163

CROWN (Creating a Respectful and Open
    World for Natural Hair) Act, 109, 110.
    see also hairstyles
C-suite gap, 134
cultural competency
    in counseling, understanding role of, xxiii
    increasing, xxv
cultural context model, xxi–xxii
cultural formations, introduction of, in fourth
    edition of the *DSM*, 163
cultural representation, the *DSM* and, 160–
    61. *see also* mental health disorders via a
    cultural lens, addressing
culture
    counselors' interactions with clients and
        role of, xxii
    operational definition of, in text, xv
    status quo, Black women, and, xx
current self, alignment of perceived self,
    desired self, and, 56

dating outside of one's race, 92, 93, 97–99
    creating and processing possibilities related
        to, 99
    journal prompts on, 102–3
Davidson Trauma Scale (DTS), 155
Davis, V., 24, 104
DBT. *see* dialectical behavior therapy (DBT)
deal-breakers, friendships and, 84–85
death by murder, disproportionate rate of, for
    Black children and youth, 60
decision-making, trauma and, 143
defense mechanisms
    friendships and, 89*t*
    guilt and, 127
    trauma treatment and, 142
    types of, 181*t*
    understanding, breaking generational cycles
        and, 64
defensive body language, trauma, acute stress
    disorder, and, 152
defensive countertransference, 144
deflecting, guilt and, 127
Delta Sigma Theta, 77
dementia, 162
democracy, American dream and, 33
dependence, in five-dimensional framework of
    mattering, 95
depression
    addressing family lineage of, 77–78
    anxiety comorbid with, careful consider-
        ation of, 173–74

Black children and youth and dispropor-
    tionate rate of, 60
Black women and overdiagnosis of, 135
historical background on, 162
incongruences for Black women and,
    164–65
prevalence of, 161
researching history and political influence
    related to, 162–63
depressive disorders, 142, 179
    due to another medical condition, 173
    eight types of, 173
DEQ. *see* Distressing Event Questionnaire
    (DEQ)
desired self, alignment of perceived self, cur-
    rent self, and, 56
diagnosis, proper, cautionary note on, 173, 175
Diagnostical and Statistical Manual (DSM),
    112, 137–38, 150
    anxiety officially recognized in, 174
    cultural representation and, 160–61
    PTSD described in, 151
    reviewing history and changes of particular
        disorders in versions of, 162–63
    see also DSM-5-TR
dialectical behavior therapy (DBT), 13
Different World, A, 111
direct aggression, 150
disability, disorder *vs.*, 161
discrimination, xviii
    Black women and, *vs.* Black men or white
        women, 147
    race-based hairstyles and protection from,
        109
    workplace, 39
disinhibited social engagement disorder, 155
disorder, disability *vs.*, 161
disruptive mood dysregulation disorder (chil-
    dren based), 173
dissonance, 54, 123
Distressing Event Questionnaire (DEQ), 155
diversity, 105
Divine Comedy (Dante), 134
divorce
    Black women and, 6
    question of children and, 8–9
Dixon, E., 65
doctoral degrees, Black women and earning of,
    statistics on, 29
domestic violence
    breaking generational cycle of, 50
    question of children and, 8, 9

double consciousness
 addressing in therapy, 108
 coining of term for, 107
double minority status, of Black women, xiv,
  xvi, xx–xxiii, 24, 92, 145, 186, 187
doubt, 129–31
 journal prompts on, 140
 patterns and, 130
 root of, 129
 therapist's tip on, 130–31
dreadlocked, origin of term for, 109–10
dreams for your life, journal prompts on, 183
*DSM. see Diagnostical and Statistical Manual
  (DSM)*
DSM-5-TR, 165, 169, 179
 clinical characteristics of PTSD in, 151
 cultural inclusion changes in, considerations related to, 163–65
 cultural sensitivity sections in, 161
 culture-related diagnostic lens sections in,
   176, 187
 *see also Diagnostical and Statistical Man-
   ual (DSM)*
DSM III, depression introduced as a mental
  disorder in, 162
DTS. *see* Davidson Trauma Scale (DTS)
dual masks, 107–8, 119
Du Bois, W. E. B., 35, 107
DuVernay, A., 24
dysthymia, 169

earnings
 average for Black women *vs.* U.S. average
   for women, 147
 for Black women *vs.* Black men, 18
ecological systems theory, 76
education
 Black women *vs.* Black men and, 18
 in the United States, 27–29
educational access
 Black women, transformational change,
   and, 26
 discrimination against Black Americans
   and, xviii
educational attainment rate, Black women
  and, pros and cons of, 25–27, 28
educational degrees, Black women and gains
  and losses related to, 29
educational knowledge, occupational knowledge *vs.*, 80
EEOC. *see* Equal Employment Opportunity
  Commission (EEOC)

ego-extension, in five-dimensional framework
  of mattering, 95
Ehrhardt, A., 17
elders in the Black community, respect and
  deference given to, 65
ELS. *see* Evaluation of Lifetime Stressors (ELS)
Emancipation Proclamation, 91–92
EMDR. *see* eye movement desensitization and
  reprocessing (EMDR)
emotional connection, therapeutic relationship and values related to, xxii
emotional expression, 17
 scheduling time with partners, 59
 skill deficits related to, 56
emotional labeling, 139*t*
emotionally unavailable parents, 64
emotional tracking, 139*t*
emotional vocabulary, increasing, 126, 128
emotions
 for all, Black women and, 187
 common, that Black women avoid/are not
   allowed to experience, 132–35
 consistent happiness, 134–35
 as a core belief, 131–32
 correlating to thoughts, 139*t*
 doubt, 129–31
 feeling wheel and, 136
 grace, 132–33
 guilt, 127–29
 related to friendships, 73
 shame, 124–27
 therapeutic guide for, 138*t*–39*t*
 therapist's introspection on, 138*t*
 trauma and, 143
 working with, 123–40
empowerment, servant *vs.* serving and sense
  of, 28
empty chair technique, 64, 118*t*
end-of-session check-ins, various types of, 137
enslavement, ancestral, Black Americans with,
  xviii. *see also* slavery
envy, 134, 135
Equal Employment Opportunity Commission
  (EEOC), 39, 41
equality, American dream and, 33
Erikson, E., psychosocial theory of, 76
Estriplet, T., 176
ethical codes, advocacy for our clients and,
  34–35
ethnoracial groups
 DSM-5-TR, cultural inclusion-related
   changes, and, 164

Eurich, T., 79
evaluation, in Bloom's taxonomy, 31, 32
Evaluation of Lifetime Stressors (ELS), 155
existential therapy, clinical focus, sample therapeutic SMART goal, technique or intervention, 46*t*
expatriate community, 96, 97
Exploring Lifespan Development (Berk), 76
extinction, 118*t*
eye movement desensitization and reprocessing (EMDR), clinical focus, sample therapeutic SMART goal, technique or intervention, 158*t*

family, creating legacy of work *vs.*, insights from a client: DX, 29–30. *see also* coparenting; marriage; parenting in a healthy way, engaging in
family wealth, household income *vs.*, 34
Fanon, F., 107
fatigue, two marginalized identities of Black women and, 164–65
fear, anxiety *vs.*, 174
Federal Reserve 2019 Survey of Consumer Finances, 34
feeling, mental state *vs.*, 129
feeling wheel
    in gestalt therapy, 20*t*
    in rational emotive behavioral therapy, 139*t*
    shared emotional awareness and expression and, 136
    utilizing, 126
    see also emotions
Feinberg, M., 66
Feinberg's Internal Structure and Ecological Context of Coparenting model, 66
Feinstein, R. A., 11
femininity, culture of, xx
feminist therapy, 13
    clinical focus, sample therapeutic SMART goal, technique or intervention, 21*t*, 100*t*
    nontraditional lifestyle choices and, 21*t*
fictive kinships, interdependence and, 74
fictive relationships, catalyst questions, 75–76
financial literacy, Black women and, 126. *see also* household income; money; wealth
"first, the," experiences and harm of, 26
5 Love Languages, The (Chapman), 73
5 Whys technique, 139n1
forgiveness, journal prompts on, 140
formal learning, socialized reality of segregation and intersecting with, 125–26

Frames of Mind: The Theory of Multiple Intelligences (Gardner), 55
Frankl, V., 162
freedom
    definitions of, 91
    feelings of, journal prompts on, 101, 102
    see also newfound freedom, embracing
Freud, S., 64, 131, 144, 162
Frey, W. H., 105
friendships, understanding, 72–90
    attachment formation and, 72–73
    deal-breakers and, 84–85
    early friendships, 80
    emotions related to, 73
    fictive relationships, 75–76
    from first friend to the current friend, 78–79
    friendship that we have with ourselves, 78
    history and, 74
    human development theories and, 76–77
    insight from a client: KJJ, 77–78
    journal prompts, 89–90
    navigating the overlap of friends, 85–86
    philosophy of friendships: reason, season, lifetime, 83–84
    self-awareness and, 79–82
    skills for maintaining healthy friendships, 85
    therapeutic guide for, 88*t*–89*t*
    therapist's introspection on, 87*t*
    what the Black woman brings to a friendship, 82–83
Frijda, N. H., 143
funding gap, 134
Fürisch, E., 82

Gardner, H., 55, 61
gaslighting, guilt and, 127
Gelso, C. J., 144
gender
    Black parenting styles and intersection with, 60
    Black women and, xix–xx
    friendships and factors related to, 77
    interracial marriages and, 98
    intersections of race and, for Black women, xiv, xvi, xx–xxiii, 24, 92, 145, 186, 187
    microaggressions and, 145
    socialization messages received and cultural identity of, 161
gender-based toys, 18
gender roles, coining of term for, 18
General Assembly of Virginia, Racial Integrity Act passed by, 98

generalizations, 105. *see also* stereotypes
generalized anxiety disorder, 37, 175
generalized language, marginalized persons
  and, 180
generational cycles, breaking, 49–71, 94
  awareness, intention, and consistency
    needed for, 55, 56, 66, 67
  childhood messages and core beliefs that no
    longer apply, 51–54
  coparenting relationships, 66–67
  creating harmony within generational
    cycles, 52
  creating new skills, 62
  engaging in parenting in a healthy way, 60–61
  financial literacy and, 126
  friendships and, 73
  grandmother teaching her granddaughter
    how to ride a bike analogy, 49–50
  insight from a client: TTT, 58–59
  journal prompts, 69–71
  learning new skills, 54–56
  taking a stand against outdated parental
    ways, 64–65
  therapeutic guide, 68t–69t
  therapist's introspection, 67t
generational wealth, definition of, 34
genograms, in analytical psychology therapy, 68t
gestalt therapy
  clinical focus, sample therapeutic SMART
    goal, technique or intervention, 20t, 118t
  empty chair technique in, 64, 118t
Ghana, Akan people of, xix
girls
  early maternal socialization of, 10–11, 22
  gender stereotypes and, 76–77
Global Psychotrauma Screen, 155
grace, 132–33
  definition of, 132
  insight from a client: KM, 133
  journal prompts on, 140
Great Migrations, two, Black people and sto-
    ries within context of, 92–93, 94
grief
  coparenting and processing of, 67, 71
  friendship issues and, 81, 90
  losses tied to newfound freedoms and, 95
Griffin, R. A., xxi
guided discovery, 138t
guilt, 127–29, 167
  root of, addressing, 127–29
  should and, 125
  see also shame

hairstyles
  Black girls, media-based beauty standards,
    and, 53–54
  Black women, racial discrimination, and,
    111–12
  clinician's role in advocacy around, 109
  CROWN Act and, protection from discrim-
    ination related to, 109
  insight from a client: MP, 111–12
  journal prompts on, 119–20
  straightening hair, Black women and rein-
    forced experience of, 107, 110
Hamer, Fannie Lou, forced sterilization of, 11
happiness
  consistent, Black women and, 134–35
  joy and enjoyment *vs.*, 134
harmony, creating within generational cycles,
    52
Harper's Weekly, 27
Harris-Perry, M., 107
Harvard Business Review, on workplace lone-
    liness, 37
Hayes, J., 144
HBCUs. *see* Historically Black Colleges and
    Universities (HBCUs)
heart disease, panic disorder and, 178–79
Height, D., 24
Hernandez, P.
  expands on cultural context model, xxi–xxii
  intersectionality as defined by, xx–xxi
heterosexual gender roles, addressing, 17–18
hippocampus, trauma and, 143
hiring, hairstyle modifications and, 111
Historically Black Colleges and Universities
    (HBCUs), 111, 116, 133
historical stereotypes, core beliefs and, 112–15
hobbies, Black women, depressive symptoms,
    and change in, 165
homeownership, Black women and percent-
    age increase in, 26
home state, moving away from, 92, 93, 94–95,
    99, 102
homework assignments, 21
hooks, b., xxi, 104
hope, raising children and, 54, 55
household income
  family wealth *vs.*, 34
  median, for Black Americans *vs.* for white
    Americans, 33–34
  see also financial literacy; money; wealth
housing, discrimination against Black Ameri-
    cans and, xviii

human development theories, friendships and, 76–77
humanistic theoretical concepts, 151
humanistic therapeutic approach, to trauma treatment, 153–54
Hurston, Z. N., 104
hypervigilance, trauma, acute stress disorder, and, 152
hysterectomies, unknown, 11
hysteria, women and original diagnosis of, 131

identification (attach to something positive), 64
IES-R. *see* Impact of Event Scale Revised (IES-R)
ignorance, misperception and, 132
illiteracy, slavery and, 27
imagery-based exposure therapy, 138*t*
imagination, self-doubt and, 130
Imago, 13
Imes, S., 39, 129
"I" messages, boundary-setting and, 65
Impact of Event Scale Revised (IES-R), 155
importance, in five-dimensional framework of mattering, 95
imposter syndrome, 130
    catalyst questions, 40
    coining of term for, 129
    definition of, 39
    journal prompts for, 47
individualism, collectivism *vs.*, survival and, 105
individuality, American dream and, 33
individual psychology, clinical focus, sample therapeutic SMART goal, technique or intervention, 46*t*
Indonesia, Khasi tribe and Minangkabau people of, xix
induced countertransference, 144, 145
industrial accidents, 141
inequality, intersectionality and various forms of, 24
infant mortality
    discrimination against Black Americans and, xviii
    disproportionate rates of, for Black children and youth, 60
infidelity, 149–50
insecure attachment styles, breaking generational cycle of, 50
insecurity, navigating lack of workplace knowledge and, 39–40

Insight (Eurich), 79
inspiration, envy *vs.*, 134, 135
intake form, tracking trauma on, 147
intelligence, eight different kinds of, 55
interdependence, fictive kinships and, 74
intergenerational trauma
    addressing in Black families, 64–65
    definition of, 64
intermediate beliefs, core beliefs and, 51
international living. *see* moving abroad
international teletherapy, 96
interpersonal intelligence, 55
interracial relationships, 92, 93, 97–99
intersectionality
    coining of term for, 24
    definition of, xx–xxi
    operational definition of, in text, xv
    power, relational safety and, within mental health therapy context, xxii
    of race and gender, double minority status of Black women and, xiv, xvi, xx–xxiii, 24, 92, 145, 186, 187
intimate partner violence (IPV), Black women and, statistics on, 146
intrapersonal intelligence, 55
introspection, journal prompts and, xxiv
introspective and reflective processing, 17
involuntary minority
    defining, in two specific ways, xvii
    voluntary minority *vs.*, xvii–xviii
Inyx Therapy Group, 171
IPV. *see* intimate partner violence (IPV)

Jack and Jill of America, 77, 111
Jackson, J., 141
Jacobsen, J., 178
jargon, mental health, correcting improper use of, 174
Jim Crow era, 108, 132
job interviews, hairstyle modifications and, 111
Jollans, L., 170
journaling, about moving abroad, 97
journal prompts, 186
    for breaking generational cycles, 69–71
    for creating a legacy for work, 47–48
    for embracing newfound freedoms, 101–3
    on friendships, 89–90
    for mental health disorders addressed via a cultural lens, 182–83
    for moving beyond stereotypes, 119–20
    on nontraditional lifestyle choices, 21–23

reflection and introspection and, xxiv
on stereotypes, 119–20
trauma treatment-related, 159
for working with emotions, 140
joy and enjoyment, happiness *vs.*, 134
judgment, shame and notion of, 124
Jung, C., 166
Junge, C., 84

Khasi tribe, xix
King, Martin Luther Jr., 37, 106
knowledge, in Bloom's taxonomy, 31

language development, in girls *vs.* in boys,
76, 77
Latino Americans, interracial marriages
between white Americans and, 98
laziness stereotype, 169
leadership gap, 134
learning
again, unlearning and, 186
remaining dedicated to, 14
Lee, A., 64
legacies, creating through work, 25, 28–29
being "the only" at work and, 37–38
crabs in the barrel toxic mentality and, 43, 44
having more money than previous generations, 33–35
journal prompts for, 47–48
microaggressions and sexual harassment
and, 41–42
navigating lack of workplace knowledge
and, 39–40
research on Black women at work, 38
talented tenth issues and, 35–36
therapeutic guide, 45*t*–46*t*
therapist's introspection, 44*t* –45*t*
Leisure, E. C., 12
lessons learned, marriage questions and, 22
LGBTQ+ movement, uniqueness of identity
of trans women and, xvi
liberty, American dream and, 33
Likert scale approach, to end-of-session check-
ins, 137
limbic system, 129, 146, 151
Lincoln, A., 91
linguistic intelligence, 55
Links, The, 77
listening, objectively and subjectively, to your
Black women clients, xxiii
Lloyd, B. C., 41

logical-mathematical intelligence, 55
loneliness
epidemic of, studies on, 37
friendship issues and, 86
Lorde, A., 123
loud ghetto girl stereotype, 106
love languages, Black children and lack of
fullness of, 73
Loving, M., 98
lynching, 93
Lyte, MC, 72

macroaggressions
of educational system built for white men, 28
percentage of Black women with experience of, 41
major depressive disorder, 78, 127, 162, 168, 173
loneliness and, 37
major depressive episodes *vs.*, 162
minority persons with two or more marginalized intersections and, 164
perfectionism and, considering link
between, 165–66
postpartum depression and, 170
prevalence of, in United States, 169
Malcolm X, 37, 106
mammy stereotype, 82, 106
manipulation, guilt and, 127
marginalization
Cultural Context Model and experiences
of, xxi
minimizing, moving abroad and, 95
marginalized communities
community funds and, 42
lived experience of people in, xvi
stereotypes, survival, and, 116
marginalized identities
group, microaggressions and, 41
intersection of gender roles and, 18
marriage
generational messages about, 69
healthy, skills for, 6
journal prompts on, 22
managing your own perceptions about, 7–8
opting out of, Black women *vs.* Black men
and, 18
question of, 5, 6–8
marriage gap, 134
marrying outside of one's race, 92, 93, 97–99,
102–3
Martorell, G., 10

martyrdom, 170
  Black women, depression, and, 165, 166–68
  insight about, from a client: CM, 167–68
master's degrees, Black women and earning of,
    statistics on, 29
maternal mortality, Black women *vs.* white
    women and, xviii, 11, 176
maternal socialization of girls, examples of,
    10, 22
matrilineal societies, xix
mattering
  five-dimensional framework of, 95
  moving abroad and concept of, 97
McDowell, T., xxii
McKinsey and Company, beauty business
    study, 110
McManus, E., 164
media portrayals
  healthy representation in, importance of, 82
  insight from a client: JST, 83
mental health, friendships integral to, 87
mental health clinicians, working with Black
    women and intentions of, 14
mental health disorders via a cultural lens,
    addressing, 160–83
  anxiety, 174–79
  avoidance, 169
  cultural formations, 163–65
  depression, 161–62
  journal prompts, 182–83
  martyrdom, 166–68
  perfectionism, 165–66
  therapeutic guide, 181*t*–82*t*
  therapist's introspection, 180*t*
mental health taboos, unhelpful therapeutic
    space and, 161
mental state, feeling *vs.*, 129
mental status exam (MSE), 170, 171–73
mentors and mentorship, 40, 48
Me Too movement, 41
Meyers, D., xx
Mezzich, J. E., 163
microaggressions, 133, 145–46, 150, 151, 164,
    165
  definition of, 41, 145
  of educational system built for white men, 28
  percentage of Black women with experi-
    ence of, 41
  sexual harassment and, 41–42
*Microaggressions in Everyday Life: Race, Gen-
    der, and Sexual Orientation* (Sue), 145

Minangkabau people, Indonesia, xix
Mindful Attention Awareness Scale, The
    (Brown & Ryan), 82
mindfulness, 118*t*
Minnesota Multiphasic Personality Inventory-
    2-Restructured Form (MMPI-2-RF), 155
miracle question
  description of, 62
  embracing newfound freedoms and, 101*t*
  end-of-session check-ins and, 137
  moving abroad and, 96
  utilizing, 63
miscegenation, 98
misogyny, 143, 164
misperception, ignorance and, 132
Mississippi Scale for Combat-Related PTSD
    (M-PTSD), 155
mistakes, 132
Mocha Moms, 77
modeling approach, end-of-session check-ins
    and, 137
money
  Black women and concept of, 126
  having more than previous generations,
    33–35
  management skills, learning, 34
  see also financial literacy; household
    income; wealth
Money, J., 17, 18
"Money Attitudes, Financial Capabilities, and
    Impulsiveness as Predictors of Wealth
    Accumulation" (Fenton–O'Creevy &
    Furnham), 26, 28, 34
mood disorders, 151, 162
Morrison, T., 91
Mosley, E. A., 41
Mosuo people, China, xix
mother and child rituals, in ancient societies,
    10
mother-based organizations, as safe havens, 77
motherhood, journal prompts on, 22–23
mothering, culture of, xx
mother role, exploring: catalyst questions for,
    9–10
motivational interviewing, xxiii, 12, 35, 177
moving abroad, 92, 93, 95–97, 99
MPSS-SR. *see* PTSD Symptom Scale: Self-Re-
    port Version (MPSS-SR)
M-PTSD. *see* Mississippi Scale for Com-
    bat-Related PTSD (M-PTSD)
MSE. *see* mental status exam (MSE)

multicultural counseling and therapy, clinical
focus, sample therapeutic SMART goal,
technique or intervention, 88*t*
multiple intelligence theory, 55, 61
murders by police
Black people *vs.* white people and, 147
discrimination against Black Americans
and, xviii
Murthy, V. H., 37
muscle tension, trauma, acute stress disorder,
and, 152
musical intelligence, 55

narrative therapy
clinical focus, sample therapeutic SMART
goal, technique or intervention, 88*t*, 139*t*
working with emotions and, 139*t*
National Center for Education Statistics, 29
National Health Interview Survey, 55
National Pan-Hellenic Council, 111
National Survey of Children's Health, 55
Native American women, early formal education for, 27
natural disasters, trauma caused by, 141, 146
naturalist intelligence, 55
natural selection, social stereotypes and, 104
neglect, 146
breaking generational cycle of, 50
tracking via intake, 147
neighborhood groups, as safe havens, 77
neuromarkers, postpartum depression, persistent depressive disorder, and, 170
newborns, mothers separated from, during
slavery era, 74–75
newfound freedom, embracing, 91–103
dating or marrying outside of one's race, 92,
97–99
journal prompts for, 101–3
moving abroad, 92, 95–97, 99
moving away from the home state, 92,
94–95, 99
therapeutic guide for, 100*t*–101*t*
therapist's introspection on, 100*t*
new skills, requirements for learning, 62
*Nobody Knows the Trouble I've Seen: The
Emotional Lives of Black Women* (Burnett-Zeigler), 55, 56
nontraditional lifestyles, choosing, 5–23
addressing heterosexual gender roles, 17–18
Black women and increase in, 5
children, question of, 5, 8–14

church attendance, question of, 5, 14–17
evolution of options and decisions and, 19
journal prompts, 21–23
marriage, question of, 5, 6–8
therapeutic guide, 20*t*–21*t*
therapist's introspection, 19*t*
nonverbal communication, doubt and, 131
Noonan, C., 37
nurturance, as afterthought to survival, 60–61,
73

object relations theory, 73
observation, doubt and development of, 129
obsessive compulsive disorder, 162
occupational knowledge, educational knowledge *vs.*, 80
OECD. *see* Organization for Economic Cooperation and Development (OECD)
Ogbu, J., involuntary minority as defined by,
xvii
"only, the," at work
Black women contending with, 27, 29,
37–38
insight from a client: IW, 43–44
oppression, weaponization of Black women
and, xvii
Organization for Economic Cooperation and
Development (OECD), 39
other specified anxiety disorder, 175
other specified depressive disorder, 173
outdated parental ways, taking a stand against,
64–65
overdiagnosis, avoiding, 174
oxytocin, language acquisition and, 77

panic attack specifier, 175
panic disorder, 175
catalyst questions for, 179
cultural differences for Black people and,
176
heart disease and, 178–79
Papalia, D. E., 10
parenting in a healthy way, engaging in, 60–61
coparenting relationships, 66–67
creating new skills for, 62
creating space for a new parenting style, 61
taking a stand against outdated parental
ways, 64–65
parenting skills and parenting styles, journal
prompts on, 70
Parenting Stress Index (PSI), 155

parents
    anxiety in offspring and anxiety in, 175
    hope in, as key factor in child development, 55
Park, C. L., 15
Parks, R., 49
patriarchal societies, origination of, xix
patriarchy, xvii, 93
    incongruent experiences of Black women and religion due to, 15
    religion and role of, in lives of women, xix
patterns, competence and, 130
Pavlova, B., 175
pay gap, 134
PCL-5. *see* PTSD Checklist for *DSM-5* (PCL-5)
PDS. *see* Posttraumatic Diagnostic Scale (PDS)
Penn Inventory for Posttraumatic Stress Disorder, 155
perceived self, alignment of desired self, current self, and, 56
perfectionism
    Black women, depression, and, 165–66
    journal prompts on, 182
permissive parenting style, 60
persistent depressive disorder, 173
    neuromarkers and, 170
    prevalence of, in United States, 169
person-centered therapy
    clinical focus, sample therapeutic SMART goal, technique or intervention, 20*t*, 117*t*
    nontraditional lifestyle choices and, 20*t*
Pew Research Center, 76
    on interracial marriages, 98
    religious landscape study, 14
physical abuse, tracking via intake, 147
Piaget, J., 76, 105
pleasure, protection *vs.*, 166
"Politics of Self-Respect, The" (Meyers), xx
positive visualization, 139*t*
postpartum depression
    Black women's higher percentages of, 176
    persistent depressive disorder, neuromarkers, and, 170
Posttrauma Risky Behaviors Questionnaire, 155
Posttraumatic Diagnostic Scale (PDS), 155
post-traumatic stress disorder (PTSD), 155
    acute stress disorder and, what they look like for Black women clients, 151–52

    acute stress disorder and, what they sound like for Black women clients, 152–53
    hairstyle issues in the workplace and, 112
poverty rates, Black women and, 147
power, intersectionality, relational safety and, within mental health therapy context, xxii
powerful magician archetype, 177
predominantly white institution (PWI), 133
prefrontal cortex, trauma and, 143
pregnancy
    anxiety disorder developed during, 175, 176
    Black women and requirement for, 11
premenstrual dysphoric disorder, 173
presence, being seen and, xvi–xvii
pressure technique, 127–29, 139n1
preterm birth deliveries, 176
pride, shame and, 114
Primary Care PTSD Screen for DSM-5, 155
probing questions, 12
problem-solving process, 7, 17
    coparents and, 66
    creating therapeutic goals for, 59
    skill deficits related to, 56
    steps in, 57
product inventory-based pregnancy, 11
professional roles and titles, Black women *vs.* Black men and, 18
promiscuous woman, 82
protection, pleasure *vs.*, 166
"protective hairstyles," 116
PSI. *see* Parenting Stress Index (PSI)
PSS-1. *see* PTSD Symptom Scale-Interview (PSS-1)
psychoanalytic psychotherapy, clinical focus, sample therapeutic SMART goal, technique or intervention, 89*t*, 181*t*
psychoeducation, 174
Psychology of Religion and Spirituality journal, 15
psychopharmacological therapy, clinical focus, sample therapeutic SMART goal, technique or intervention, 182*t*
psychosocial theory (Erikson), 76
PTSD. *see* posttraumatic stress disorder (PTSD)
PTSD Checklist for *DSM-5* (PCL-5), 155
PTSD Symptom Scale-Interview (PSS-1), 155
PTSD Symptom Scale: Self-Report Version (MPSS-SR), 155
PWI. *see* predominantly white institution (PWI)

question prompts, 13, 64
questions
asking, during our sessions with clients, 35
specific, about microaggression and sexual
harassment, 42
see also catalyst questions; miracle question

race
Black parenting styles and intersection with,
60
Black women and, xvii–xix
intersections of gender and, for Black
women, xiv, xvi, xx–xxiii, 24, 92, 145,
186, 187
microaggressions and, 145
socialization messages received and cultural
identity of, 161
race-based organizations, 92
"Racial Differences in Parenting Style Typologies and Heavy Episodic Drinking Trajectories" (Clark, et al.), 60
Racial Integrity Act, 98
"Racial Microaggressions in Everyday Life:
Implications for Clinical Practice" (Sue,
et al.), 145
racism, 93, 143, 164
Black parenting styles and, 60
Black women and, *vs.* Black men or white
women, 147
racist stereotypes, rejecting, 109–12
Rae, I., 49
rape, 141
rape-based pregnancy, 11
RAS. *see* reticular activating system (RAS)
rational emotive behavioral therapy (REBT), 13
clinical focus, sample therapeutic SMART
goal, technique or intervention, 139*t*
rationalization (excuse and justify mistakes),
64, 65
reaction formation, core beliefs and, 78
reactive countertransference, 144–45
reality television, friendship models portrayed
on, 82
reality therapy, clinical focus, sample therapeutic SMART goal, technique or intervention, 45*t*
REBT. *see* rational emotive behavioral therapy
(REBT)
reciprocity, in friendships, 79
reflection, journal prompts and, xxiv. *see also*
journal prompts

Reflection Rumination Questionnaire (Trapnell & Campbell), 82
relational safety, power, intersectionality and,
within mental health therapy context, xxii
religion
Black Americans and positive *vs.* negative
tendencies related to, 15
Black parenting styles and intersection with,
60
Black women and role of, xix, xx
role of patriarchy in lives of women and, xix
spirituality *vs.*, 14–15
religious communities, patriarchal practices
in, examples of, 15
religious institutions, great exodus from, factors related to, 14
religious or spiritual practices, journal prompts
on, 23
replacement building activities, spirituality
and religion issues and, 16–17
research population, Black people not
included in, 160, 169
resentment, guilt and, 127
restorative conversations, 7
coparents and, 66
lack of, 56
process for, steps in, 57–58
reticular activating system (RAS), trauma and,
143
Revolutionary War, Black people and history
of fighting in, xviii
Riina, E., 66
Rogers, C., 162
role models, lack of, 40
role-plays, 12, 114
Rowan, J., 144

safe havens, friendships for Black women and
goal of, 77
safety
advocacy and creation of, 136
community-based structures and sense of, 92
Great Migration and fear of, 93
suppression *vs.*, 132
sage archetype, martyrdom and intersection
with caregiver archetype, 166
Sage Journal, 38
Saleem, F. T., 60
sandtray therapy
definition of, 20n2
nontraditional lifestyle choices and, *20t*

sandwich approach, 137
Sankofa, the, in Ghanian Akan Adinkra history
    and symbolism, 74
scaffolded conversations, 12
schemas
    patterns and, journal prompts for, 119
    Piaget and coining of term for, 105
    stereotypes and, 104–7
Schlossberg, N. K., 95
Schwyck, M. E., 78
Screen for Posttraumatic Stress Symptoms
    (SPTSS), 155
secondary trauma, 154
segregation, xviii
    intersection of formal learning with reality
        of, 125–26
    self-selected, 92
selective mutism, 174, 175
self-actualization, Black women and goal of, xiv
self-awareness, 84
    assessments, 81–82
    catalyst questions for, 81
    friendships and, 79–81, 86
    grace and, 133
    happiness and, 134
    increasing, 80, 128
    stereotypes and need for, 114
Self-Awareness Outcomes Questionnaire (Sut-
    ton et al.), 82
self-blame, 125
self-care
    boundaries and, 125
    professional development and, for thera-
        pists, 188
    therapeutic relationship and values related
        to, xxii
self-concept, 78
self-determination, Black women in the work-
    force and, 25
self-doubt, 129
self-esteem, 78
self-grace, journal prompts on, 140
self-monitoring, 118*t*
self-numbing, trauma, acute stress disorder,
    and, 152
Self-Reflection and Insight Scale, The (Grant
    et al.), 82
self-regulation, 78
self-sabotage, trauma, acute stress disorder,
    and, 152
self-talk, 78, 79, 140
sellouts, accusations of being, 107

sensory recall, trauma and, 143
sentence starters, 12, 59, 64
separation anxiety, 174, 175
servants *vs.* serving, sense of empowerment
    and, 28
sexism, Black women and, *vs.* Black men or
    white women, 147
sexual abuse, tracking via intake, 147
sexual assault, Black women *vs.* white women
    and, 146
sexual harassment, microaggressions and, 41–42
sexual orientation
    microaggressions and, 145
    reviewing history and changes related to, in
        versions of *DSM*, 163
SFT. *see* solution-focused therapy (SFT)
shame
    catalyst questions related to, 127
    definition of, 124
    distortion of, 125
    journal prompts on, 140
    should and, 125
    subtle signs and statements of, addressing, 114
    see also guilt
should
    blame and root of, 125
    as a cognitive distortion, 125
side-by-side play, babies and toddlers and, 84
simple approach, to end-of-session check-ins, 137
single and sad woman, 82
single lives, Black women and, 26
SI-PTSD. *see* Structured Interview for PTSD
    (SI-PTSD)
sister circles, 77
Sisters of the Order of Saint Ursula, 27
skill-based learning, creating an environment
    for, 7
skills, learning new, 54–56
skill set deficits related to communication,
    problem solving, and restorative conver-
    sations, 56
skin, bleaching, 107
slave breeding pregnancy, 11
slavery, xviii, 24, 108, 132
    Black parents' authoritarian style as a
        response to, 60, 61
    Black women as caretakers and, 166
    forced childbirth and, 11
    friendships during, importance of, 74
    illiteracy and, 27
    mothers separated from newborns during,
        74–75

SMART (Specific, Measurable, Achievable, Relevant, and Time-bound) goals
  in analytical psychology therapy, 68*t*
  in behavioral therapy, 69*t*, 118*t*
  in cognitive behavioral therapy, 181*t*
  in cognitive therapy, 138*t*
  in creative arts therapy, 158*t*–59*t*
  definition and directness of, 20n1
  in EMDR, 158*t*
  in existential therapy, 46*t*
  in feminist therapy, 21*t*, 100*t*
  in gestalt therapy, 20*t*, 118*t*
  in individual psychology, 46*t*
  making and using, 187–88
  in multicultural counseling and therapy, 88*t*
  in narrative therapy, 88*t*, 139*t*
  in person-centered therapy, 20*t*, 117*t*
  in psychoanalytic psychotherapy, 89*t*, 181*t*
  in psychopharmacological therapy, 182*t*
  in rational emotive behavioral therapy (REBT), 139*t*
  in reality therapy, 45*t*
  in solution-focused brief therapy, 101*t*
  in strategic family therapy, 68*t*
  in strength-based therapy, 101*t*
  in trauma-focused cognitive behavioral therapy, 157*t*
social anxiety disorder, 174, 175, 177
social class, Black parenting styles and intersection with, 60
social Darwinism, social stereotypes and, 104
social inclusion, stereotypes and, 116
social learning, 76
social rules of engagement, 132
social stereotypes
  journal prompts on, 120
  social Darwinism and, 104
sociocultural theory (Vygotsky), 76
Socratic questioning, xxiii, 138*t*
solution-focused therapy (SFT), 160
  clinical focus, sample therapeutic SMART goal, technique or intervention, 101*t*
  miracle question and, 62, 63
SOLVE technique, 181*t*, 182n1
sororities, as safe havens, 77
Souls of Black Folk, The (Du Bois), 107
spatial intelligence, 55
spirituality
  definition of, 14
  journal prompts on, 23
  religion *vs.*, 14–15

SPTSS. *see* Screen for Posttraumatic Stress Symptoms (SPTSS)
stereotypes
  addressing, 94
  Black women facing from other Black people, 107
  catalyst questions for exploring, 106, 108
  development of, 116
  dual masks and, 107–9
  hairstyles and, rejecting, 109–12
  historical, core beliefs and, 112–15
  journal prompts on, 119–20
  moving beyond, 104–20, 185
  racist, rejecting, 109–12
  schemas and, 104–7
  social Darwinism and, 104
  social inclusion and, 116
  survival and, 116
  Therapeutic Guide for, 117*t*–18*t*
  therapist's introspection on, 117*t*
  see also bias(es)
stereotypical gaze, 164
sterilization without consent, Black women and, 11–12
stories, in narrative therapy, 139*t*
strategic family therapy, clinical focus, sample therapeutic SMART goal, technique or intervention, 68*t*
strength-based therapy, clinical focus, sample therapeutic SMART goal, technique or intervention, 101*t*
stressor-related disorders, 151–53, 155
strong Black woman persona
  historical stereotypes and formation of, 114–15
  trauma and, 56
Structured Interview for PTSD (SI-PTSD), 155
"Study of Negro Problem, The" (Du Bois), 35
sublimination (divert negative into acceptable), 64
substance/medication-induced anxiety disorder, 175
substance/medication-induced depressive disorder, 173
Sue, D., 41, 145
suppression, safety *vs.*, 132
Supreme Court, first Black woman sworn into, 136
Surowiec, A., xix
survival, 116
  collectivism *vs.* individualism and, 105
  community and, 106
  dual masks and, 107–8

survival (*continued*)
  social stereotypes and, 104
survival aggression, 148–50
survival messages, parents in oppressive circumstances and, 64
susu (or *sou-sou*), 42
synthesis, in Bloom's taxonomy, 31, 32
systematic desensitization, 118*t*

TAA. *see* Trauma Assessment for Adults (TAA)
talented tenth
  coining of term for, 35
  expectation and/or pressure to open doors
    for others and, 35–36
Taylor, S. L., xiii
team building, 17
teletherapy, international, 96
TF-CBT. *see* trauma-focused cognitive behavioral therapy (TF-CBT)
theoretical orientations, therapeutic
  approaches *vs.*, 160–61
therapeutic-aligned inquiry formats, xxiii
therapeutic approaches, theoretical orientations *vs.*, 160–61
therapeutic guide
  breaking generational cycles, 68*t*–69*t*
  creating a legacy through work, 45*t*–46*t*
  embracing newfound freedoms, 100*t*–101*t*
  friendships, 88*t*–89*t*
  mental health disorders addressed via a
    cultural lens, 181*t*–82*t*
  moving beyond stereotypes, 117*t*–18*t*
  nontraditional lifestyle choices and, 20*t*–21*t*
  two main parts of, xxiv
  working with emotions, 138*t*–39*t*
therapeutic relationship, Black woman and
  safe haven of, 7
therapeutic silence, 12
therapists
  alignment between intention and knowl-
    edge of, xv
  becoming, author's personal journey to,
    xiii–xiv
  professional development and self-care for,
    188
  well-intended, but culturally incompetent,
    14
  see also therapist's tips
therapist's introspection
  on Black women and diagnostic mental
    health disorders, 180*t*

  on Black women and their engagement
    with work, 44*t*–45*t*
  on breaking generational cycles, 67*t*
  on embracing newfound freedoms, 100*t*
  on friendships, 87*t*
  on moving beyond stereotypes, 117*t*
  on trauma, addressing, 156*t*–57*t*
  on working with emotions, 138*t*
therapist's tips
  advocacy, 135
  Bloom's taxonomy, 30–31
  clinician's role in advocacy, 109
  coparents, 66
  correcting improper use of mental health
    jargon, 174
  countertransference, 144–45
  creating and processing possibilities, 99
  creating harmony within generational
    cycles, 52
  creating space for a new parenting style, 61
  description of, xxiii
  diagnosing the correct trauma disorder,
    154–55
  direct and difficult questions, asking, 18
  on doubt, 130–31
  eight depressive disorders, knowing the
    difference, 173
  on feeling wheel, utilizing, 126
  on humanistic therapeutic approach, utiliz-
    ing, 153–54
  imagination exercise–separation from a
    child, 74–75
  on important skills, 7
  managing your own perceptions on mar-
    riage, 7–8
  mental status exam, 171–73
  microaggression and sexual harassment, 42
  on the miracle question, utilizing, 63
  pressure technique, 127–29
  question prompts, 13–14
  research depression history and political
    influence, 162–63
  research on Black women at work, 38
  on sandwich approach, utilizing, 137
  self-awareness assessments, 81–82
  skills-communication, problem solving, and
    restorative conversations, 56–58
  skills for maintaining healthy friendships, 85
  suffering of angry and aggressive Black
    women, 151
  tracking trauma via intake, 147–48

trauma assessments and tools, utilizing, 155–56

twelve anxiety disorders and knowing the difference between, 175

on workbooks and worksheets, utilizing, 54

thought recording, 138*t*

THQ. *see* Trauma History Questionnaire (THQ)

Title IV of 1972, 25

toddlers, friend-based connections between, 84

toys, gender-based, 18

trailblazers, challenges faced by, 94

trailblazing, obstacles arising in process of, 25

transformed life, pros and cons of, 186–87

trans women
    Black, stereotypes of, 106
    included in the definition of women, xv–xvi

trauma, 141–59
    definition of, 141
    direct aggression, 146–47, 150
    disproportionate rate of, for Black children and youth, 60
    healing from, 94
    historical, parenting style and, 64
    humanistic therapeutic approach to, 153–54
    intergenerational, addressing, 64–65
    journal prompts related to, 159
    microaggressions, 145–46, 150, 151
    personal freedom and healing from, 156
    race-based, parenting style and, 64
    survival aggression, 148–50
    therapeutic guide for, 157*t*–59*t*
    therapist's introspection on, 156*t*–57*t*
    tracking via intake, 147
    treating, 141–43
    unaddressed, future trauma and, 142

Trauma Assessment for Adults (TAA), 155

Trauma Assessment for Adults (TAA)-Self-Report, 156

trauma assessments and tools, utilizing, 155–56

trauma disorders, 150–53
    acute stress disorder, 151–52
    diagnosing correct, 154–55
    posttraumatic stress disorder, 150, 151–53

trauma-focused cognitive behavioral therapy (TF-CBT), 112
    clinical focus, sample therapeutic SMART goal, technique or intervention, 157*t*

Trauma History Questionnaire (THQ), 155

Trauma-Informed Mental Health Assessment, 156

Trauma Symptom Inventory (TSI), 156

Traumatic Stress Schedule (TSS), 156

TSI. *see* Trauma Symptom Inventory (TSI)

TSS. *see* Traumatic Stress Schedule (TSS)

Unbought and Unbossed (Chisholm), 25

understanding, in Bloom's taxonomy, 31

unemployment, 93

unhealthy skills, avoiding demonizing teacher of, 56

uninvolved/neglectful parenting style, 60

United States
    depression in, prevalence of, 169
    drop in annual number of births in, 1990-2020, 11
    education in, 27–29
    ending of slavery in, 91–92
    race and gender statistics in, 25
    role of religion in lives of Black women *vs.* Black men in, xx

United States Army population, percentage of Black Americans in, xviii

universal cultural truths, counselors and openness to, xxii

unspecified anxiety disorder, 175

unspecified depressive disorder, 173

U.S. Census Bureau
    drop in marriage rate data, Black women and, 6
    Great Migration data, 93
    interracial marriage statistics, 98

U.S. State Senate Committee on Small Business and Entrepreneurship, on Black women business owners, 25

values, Black parenting styles and intersection with, 60

vice presidency of the United States, first Black women voted into, 136

Vietnam War, 150

village, connected, friendships and, 73, 74

violence, mental health disorders and exposure to, 147

voluntary minority, involuntary minority *vs.*, xvii–xviii

Vygotsky, Lev, sociocultural theory of, 76

Walker, A., 5, 25

war, 141

War of 1812, Black people and history of fighting in, xviii

wealth
  definition of, 34
  generational, 34
  see also financial literacy; household
    income; money
wealth-building opportunities, discrimination
  against Black Americans and, xviii
wealth gap, 34, 134
weaves, unwanted, 107, 110
"welfare queens" label, 114
Whelan, R., 170
white Americans
  data on interracial marriages and, 98
  median household income for, 33–34
white family wealth, Black family wealth *vs.*,
  34
white men
  earnings for Black women *vs.* those for, 164
  educational system in the United States
    and, 27
whiteness, beauty standards centered on, 51
white women
  maternal deaths and Black women *vs.*, 11
  reported rates of gender-based harassment
    and, 41
wifehood, culture of, xx
wigs, unwanted, 107
Wiley Online Library, 38
Williams, D. K., 14
Winfrey, O., xiii, 91, 123
woman, operational definition of, in text, xv
womanhood, culture of, xx
women
  hysteria in psychological history and, 131
  religion and role of patriarchy in lives of, xix

WHO on impact of direct aggression on,
    147
  see also Black women; white women
Women's Liberation movement, intersection
  of Civil Rights movement and, 26, 28,
    34, 93, 135
women's suffrage, 126
Wong, L. C. J., culture and therapeutic relationship study, xxii–xxiii
work
  Black women, history of slavery, and rela-
    tionship with, 24
  Black women being "the only" at, 27, 29,
    37–38, 43–44
  creating legacies through, 5, 28–30, 44*t*–45*t*
  research on Black women at, 38
  see also legacies, creating through work
work *bestie* persona, 85
workplace
  hairstyle modifications and, 111–12
  knowledge, navigating lack of, 39–40
workplace discrimination
  Black people and experience of, 41
  prohibition against, 39
World Health Organization (WHO)
  on direct aggression toward women, 147
  on loneliness as a social epidemic, 37
  on prevalence of depression, 161, 169
World Wars, Black people and history of fighting in, xviii
wrongful convictions, Black people and, statistics on, 146

Yabusaki, A. S., diversity, privilege, and dialogue research, xxii

About the Author

As a leading professional in the mental health field, **LaNail R. Plummer, EdD, LCPC-S,** and her team of 30 Black/women of color, are committed to improving the lives of others through the mental health education and coaching. A U.S. Army veteran and the CEO and founder of Onyx Therapy Group—an organization she founded in 2013—Dr. Plummer has 20 years of experience working with a multitude of clients and specializing in the care of young women, Black and Brown communities, and members of the LGBTQ+ community. Headquartered in Washington, DC, Dr. Plummer and her team service the DC area as well as Maryland, Virginia, Pennsylvania, Louisiana, and South Africa.

As the creator of the Culturally Integrated Clinical Supervision Model, Dr. Plummer is dedicated to providing education, direction, and guidance to make sure that all marginalized people and professionals are treated with care and mindful intention, so as to promote psychological safety and healing.

Dr. Plummer is the department chair of counseling at Trinity Washington University (DC) and has developed a course for counseling entrepreneurs titled "Entrepreneurship in Mental Health."

Dr. Plummer is the mother of two adult children, Alyssa Eve and Bradshaw Jr., and is married to her wife, Maegan. She is a proud member of The BOW Collective and Delta Sigma Theta Sorority, Inc.